LORD JUSTICE BIRKETT

LORD JUSTICE

BIRKETT

DENNIS BARDENS

Illustrated

LONDON
ROBERT HALE LIMITED
63 Old Brompton Road, S.W.7

© Dennis Bardens 1962
First edition October 1962
Reprinted October 1962
Reprinted November 1962
Reprinted January 1963
Reprinted February 1963

For

MARIE

Printed in Great Britain by Richard Clay and Company, Ltd.,
Bungay, Suffolk

PREFACE

THIS IS AN attempt to present what appear to me to be some of the main facts of the life of Lord Birkett, one of the greatest advocates of this age.

It is clear that, as Lord Birkett led so long and crowded a life and was involved in so many sensational and dramatic court cases, it would take a library of books to cover them completely. To attempt to include everything within the compass of a single volume would be to so reduce each phase as to make the book appear to be a catalogue; a single year of Norman Birkett's life, let us say 1928, would provide material for several books, and one single case in that year has itself been made the subject of a book. That there are numerous omissions is, therefore, axiomatic.

The second point I would like to make is that this biography does not carry the express or implied approval of the Birkett family. Except where I quote individuals, the views and assessments are mine alone.

I would like to thank the many informants who responded to my appeal to those who knew Lord Birkett, and to the *Guardian* and *Birmingham Post* for publishing it. I am also indebted to the New York office of *Time* and *Life*, to Mr. Stanley Pryor, Mr. Reginald Elms, Mr. Victor Hull of the British Museum, Mr. E. A. P. Hart of the Inner Temple Library, Mr. Don Hyndman of the American Bar Association, Miss Dawn Tindle, Librarian of the Reform Club, Mr. Sidney Campion, Mr. Geoffrey Williamson, Mr. H. S. Manning, Mr. J. F. Chadderton, Mr. Timothy Donovan, Mr. Claude Westell, Mrs. Elizabeth Baines, Mr. Albert B. Zimmerman and Mr. F. E. Cook, County Librarian of Lancashire County Council, for much valuable assistance, to Dr. George Morey, LL.D., for kindly reading the manuscript and Mrs. Vivienne Semmence for help on research.

Lord Birkett once said that his favourite epitaph was a line from Thomas Hardy: 'You was a good man and did good things.' It aptly summarises his own life. Writing a biography is a sort of retrospective reporting; and I can truthfully say that of the scores of people who have known Norman Birkett at different stages of his life, not one has adduced a single fact which detracted in the slightest from the popular picture of Lord Birkett as the best type of Englishman, with his love of tradition, of the open air, his humour and love of fair play. Inevitably, success attracts envious detractors during a man's lifetime, yet even here Norman Birkett, despite his outstanding success at the Bar, had fewer than most people of comparable status. It was moving, and at times actually sad, to hear and read of the indelible impression he made upon his friends, in memories which often remained fresh even after fifty or sixty years.

DENNIS BARDENS

Reform Club,
Pall Mall, S.W.1

CONTENTS

ILLUSTRATIONS

CHAPTER I

Childhood in Lakeland

WHEN LORD BIRKETT of Ulverston died in London on February 11th, 1962, a sense of irrevocable loss pervaded the Lakeland town of Ulverston. The boy whose eloquence had moved them seventy years ago had, only a few days before his death, charmed and won over the House of Lords by his impassioned plea to spare the beautiful Lakeland district the discord and ugliness of urban spoliation.

Norman Birkett, as he loved to boast, was an Ulverstonian born and bred. Only a year ago, when opening Ulverston's new library, he told the residents, in a speech which is a marvel of euphony, rhythm and wit, of his heart's response to his old town: 'I know every street in it. I know every building in it. The moment I catch sight of the Monument I say to myself, "At last I am home again."'

His listeners knew that this was no studied compliment. Throughout his life Lord Birkett read his local paper, the *Ulverston News*, with as much avidity as his *Observer* or *Guardian*. He went 'home' as often as he could, this draper's son who became the greatest of English advocates, a Judge of the King's Bench Division and a Lord Justice of Appeal. Woolworths may have spread themselves, the horse sales may be less frequent, the smithy's forge may have made way for the cinema, but the natural beauties of his beloved Lakeland, which 'man did not make and cannot mar', are there still, with the vistas and subtle, changing moods. The town to this day has the same integrated, self-sufficient air as though its people are sure of their world and its values, and know just what they are about. Birkett's drapery store still dominates County Square, although Harry Birkett, Norman's cousin, who carried on the business until he retired to Kendal, sold out to the Co-operative Society. Ulverston still has a grey, mature look.

It was in Ulverston that Norman Birkett acquired his early religious leanings, his love of oratory, of natural beauty, poetry and reading. In its free, forthright and varied society, where application and individuality were the rule rather than the exception, he learned to be interested in other people, in their diverse destinies, their joys and sorrows. There, I feel, he learned his sense of personal responsibility towards all human beings.

The Ulverston he knew typified a way of life and an attitude to living which has vanished never to return; the sense of purpose, of belonging to an Empire on which the sun would never set; the seemingly endless possibilities of human endeavour; the security and warmth of family life; wholesome access to fields and mountains, lakes and rivers; the rhythm of the seasons; and the fervent, unquestioned, heart-warming religious faith which in those days permeated every detail of daily life. Ulverston fashioned Norman Birkett's character and outlook indelibly, to the benefit of his town and of his country.

Norman Birkett was born on September 6th, 1883, in the comfortable home which served until in later years they moved to Nithsdale, a handsome detached house at Kilner's Park, near by.

His father, Thomas Birkett, was a good Christian tradesman (both appellations were considered respectable then) whose acumen and industry enabled him to keep his wife Agnes and his four children (Norman was the third, Edith and Gilbert preceding him; Ellen was born later) in fair comfort. They could, for example, afford a nursemaid, now Mrs. Agnes Muncaster, who at the age of ninety-two still has memories of taking the Birkett children to pick daffodils and bluebells. She still recalls how 'Norrie' and the others came with her one sunny day to Newland Bottom, and how Norrie, then five years old, flopped out with fatigue and heat and had to be carried pick-a-back all the way to Ulverston.

Thomas Birkett, whose family had been in the area for generations, was the son of a cooper. He owned two prosperous drapery shops in Ulverston, one in New Market Street and the other—the larger one—on the corner of County Square, three stories high and employing eight assistants. He was a tall, sandy-haired man of driving energy and sound principles, who took a lively interest in local affairs. He was a pillar of the local Wesleyan community, became a councillor and eventually Chairman of the Rural District Council.

'Birkett's Stores' were a landmark for generations to come and to go. Legions of little boys went there for their school outfits.

Workmen from surrounding villages and farms bought their dungarees, mole trousers or painter's jackets there. His values were competitive, even for those times. Men's and youth's trousers 'for immediate wear' cost from 6s. 6d. to 13s. 6d. He would sell you a good tweed suit for 18s. 6d., and there were boys' tweed suits 'from 2s. 6d.'. Ladies' corsets cost from 1s. 11d. Service was prompt too; a mourning suit would be made to measure within six hours.

In later years newspapers liked to write about 'the draper's boy' who made good, and certainly Birkett himself did little to discourage this romantic legend. Make good he did, but it is nonsense to describe him as a draper's boy; applied to the Victorian period, it evokes Dickensian visions of an under-nourished lad working endlessly for a pittance and probably sleeping under the counter. The Birketts lived in good, solid, upper-middle-class comfort and materially lacked nothing.

Ulverston was at this time (as it is now) a thriving market town conveniently centred in the Lake District, the district hallowed by Wordsworth, Coleridge, Southey and Ruskin, whose works young Norman was later to imbibe and whose response to the beauties of Lakeland he was to share. For Ulverston is within easy access of Lakes Windermere, Ullswater, Grasmere and Coniston, Derwentwater, with their ever-changing moods, brooding waters and unforgettable charm. It was a cheerful town, within close proximity, too, of the sea and hills.

There were tanneries and chemical works, corn-mills, a paper factory and an iron furnace constructed in 1876. The actual parish consisted mainly of slightly undulating country, with a general rise from the Leven estuary westwards. North of the town the surface rises more rapidly, and Hoad Hill to the northeast, crowned by the monument to Sir John Barrow, after whom the town of Barrow is named. He was born in 1764 in a cottage in Dragley Beck, a hamlet south-east of Ulverston, and was secretary to the Admiralty for forty years. South-east, too, lie the site and park of Conishead Priory.

The canal, cut by Rennie of Waterloo Bridge fame, links the town with Morecambe Bay, across which on a clear day Morecambe, Lancaster and Blackpool may easily be seen. On the slope of the hill stood the spacious and lofty St. Mary's Church with its sixteenth-century tower and the Norman door saved when the original building was destroyed in a storm. A monument in it implores the passing tribute of a sigh for the soul of William Dobson, Gentleman Usher to Queen Elizabeth the First.

Ulverston was a thriving centre of Nonconformist religion. About a mile south of the town lay Swarthmoor Hall, where George Fox, founder of the Quaker movement, came in 1652 and which is to Quakers what Epworth Rectory is to the Methodists. It was also the home of one of the greatest Lancastrian women, Margaret Fell. At the age of seventeen she went there to live as the wife of Judge Fell, and it was while her husband was on circuit that George Fox, who had been preaching in barns and fields, called and converted her. Judge Fell was not a Quaker, but gave shelter to victims of persecution. When he died Margaret Fell married George Fox and herself suffered, including four years in a dungeon at Lancaster Castle, for her beliefs.

To Swarthmoor, too, came the great evangelists Wesley, who preached there in 1752, and Whitfield, two years earlier, and people flocked from the surrounding countryside to hear them. In Norman's time the town of Ulverston (pronounced Ooston) could boast the old Wesleyan Chapel built in 1814, a mission chapel opened in 1875, a Congregational Church, a Baptist House and two Friends Meeting Houses. By the time Norman Birkett was born the Industrial Revolution was nearly a century old, an increasingly literate working class had become more vocal in its demand for reform—the Corrupt Practices Bill, which cleaned up Britain's electoral system, was passed in 1883—and in North-West England the drift from the Church of England to the free churches had become an avalanche. The established church had become synonymous with privilege entrenched; in the homelier chapels there was less ritual and more fervour; a man could feel he was standing on his own feet, spiritually speaking. In Ulverston religion for most residents had to be homespun—sound and good, like the linens and checks and ginghams once sold there, but not too fancy.

The tremendous influence of the Wesleyan faith on the life and character of Norman Birkett simply cannot be over-estimated. From the earliest age his mother and father took him to the chapel at the bottom of the hill, not far from the town centre, where musicians and artists of note came at least once a year to celebrate

the choir festival. And on Sunday afternoons Norman, with his
brother Gilbert and his sisters Edith and Ellen, would go to
Sunday school.

At these classes Norman learned the Bible by heart. Even at an
early age his phenomenal memory was proved by his ability to
recite long passages. He learned to sing, and was considered a
good singer. With as much willingness as can be expected of a
young boy, he imbibed his weekly dose of religion. His father,
and a friend, Mr. Schofield, loved the Sunday school. Once Mr.
Schofield, having missed his usual transport from Ambleside,
walked the entire distance to Ulverston—about forty miles—so
that he would not be late for Sunday school the following
morning.

From the earliest age, Norman was polite and considerate of
others—but his mop of sandy hair, blue eyes and frank, carefree
approach showed an independent spirit. He had the healthy boy's
appetite for mischief. One old resident has told me that on one
occasion the Birkett family were seated on one side of the aisle and
some of Norman's friends on the other side. Norman and his
brother made paper-boats and attached string to them, and during
a particularly long prayer, while Mr. Birkett senior usually dozed
off, they 'sailed' their captive boats to and fro across to their
friends. But the Sunday came when Thomas Birkett opened his
eyes at the wrong moment. What he said and did in the privacy
of Nithsdale was never revealed, but it worked; the brothers never
offended in this way again.

The same informant remembers the Birkett brothers arriving
for a Christmas party, immaculately dressed but their faces
flushed and tense with secret purpose. They studiously ignored
jellies, cakes and sandwiches and, instead, consumed cup after cup
of tea, almost choking with laughter as each tried to race the
other. It was a competition to see who could drink the most tea.

There was a spaciousness, a security and a wholesomeness about
his early life. There was scope for boyish exuberance, and although by modern standards, Ulverston before the twentieth century could be called secluded, it was far from dull. The environment bred individualism. When Norman was born a character
known locally as the 'Skiddaw Hermit' was famous in the town.
With his tousled hair, patriarchal beard, he lived perpetually,
winter or summer, sleet or sunshine, in nothing but a shirt and a

pair of trousers. His home was a canvas tent 3,000 feet up in the Troutbeck Valley, the tent base packed well with bracken and dried twigs and heavy stones. His only companions were field mice, which he befriended.

The hermit would stride through Market Street with a painter's canvas under his arm, sometimes offering pamphlets he had written on the corruption of society and the joys of nature. The hermit could play with words: 'I can enjoy a walk through the forest, but even there the vile hand of tyranny is at work . . . there is something about true taste for the works of nature . . . which has a marvellous tendency to purify the mind from all meanness and lead the thoughts to exalted and pleasing conceptions of God.' Once he strode into a Lakeland chapel during the service, walked with measured tread to the pulpit, turned to the congregation and informed them: 'Ye are all going to Hell!', then quietly left.

The tradesmen of Ulverston knew everyone, everyone knew them, and they knew each other. They included some colourful types, such as H. W. Mackereth, the Barnum of the pharmaceutical world whose Alexandrian Senna, Reciprocity Soap (3s. 9d. for 14 pounds), Manx Shrub balsam for rheumatics, Sweet Essence of Rhubarb and Macpemul ('arrests all tendency to weakness and decay') could be found in cottage or castle. He was also an agricultural seedsman, florist, insurance agent, mineral-water dealer, oil and paint merchant, photographic chemist, and a wine and spirit merchant. He could give you a hangover or cure it.

There was Hodgson the butcher, the memory of whose home-cured bacon and pickled tongues could make the mouth water fifty years later, and the courtly Mr. Atkinson, whose bookshop was for Norman an enchanted cave; it was to Atkinson's that Thomas Birkett took his small son to buy his first book, having granted him the privilege of a shelf of his own. All his life Norman Birkett was to treasure those first volumes, such as Sir Edmund Gosse's *Father and Son*, and to the last they had pride of place in his bookcase.

There was Mrs. Bolton at the saddler's shop, who seemed for ever dressed in black and hurrying somewhere with an enormous basket, Parkers the grocers and Downwards the Chemists, with its eighteenth-century window. Downwards' ideas of advertising were as bizarre as those of his friendly rival, Mackereth. An advertisement for his Holly Cream (to make the skin smooth) shows a naked cherub and an old witch warming their hands at a brazier in the snow-covered countryside. And there was Robert Quine, whose dashing horse-drawn two-wheeled cab brought delicious bread and cakes to the home.

The Birkett family was popular, then as now, in Ulverston, and not simply because Thomas Birkett was a respected local trades-man who took a lively interest in town affairs. Norman's grand-father, Matthew Birkett, who lived at a cottage at Croft End where his golden-haired daughter kept house for him, and whose apple-trees Norman used to climb, remained a subject of lively reminiscence: 'Well, he was no daft'n, wasn't Matthy!' an old-timer would say, and nodding heads would endorse this sage judgement. A headstone in Haverthwaite commemorates his death in 1894.

The Birkett children went to the Wesleyan Day School in Ulverston, built on ground adjacent to the Wesleyan Chapel after the 1870 Education Act as an alternative to the Church of England School. It was mainly attended by the children of Non-conformist families, Congregationalists, Baptists and Wesleyans. Here Norman Birkett received a good grounding in the elements of education, showing particular aptitude for English and much aided in his studies by a phenomenal memory. Norman Birkett is remembered as a friendly, gregarious boy, often up to mischief, yet never one to criticise unkindly, to be snobbish or capable of any mean act. At Nithsdale people were always coming and going; a lay preacher on the Wesleyan circuit would be put up for the night; or a business friend would come home to dinner or a dis-cussion; the talk might be on the impossibility of transubstantia-tion, the merits and demerits of Home Rule for Ireland, the state of the local mangold crop or the ideas of Ruskin, whose family, by his express wish, preferred him to be buried in Coniston church-yard rather than Westminster Abbey.

And the outings—so many and so varied. The annual Wesleyan tea was a jolly, social affair bringing families together from all over Westmorland. There were visits to Conishead Priory, shrouded in woods; picnics on Windermere, the largest lake in England ringed by pleasant, wooded hills and with the mountains behind; Grange-over-Sands, in spring and summer ablaze with

flowers; Keswick, on the shores of Derwentwater, said by some to
be the loveliest lake of all; and Greta Hall where Southey and
Coleridge, Hazlitt, de Quincy, Wordsworth and Shelley and
Charles Lamb all stayed at one time or another. Few beauty spots
can claim association with so many poets and literary men. There
was boating and swimming and fishing and cricket and—of all
places in the world Lakeland is most rewarding for this—walking.
Rambling and roaming at will among the lakes and mountains,
woods and fields, was one of Norman's greatest joys. He did not
assay much rock-climbing, probably because of the fact that although wiry, energetic and cheerful, there were times when his
health was decidedly erratic.

Norman had inherited his mother's chest complaint. At one
time, on the doctor's advice, he slept in the garden so that his
lungs might strengthen, and in later years, to a close friend, he
talked of the grief which his 'silly chest' caused him when he
failed a medical examination.

This chest trouble, which at one time threatened to become a
permanent menace to health and activity, he seldom referred to,
accepting with confidence the verdict that it would 'clear up in
time'.

Norman had plenty of friends—James Bowe, son of the local
Inspector of Taxes, who later became a barrister with chambers in
the Middle Temple; Tim Riley; Dick Grenfell—who was a popular choice as a referee for the fights, mostly good-humoured, that
happen naturally wherever boys foregather. As for his bad chest,
he never used it as an excuse for avoiding strenuous activity or uncomfortable duty. One old resident, indeed, recalled to me that
'there was something rather challenging about his appearance
with his reddish hair and boisterous carefree manner'. On the
cricket field he would run and bat with the best of them, never
shining, perhaps, although he loved the game all his life, but
bringing to it a zest and honest enjoyment which those who
played with him still remember with pleasure.

CHAPTER II

Copperknob at School

WHEN NORMAN BIRKETT was still a lad his father was left a widower with the four young children to look after. For a time the elder daughter, Edith, kept house for the family. Then Thomas Birkett married again, to Agnes Dodding, who was living in Ulverston at the time as a companion to a local resident, Mrs. Worsdell. In due course another daughter, Mary Birkett, was born. It was a happy and united family, and Norman was a great favourite with his step-mother.

At the age of twelve Norman left the Wesleyan Day School and, like his brother Gilbert, was enrolled as a pupil of the Higher Grade School in Barrow, ten miles away.

Although in later life Norman Birkett used to say that his one regret was that he did not go to a Public School, his educational grounding at Barrow was sound, thorough and successful in its results.

The foundation stone had been laid seven years previously, and the style of architecture described as 'Victorian Classic'. The basement, euphemistically called the ground floor, contained a large science lecture hall communicating with a laboratory. There was provision for tuition in most subjects taught in a technical school—chemistry, metallurgy, pattern-making, turning, fitting, forging, engineering, plumbing and sanitary instruction. The first (i.e., ground) floor accommodated the large assembly hall and four classrooms, its 'handsome glass partitions' as the *Barrow Herald* rhapsodised, permitting 'the complete oversight of the Headmaster...' Of this facility 'Boss' Harris, the bearded, patriarchal Headmaster, made the fullest possible use; his punishment of refractory pupils was swift and salutary.

'Boss' or Jimmy Harris, regarded with a mixture of awe and veneration by generations of Barrovians, typified the practical type of plodding Victorian idealist. He thoroughly believed in the equity and usefulness of educating all classes of children—an idea certainly not considered axiomatic then—and was not put off by the difficulty of some of his material.

When Norman joined Harris was nearly forty, but looked older because of his heavy black beard, thinning hair, the thin, gold-rimmed spectacles, stiff wing collar, black bow-tie and heavy black jacket. A thick gold chain, leading to a hidden pocket watch, jangled against an ample stomach as he walked. He was a monument of dignity, even when, according to one pupil 'he went to quell a ruction with his cane whacking right and left, his words being puffed out and his squeaky voice almost becoming a roar'. Another pupil describes him as 'paunchy and peppery and set in his views'.

Harris visited the classes often, watching deficiencies and improvements with the liveliest interest and insisting on each teacher keeping a diary. If he kept a tight rein upon masters and pupils it was because he thought education came first, and that for most of his pupils it was their only chance to lift themselves above poverty and squalor. For Barrow, which at the turn of the nineteenth century had only 200 inhabitants, had grown at a fantastic rate. With the choice of Barrow as the headquarters of the Furness Railway Company, the decision to manufacture iron and steel and the exploitation of nearby mines, labourers poured in from everywhere —miners from Cornwall, navvies from Ireland, ironworkers and shipbuilders. Now it was a flourishing industrial town, with all the evils of rapid growth; squalid slums, overcrowding, improvidence, poverty and drunkenness.

It was to save his boys (there was also a girls' school attached) repeating the follies of their parents that 'Boss' Harris invited a Band of Hope lecturer to come and lecture the boys on the effect of alcohol on the human body. Essays on teetotalism were written and prizes awarded.

Pride of Empire was a constant theme. The school took a leading part in the elaborate Jubilee celebrations of 1897, and the pupils themselves subscribed their pennies to buy the bust of Queen Victoria whose reign was the longest in British history. Norman was among the boys who assembled in the central hall to watch the unveiling.

That the sun would never set upon the Empire, and that the Boers were as ill advised as they were ill mannered to hamper the extension of British imperialism in South Africa, were unarguable propositions. The School Board might skimp on some expenses, but flagpoles were always a priority. They were not always used, however, to flaunt imperialism. Norman Birkett long remembered that sad day in 1898 when the Union Jack flew at half-mast to mourn the death of Gladstone. Mr. Brooks, a brilliant mathematics master from Somerset, with a fondness for wielding the stick, turned to Norman and said: 'The greatest man in all England is dead.' Birkett had read many of Gladstone's famous speeches, and had always admired him. By a strange coincidence he was, years later, to defend the reputation of 'the greatest man in all England'.

Norman Birkett was a 'train boy'—one of the forty-six boys (there were seventeen girls, too) who came into the Higher Grade School from outside of Barrow. The daily journeys made a welcome break in routine, with their metamorphosis from the quiet market town of Ulverston to the bustle and din and dust of Barrow. The foreman porter at Ulverston station, by common consent the target for everyone's high spirits, would tremble in his shoes as the children came racing towards the station. Norman, his sandy hair waving in the breeze, his satchel banging on his back as he ran, was usually the leader of any mischief. With shouts and whistles, with ear-splitting catcalls, laughs and banging of doors, the pupils invaded the train, and the journey got more boisterous as it collected more boys at every stop.

The train, in fact, was a kind of club on wheels. Norman usually travelled with Fred Briscoe of Ulverston and Coupland from Cartmel Fel. Satterthwaite came in from Coniston, J. W. and Harry Park from a remote country rectory at Woodland, Sam Coade from Millom.

Elderly people, not without reason, were apprehensive about using this line at school times. One day however an old lady on Ulverston platform said to the boys: 'I'm fond of boys; I'll travel with you.' The railway coaches were divided into compartments which were entered by a door with a sash window. Passengers sat on a seat, facing each other. Birkett sat facing the old lady, looking the picture of innocence, but his head busy with schemes.

The boys insisted on having the sash down, to the lady's anxiety; two of the boys were leaning out, while a third tried to get a view over their heads, the lady being frantic in case the catch broke and the boys were thrown on to the track. When the train entered the Lindal Tunnel there was pandemonium in the darkness.

On emerging from the tunnel the train door was open and
Birkett was missing! The lady was in hysterics. The train then
entered Furness Abbey tunnel, and when it emerged there was
Birkett in his seat again, as quiet and innocent as though nothing
had happened at all. He had been hiding in the luggage rack
above the old lady's head.

'In those days,' one old pupil, Harry Backhouse, told me, 'the
railway coaches were lit by an oil lamp let into a hole in the roof.
They could be taken out for cleaning and they were anchored by
a short length of chain. One day Birkett removed the lamp and
put his head through the hole. To do this the boys held him up,
but he was too heavy for them, and they let go of him. Unfortunately for poor Norman, his head wouldn't go through the
hole because his ears were in the way. He was lucky not to get
them torn off by the weight of his body.' As he put it later in
mimicry of the Ulverston dialect: 'Me lugs were in t'way.'

Sometimes Norman would regale his companions with whole
chapters of the Bible, or Dickens, learned by heart and declaimed
with confidence and conviction. His brilliance in this respect is
remembered by pupils who travelled with him as 'train boys'.
The previous evening's homework had included the life of some
famous man. Birkett, naturally enough, had chosen his favourite
hero, Gladstone. As he entered the railway compartment he
showed his mates three pages of closely written foolscap which he
had compiled.

When the train started, 'Norrie' mounted on the seat, supported himself in the swaying carriage by grasping the luggage
rack with one hand and—entirely without reference to his written
notes—delivered his eulogy without hesitance, and in so eloquent
a way that the boys were literally spell-bound. There cannot be,
and cannot have been, many schoolboys who can reduce their
companions to absolute silence for fifteen minutes by reciting
their homework.

'If he could do that at the age of seventeen,' my informant com-
mented, 'no wonder he could impress juries in later life.'

Despite this serious streak and willingness to learn, Norrie or
Copperknob, to give him his other nickname, was 'a lad of the
lads'. By no means quarrelsome himself, he was not wanting in
spirit, and as fights were a frequent occurrence on the outward

and homeward journeys, he was in much demand as a referee. At one time the train lads would entice Norman into a carriage where James Phillipson was already seated, well knowing that, for no known reason, the two were at daggers drawn. Two fights ensued, but after a while both parties saw through the trick and avoided each other. One pupil, Miss Iddon, remembers how, 'Norman took it on himself to look after me as one of the girls was rather a bully.'

Birkett's quick wit and sense of humour were admirably demonstrated when he played the part of Ariel in a performance of Shakespeare's *Tempest*. The boys were assembled in the Science Lecture Theatre, where row upon row of desks mounted upwards. Unheard and unseen by boys and masters, Norman crawled along the gangway to the top row, hid himself in a corner and, when it came his turn to speak, astounded the house as his voice, so perfectly timed, so impish and sprite-like (as it should have been), appeared to come from nowhere. For a second everyone was speechless; then, as they realised what had happened, laughter broke out, followed by loud applause.

Another informant put it this way: 'He was such a *balanced* boy —such a compound of mischief and responsibility, politeness and spirit, courage and compassion, charm and simplicity. He could behave himself without being a prig. He could assert himself and yet consider the feelings of others. He had exceptional intellect and yet could enjoy the rough-and-tumble of a boy's life.' Could any boy ever wish for a better tribute?

Like most of the others, Norman would bring his lunch in a basket and eat it in the coffee house at the top of Higher Grade Hill, washing it down with coffee or ginger beer. In the evening pupils had usually about twelve minutes in which to catch the train from Barrow Station, and it was literally a race. Uttering blood-curdling whoops like Indians on the warpath, boys and girls tore down the streets at the back of Dalton Road, towards the central station. The more timorous residents sought instant refuge in doorways at the mere sound of the oncoming stampede.

On the way home Norrie would enjoy a cigarette, despite his father's strict instructions not to smoke. As the train neared Ulverston, however, he would put his head out of the window so that the wind would blow away any odour of tobacco that might linger in his shock of ginger hair. On one occasion he was nearly caught by Mr. Ramsden, Manager of the Furness Railway, and a friend of Norman's father. Mr. Ramsden was sitting in the guard's van, where the projecting window enabled the guard to see the full length of the train while seated. He just spotted the ginger-headed boy taking a few frantic puffs at the fag end before throwing it away and allowing his shock of hair to wave in the breeze. When the train drew in Mr. Ramsden hurried down the platform determined to catch and expose the culprit. But Norrie's keen eyes had spotted him in the guard's van, too, and before the train drew to a halt he had opened the carriage door, leapt down, racing away down the subway and home to safety.

His determination to smoke, however, landed him in real trouble with Mr. Birkett senior. One autumn evening, in a spirit of 'dare' he bought a pipe and some shag at 4d. an ounce. He smoked the pipe right up to the door of his home and then, being a novice, thrust the still-smoking pipe into his jacket pocket. He walked straight into the room where his father was seated, and almost immediately was startled by the question: 'Norman, have you been smoking?' There was little point in denying it, as a second later his pocket was on fire. Norman told the joke against himself, but did not reveal by what secret alchemy Mr. Birkett cured him of the habit. He was not seen to smoke again in the carriage after that.

One journey back from school was, for Norman and quite a few others, for ever memorable.

School used to finish at half-past four, and there were several blackboards full of homework which had to be copied down before the train home was caught. It was arranged that each boy should copy a different set of questions and share them out in the train or the railway waiting-room if the train wasn't in.

One day a boy called Lloyd, who had his knife into them, got all the homework questions from the other boys and then refused to give them details of the history questions. This meant that all but Lloyd would go to school without their history, and the teachers would not accept any excuses.

The boys were ablaze with consternation and anger, but Lloyd, hoping to escape their just vengeance, avoided them and got into a compartment where there was a commercial traveller, thinking that in the presence of a grown-up the others would not try any rough stuff.

This coach had a corridor, and the boys got into the next compartment and held a council of war. The plan was, when the train entered Furness Abbey Tunnel for the boys to sneak along the corridor, rough up Mister Lloyd and grab his cap and schoolbag. This they did, but were rather surprised at the fight their victim put up, and they all bore marks of the fray.

When they reached their own compartment and were out of the tunnel they found they had a neat attaché case and a smart check cap. At that moment a battered commercial traveller, minus his collar and part of his shirt, entered their compartment and gave them 'the finest hiding they'd ever had'.

It was at the Higher Grade School that Norman Birkett cultivated that love of cricket which was to last him all his life. The Athletic Club was a vigorous and uninhibited affair, with teams composed of scholars, masters and old boys. Even 'Boss' Harris, looking uncommonly like W. G. Grace with his bushy dark beard and white flannels, would wield a bat. Each year teams were picked to play in the Furness and District Junior League.

For the rest of his life, too, Norman Birkett remembered in vivid detail the masters who shaped his daytime environment; there was 'Snobber' Brooks, the mathematics master; 'Porkie' Gower the chemistry master, whose passion for sulphurated hydrogen was ascribed to the fact that it smelt worst; and Tom Hird, whose love of literature and poetry inculcated in Norman Birkett the habit of selective and attentive reading. Nor was oratory and declamation neglected, although in his time no pupil —by common consent—equalled him in this. Was it inherent aptitude, or the effect of hearing preachers of every degree of talent declaim, week in and week out, for years? Sometimes his friends quipped that he liked to 'lecture', a failing he cheerfully admitted; the fact remains that nobody tried to stop him. If vanity there was, it was mitigated by eloquence.

'Porkie' Gower was unpopular from his habit of making personal remarks and bestowing unflattering nicknames, whereas any attempt to joke in return earned the stick.

On one occasion the boys were standing in a circle while Gower was giving a lesson when Norman was seen to be daydreaming. Gower said: 'If you think you could give this lesson better than me, Birkett, you'd better take my place.'

'I wouldn't mind having a shot at it,' said Birkett, and they exchanged places. Norman questioned several of the boys in turn, and when it came to Gower he said: 'Wrong. Come out for the stick.' But it was Norman who got the stick.

For 'Snobber' Brooks Birkett had the most profound respect, despite his notorious strictness for the first six months. Brooks was one of those teachers who had a wide knowledge of life outside of his own special subject, and was always surprising the boys with stray scraps of off-beat knowledge. Once he saw Harry Backhouse wearing a rose. 'By golly!' he said, excited, 'that's a William Alan Richardson! I didn't think they grew so far North as this'—and for half an hour he delighted the boys with a talk on rose-growing. In the middle of a geography class he once talked about the Devon and Somerset Staghounds. Later in life, to Birkett's great grief, Brooks committed suicide.

'Boss' Harris had a great love of his boys, and the more difficult they were, the more, in his rough, gruff way, he tried to help them on. A toast which he composed, and which he liked to recite at staff dinners or school outings, may not be great poetry, but does epitomise truthfully his own hopes for his pupils:

> *Here's a toast for the boy who fails*
> *If he only sincerely tries*
> *Here's a cup to the health of the fallen lad*
> *Who honestly sought to rise.*
>
> *Here's a hand to the boy who faints*
> *With the mountain top so near*
> *And* Here's *to the lad who* almost *wins—*
> *If he does his best—a cheer.*
>
> *And for him who succeeds at last*
> *A jubilant three times three*
> *If he only remembers to help along*
> *Some weaker boy than he.*

Harris was a fair man who would permit himself no favourites, but he had a good opinion of Norman Birkett, and in particular commended his essays. Norman is remembered as a good singer, and although not a musician himself, appreciated good music, especially the works of Chopin, Schumann and Beethoven.

At the age of fifteen Birkett's sense of fun almost cost him his life. One fine day in July 1898 he and a group of youngsters went bathing on Ulverston sands. They stripped near the viaduct, found the tide out and waded across the channel to the sandbank on the other side. They larked about until the onrush of the incoming tide warned them of their danger. Birkett and a few of the others started to wade across, found the tide too strong for them and the sand too slippery, and got back to the sandbank just in time. They heard somebody shouting for help and thought it was Crewsdon, who was seen to be in difficulties. They pulled him out of the channel, and were then rescued by two fishermen. One boy, the son of Councillor Penny, was missing, but was assumed to have made it successfully to the beach. Later his body was recovered. At the inquest the Coroner made caustic comments on the lack of precautions against drowning at Ulverston (in one year there had been twenty-one fatalities) and remarked that all of the boys, Norman included, had had a narrow escape from death.

Pupils who were contemporary with Norman Birkett at Barrow are not unanimous on Birkett's merit as a scholar. One tells me: '... his record there was not outstanding. But some were perhaps a little envious of his later unqualified success.' Another says: 'He was a brilliant boy in those far off days and was usually on top of the form.' What is certain is that he won the George Moore Scholarship and numerous other honours. When he left the Higher Grade School in 1898 his future plans were vague. It had been tacitly assumed that he would work in his father's shop and, perhaps, take over the business one day. His other ambition was to be a lay preacher, like his father.

For the next few years he worked hard and conscientiously in the drapery shop. He was among friendly people, in his own home town. The work left him time for private reading and study. He was able to develop and indulge in his passion for preaching. He had enthusiasm, good manners, a good educational grounding, and was pleasant and easy of address. But apart from his father's quite natural desire to see his son in his family business —Gilbert was more interested in becoming a pharmaceutical chemist—Norman's erratic health was still a factor. Beneath the surface of his cheerfulness was the sorrow of knowing that he was not as robust as other boys; he could keep pace with them, physically speaking, up to a certain point, at which his energy would suddenly ebb away. It was probably partly nervous, as well as being allied to his chest complaint. Some would use the vague cliché, 'highly strung'. It would be more correct to say that he had an artistic, sensitive and kindly nature and that in his personal quest for values he thought hard and well on the problems of life and the purpose of living.

For the next few years Norman Birkett's life was an agreeable rhythm of work at the shop, preaching in Wesleyan chapels in Ulverston and district, reading at home, social work in the town, and, for physical recreation, boating, swimming, cricket and walking.

Norman's love of walking, either alone or with a chosen friend such as Dick Grenfell (who often stayed at Nithsdale when his family came on a visit), or Jim Bowe the tax-collector's son, gave him an intimate knowledge of Lakeland. Ulverston he could really claim to know by heart, every byway and alley, every street and house and farm. But he knew, equally well, the other beauty spots, Morecambe and Heysham, Grange-over-Sands, Kendal, Penrith, Keswick, Windermere, Ambleside and Appleby. In Lakeland there was always something happening that could take one out into the open air—sheep-dog trials, cross-country racing, pole-leaping contests. There were picturesque places to explore; in Kendal, 'the gateway to Lakeland', were the ruins of an ancient castle; five miles to the south lay Levens Hall, a beautiful Tudor manor house with fantastic topiary gardens set beside the River Kent.

Windermere, the ten-mile lake which could be circled by boat, had a sylvan, gentle air about it that evoked in him a longing to write poetry and express his response to natural beauty. Many elderly people living in Lakeland today possess poems written by Norman Birkett in these days of early youth, when idealism is growing rather than dying. Those poems I have read show a deep reverence, a hunger for beauty and spiritual peace, a longing for some sense of unity with the universe. It was a mixture of romanticism and mysticism, but, in terms of poetry, an exacting medium, this emotion never quite got airborne. It scanned and it rhymed, and could be described as adequate verse which sometimes approached the lyrical; the interest of these poems is what they reveal of the state of his mind at the time. There is a persistent undercurrent of melancholy in most of them, a striving to see some reason and order in human existence. By his own admission, there were times when this sense of sadness came dangerously near to self-pity, and there were times when he was too absorbed with himself and his thoughts.

He would lose himself in useful, creative activity. He learned singing. He continued his reading of Latin and French. He learned shorthand, which was later to prove a considerable asset. One day he organised a free breakfast for the poor children of the neighbourhood, cajoling and bullying everyone he met into parting with money or food, collecting sausage rolls, buns, oranges, bags of sweets. It meant days of preparation, rushing about, argument. He worked so hard at it that although he achieved his ambition of giving the children the time of their lives (many still remember it), he made himself ill in the process. Some of the poor children heard that the young man with the sandy hair and flashing blue eyes who liked giving things away was ill. They brought him little posies of flowers, the only present they could think of that cost no money; unashamedly he took their proffered gifts and wept.

His agreeable demeanour, musical voice and ease of expression made him a popular lay preacher, and he became in demand on the Wesleyan Circuit. Even in outlying districts his face at least was familiar before he ever came to preach, for he would descend on these villages distributing leaflets advertising some special line, or perhaps a sale, at his father's shop. His appearance was so distinctive that Thomas Birkett used to joke that his son was the best advertisement his shop ever had!

One local resident has described one of Norman's earliest—he thought perhaps the first—appearance as a lay preacher. He came with another young man to take the evening service at Backbarrow. This was in line with the usual custom of trying out new preachers in remote areas. 'Country Methodists,' he says, 'like country mice, are different from the town species and, it must be assumed, more tolerant to the efforts of young preachers.' Country Methodists never knew what was coming from the pulpit, while the preacher, probably a little nervous, could not be sure that some influential notability was not sitting inconspicuously in the congregation.

But Birkett's ease and fluency were remarkable, especially for a beginner. At a later service he chose as his subject 'The Passing of Time' (a sober subject, some of his elderly listeners thought, for one so young) and once again charmed the congregation with the beauty of his diction and persuasive earnestness. On their visits to outlying spots Norman and his friends lacked nothing in showmanship. The services of a Methodist horse dealer were engaged, and the young men were driven to their appointment in a horse-drawn wagonette, singing good old Methodist hymns—'Thou Hidden Love of God', 'Ye Servants of God, Your Master Proclaim', and the opening hymn which, like the other two, remained favourites of his: 'Come, we that love the Lord, and let our joys be known'. There was a fervour and a warmth and a conviction about their evangelism; two world wars, with all the misery and social upheaval implied, still lay ahead. . . .

CHAPTER III

Cambridge Days

FROM THE AGE of eighteen to twenty-four Birkett was subject to a recurrent emotional crisis. It could be called a sort of emotional exhaustion. Perhaps his draughts of religion were too copious; perhaps his reading, extensive though it was, included too much that was serious or solemn. That he sometimes felt lonely, despite his many friends and the family circle, is undeniable; and he himself admitted, to his intimate friends, that this loneliness (his own word) sprang from too great an absorption with himself and a tendency to self-analysis that made simple acts appear too complicated.

Was the heart-warming evangelism of the Wesleyan chapel a mere anodyne to kill some secret, inner pain? To some extent perhaps, but not entirely. The pain was there and his religious faith made it easier to bear, but his Methodism was not based on this need, but upon a sound and regular reading of the Bible, a genuine interest in its teachings and a love of Wesley's numerous and wonderful hymns.

Norman was not entirely satisfactory in the draper's shop. 'I'm afraid Norrie will never make a draper,' his father used to say. One day he would be on his toes, another day would be daydreaming and inattentive. The fact was that Ulverston did not give him full scope for his ardent love of life and people. He enjoyed his preaching, and he ran a literary circle where ideas were discussed and essays, short stories and poems by the members were read. Norman Birkett often felt poetic, but was not really a poet, and the poems he published in the *Ulverston Advertiser* were the subject of good-humoured banter.

But of his eloquence, his mellifluous delivery and impeccable choice of words, there is, after the bridge of sixty years or more, unanimous agreement. One woman writes:

'When I was fourteen I was a member of Neville Street Methodist Church Sunday School at Ulverston, and how well I remember Norman Birkett coming to talk to us on the

occasion of the flower service, when all the girls of the special
choir were arrayed in white with blue hair ribbons and the boys
in blue ties with their suits. The flowers we had all brought were
arrayed in a bank, beneath the pulpit; and there was Birkett,
tall and smiling, leaning on the edge of the pulpit, swaying
slightly on his hands as he talked. . . . I know he held us all in
his hand by his compelling personality. . . .'

Norman Birkett continued to go to night school, and with the
help of a local parson, who coached him, matriculated in 1907 at
the age of twenty-four. Thomas Birkett, meanwhile, decided
that the draper's shop was no place for his son, and after talking
matters over with him, sent him away to a religious training college in the Midlands. But still the old restlessness asserted itself,
and after a while Norman told his father that he did not, after all,
want to choose the ministry as a career. The two great props of
Thomas Birkett's life had been Wesleyanism and the drapery
stores he had built up with so much patient effort; but although a
strict man, he was a shrewd and kindly one, and cheerfully
accepted his son's decision.

It was on the strong advice of a friend that Norman Birkett
decided he would like to go to Cambridge. His father agreed to
finance him, and although Law, which he now decided he wished
to study, was a great gamble, it was hardly more uncertain than
his own hitherto vague plans.

Birkett studied hard at Cambridge, where he joined Emmanuel
College, obtaining a 2nd Class in the Tripos Examination of 1910
and the LL.B. in 1911. This adequate academic achievement,
however, scarcely indicates the full degree of the impact he made
there, or the impact the place made upon him. He was universally
popular with tutors and pupils. He was quite determined to succeed, even though he had come to University rather late in life.
The drift and partial confusion of his years in Ulverston were forgotten, and he found in the atmosphere of Cambridge a new
impetus.

It can be said that at Cambridge the final seal was put upon his
love of oratory. The proceedings of the Cambridge Union fascinated him. Just as some actors are nervous wrecks off the stage
and superbly confident on it, so Norman felt happiest when he
himself was the centre of interest. In ordinary concourse he could

be shy almost to the point of diffidence, but on his feet before an audience he was in complete charge of the whole situation.

Of all memories treasured by undergraduates and graduates, I suppose recollections of Cambridge Union debates are the most satisfying of all. There, on the floor, a young man must discipline his ideas, assemble his thoughts, examine his arguments and adduce his face as effectively as possible. It is an exacting test. The Cambridge Union numbers many thousands of members from all over the University—not all of them active members, of course. The building comprises splendid rooms, including smoking rooms and a first-class library. But, of course, the real centre is the debating hall, arranged something like the House of Commons in layout and seating about 500 members. The ayes and noes sit on opposite sides facing each other, while spectators can watch from the large galleries that run round the hall.

Debate procedure had something in common with Parliament, too. Debates were held at 8.15 p.m. every Tuesday in full term, with the President in the chair. Four speakers would appear on the paper, who between them would probably take up most of the time until about ten o'clock. Their speeches, two for and two against, would provide the basis for discussions that could continue until midnight.

A newcomer stood little chance of a hearing until after 11 p.m., and would even then find himself rung down if he exceeded five minutes. Sometimes he would keep trying to catch the Speaker's eye, missing out every time because several aspirants rose at once, and only one could be asked to speak.

If, however, the undergraduate made a good first speech he was given a chance to repeat his success at later debates, and could eventually find himself selected as third or fourth speaker on the paper. If he acquitted himself well in this more exacting role the President could nominate him as a candidate for the Standing Committee, of which there were six members drawn from about twenty-five candidates. From this Committee the offices of Secretary, Vice-President and President of the Cambridge Union would be filled.

The ladder of ascendancy was, as it still is, a difficult one, and Norman had not, like so many, come from a distinguished Public School. The Union was to be a tremendous fillip to his confidence.

c

As Vice-President he moved a resolution to make Mr. Theodore Roosevelt, ex-President of the United States, an honorary member of the Union Society. It was a glittering scene, and an historic one, as Norman Birkett rose from his seat between the President and Mr. Roosevelt and made a speech which could be heard distinctly in every part of the great hall, a speech whose inflexions, euphony and rhythm impelled Mr. Roosevelt to say afterwards that it was the most gracious speech he had ever heard. It was an historic occasion because, for the first time, the name of an ex-President of the United States of America would be associated with the Cambridge Union.

Mr. Roosevelt, of course, was a Harvard man, and intimate links have long existed between Cambridge and Harvard. Emmanuel College was founded in 1584 and erected by Sir Walter Mildmay, a financier, diplomat, politician and courtier. One pupil entered at Emmanuel in 1627 was John Harvard—there is a room named after him at the College. A bachelor and later Master of Emmanuel, he went to New England, U.S.A., and died there in 1638, bequeathing to the college-in-the-wilderness half his estate and 300 books. In 1639 the College was named Harvard in his honour, laying the foundations of the oldest and most distinguished of America's universities at New Town, later renamed Cambridge, in honour of the University (about seventy of that town's founders came from Cambridge University, whose memory they thus perpetuated in the New World).

After commending to his audience 'one of Harvard's most distinguished sons' and having pointed out that of the only three honorary members of the Cambridge Union, one was Oliver Wendell Holmes (author of *Autocrat of the Breakfast-table*, born at Cambridge, Massachusetts, and a Professor at Harvard University), Birkett added 'therefore, *without further word* I move this resolution'. Having said which, he did not resume his seat, but continued to speak. The house roared with laughter, and it was some time before he could resume.

Whether this note of humour was deliberate or fortuitous one cannot say. An account of the proceedings afterwards said, 'the speech of both the proposer and seconder were delivered in the best Union Society manner'.

Granta, the University magazine, was completely impartial, even to the point of cruelty, in its criticisms of speakers. Typical comments on speakers during Birkett's term are: 'Mr. W. L. Searle threatened to be theological and embarrassed the President'; 'Sergeant Buzzfuzz was embarrassed by the weight of his own arguments'; 'Mr. Moulton...spoilt some good and original remarks by the jerkiness of his delivery'; 'Mr. Burn (Emmanuel) was incoherent'; 'Mr. E. F. Tozer (St. John's) was depressing'; 'Mr. Eyton-Jones (Jesus) had a manner which was more decrepit than his matter'.

It is clear that praise in the Cambridge Union had to be earned and that members were constantly enjoined to improve their elocution and delivery. Subjects were, of course, chosen which could provide the cut and thrust of sharp debate: 'That the *Granta* should be suppressed'; 'That this House would welcome the repeal of land taxes'; 'That this House desires... to identify itself with the cause of democracy against the House of Peers'. Very much to Birkett's taste was the subject chosen on December 6th, 1910, when there was a change of officers and visitors' debate. 'That in the opinion of this House the political liberties and true prosperity of the nation can only be assured by the return of the Liberal Government to power at the next General Election.' The motion was heavily defeated.

It is instructive to consider some of the comments on Norman Birkett made in *Granta*:

'He was educated at Barrow, and in due course it was intended he should embark upon commerce, and had it not been for the early but unwarrantable intrusion into the scheme of life of what is called "the artistic temperament" he might even be adorning the Aldermanic bench of his native town.'

It then describes him as 'one of the most interesting of all the personalities to have presided over the fortunes of the Union in recent years'.

The same article praises his memory ('it is a matter for speculation whether his power of memory exceeds that of Macaulay or Datas'). He could, it declared, quote whole pages of Dickens verbatim. There is a facetious reference to his 'love poems' which 'made the fortune of a Northern newspaper' and 'brought him hundreds of offers of marriage'. This, no doubt, was a reference to his immature efforts in the *Ulverston Advertiser*.

Some of the comments made in serious vein have a prophetic

ring. 'A vivid imagination makes him a charming companion and a subtle sympathy for all sorts and conditions of men may account for him being *a Liberal in politics and a Tory in matters of taste*' (my italics). A rather good description, in the light of his later years.

There is a hint of his future success: '... his one happiness is to lay down propositions and proceed to make them "perfectly clear".' His habit of singing in his chambers, accompanying himself on the harp and his love of cricket come in for mention. One line is strangely prophetic: '*His friends have no doubt at all that the Bar will bring him success.*' It was the unanimous hope of all students at Emmanuel that Norman Birkett should be 'called up to public charges and employments of dignity and power'.

The picture of Norman Birkett might be a little cloying if he had no weaknesses. He had none that really outweighed his virtues, but that he was now possessed of a driving ambition and a pride in success that made him inclined to lay down the law and to be dogmatic, is beyond question. Where does self-confidence end and vanity begin—who can say? It is, I think, rather revealing that he suggested to the Chairman of the Governing Body of his old school that the pupils should be given a half-day's holiday 'in honour of his attainment of the Presidency'. However, the scholars were grateful to the old boy, while his achievement was an understandable source of pride to a school comparatively new.

During his studies at Emmanuel Birkett gained a College Prize for two years in succession, on one occasion for an essay on Boswell. The Emmanuel College Debating Society also honoured him by adding his portrait to those of distinguished Emmanuel men adorning the walls of the debating chamber.

The years at Cambridge went agreeably by. There was boating on the Cam, with the gentle plashing of oars and the musical squeak of rowlocks; hymn-singing sessions in his chambers; browsing in Cambridge bookshops; monster breakfasts where everyone ate and talked to their fill; the solemnity and excitement of Degree Days in the Senate House. The mellow stone buildings, the cloisters and courtyards and gardens, so spacious and colourful, the feeling of stability, tradition and order combined to make a perfect environment for the continued development of Birkett's talents.

Like all undergraduates, Birkett made many friends, some of them, like Laurence Cadbury, to be lifelong friends. He was a frequent visitor to the home of the Westons. Weston was one of the few married undergraduates and a member of the County Lay Preachers Association; the Westons kept open house where Birkett and his friends would stay for hours, exchanging ideas, drinking coffee and eating 'deadlies', as the fancy cakes from the local confectioner were called.

Two other close friends were Harold Marley, who later became a Church of England clergyman, and 'Mallaprop'—W. W. Malleson, Vice-President of Emmanuel Debating Society, of whom it was said that he lost every minute book belonging to the societies he helped to run, and recorded proceedings on scraps of paper with which he would absent-mindedly light his pipe! He liked to sing songs of his own composition, but Birkett remembered him mainly for a daring escapade they both shared. It was arranged, in retaliation for a practical joke played on Emmanuel by Caius (they had advertised a guest speaker as Miss Carrie Nation, who proved to be a Rugger Blue in disguise), that Malleson should appear at a later debate between the two colleges disguised as a well-known Member of Parliament.

The hoax succeeded beyond everybody's wildest dreams. Malleson was a prominent member of the Amateur Dramatic Society, and slipped off to London to see Willie Clarkson, the brilliant but eccentric wigmaker who was also an expert of make-up. After four hours with Clarkson, Malleson looked every inch the sixty-year-old M.P., and as such was greeted officially, wined and dined by the college and made a speech which was well received. The Press were there, to give the hoax extra impact. The next day the whole nation was laughing at the credulity not only of the masters at Cambridge but also the pupils, who had failed to recognise, beneath his disguise, an undergraduate they had seen every day. At first there were some angry murmurs, but soon everyone surrendered themselves to the joy of a thoroughly good laugh. Even the genuine Mr. Haddock, M.P., cheerfully forgave the impersonation.

Sometimes Birkett and Weston would go and preach at Wesleyan chapels in the Cambridge area.

Birkett's Wesleyan evangelism, however, had to compete with other rival and often militant beliefs. The Master of Emmanuel, William Chawner, was believed to be an atheist. Monseigneur Robert Hugh Benson tried hard to proselytise students to Roman

Catholicism. Marley espoused the Church of England. Had he not been brought up as a Methodist, Birkett would probably have become a Quaker. He had read and studied the teachings of George Fox, and had much sympathy with Quaker ideas.

It was, therefore, a happy compromise that, on leaving Emmanuel, he went to work for George Cadbury junior, as his political secretary, while continuing to study for the Bar.

CHAPTER IV

Breakthrough into Law

THE NEXT FEW years were spent between politics and studying for the Bar. For a while Norman Birkett returned to Ulverston, but after the varied social and intellectual life of Cambridge, and more particularly the companionship, he felt again lonely and dissatisfied. Although he remained a Methodist, and continued his lay preaching, he studied other religions and beliefs, hoping to find 'unity in diversity, order in seeming chaos'. Edwin Arnold's *Light of Asia*, with its beautiful story of Gautama forsaking the luxury and power of his throne to search for truth, impressed him deeply. And the words of Paul, whom he read in the Greek, gave him new comfort: 'For all things are yours, whether Paul, Apollos, or Cephos, or the world, or life, or death, or things present, or things to come; all are yours.'

The cure for loneliness, he decided, could come only from within, not from anything external. From the Greek Testament, again, he studied until he knew by heart the sixth chapter of Matthew. The words 'Lay not up for yourselves treasure upon earth' he likened to the teachings of Gautama. At one time he had been very absorbed in himself and his private sorrows, literally weeping at poetry that seemed to echo his own mood. Then, sitting one day by the beautiful Lake Windermere, very low in spirits, he thought hard, as he afterwards told a friend, on how he could escape the trammels of self-pity and feel master of his fate. What happened at that lakeside? It was an almost mystical experience. He had been watching the sunset, with its changing pattern of amethyst and crimson, gold and green, reflected in the serene stretches of the water and flecking with light the foliage of the woods in the lower reaches. He has said that, in that moment of peace and wonder, his fears and griefs and doubts dropped away. From that moment he never looked back.

While he was waiting to be called to the Bar, Norman Birkett worked as private secretary—some described him as political secretary—to George Cadbury junior. He had become friends with Mr. Laurence Cadbury at Cambridge, and had long been sympathetic to Quaker ideas and ideals. The Cadbury family had long distinguished itself by its sound flair for commerce and its vigorous social conscience, and working conditions at Bourneville were the finest in the country. Bourneville was, indeed, a sort of Welfare State in miniature, with provisions and safeguards for the welfare and happiness of their employees far in advance of the times. In the very hey-day of Victorianism when an unbridgeable gulf separated workmen and employers, the Cadbury Brothers often joined their employees at cricket, provided sports equipment and even bought one of the new-fangled 'boneshakers' for the boys.

Richard and George Cadbury, who had joined the firm in 1850 and 1856 respectively, had continued this tradition, building houses near the works for certain employees. George Cadbury (father of George Cadbury junior, for whom Norman Birkett came to work) was an energetic opponent of slumdom, and later demonstrated how the working conditions of the workers could be improved, by acquiring, in 1893, 120 acres near the factory and building houses in harmony with the Garden City Movement, which he had pioneered. In 1900 he handed over both land and houses to the Bourneville Village Trust, with the proviso that funds and revenues must be used for the extension of the estate and the promotion of housing reform.

The Cadburys had been well ahead of their time in founding cricket and football clubs in the eighties and, at the turn of the century, founding a Men's Pension Fund, a Woman's Pension Fund and holidays with pay.

Norman Birkett was employed by George Cadbury junior personally, and not by the firm, and he played no part in the firm's business activities. At about the time he was engaged, George Cadbury junior was anxious to become a member of the Birmingham City Council. He was one of the foremost authorities in this country on town planning; so young Birkett helped his employer through a fiercely fought campaign and had the satisfaction of seeing his name at the head of the poll for the Selly Oak ward. George Cadbury was also associated with Fircroft Working Men's College, and it was part of his duty to call there every day. Birkett also went to the Junior Adult School, Cregoe Street, where George Cadbury often spoke.

Mr. Laurence Cadbury has described how Birkett's job with them literally 'started off with a bang'. On his first day he called for him in his car to take him to play tennis. At this time the horseless carriage was still partly a novelty and the car industry far from streamlined. Chassis and body were often obtained from different firms, and in this case only the chassis had been delivered. Mr. Cadbury invited the new member of the staff to share his perch on a soap-box fixed to the chassis. All went well until the somewhat ramshackle vehicle began to go down Griffin's Hill. The wind clawed up the bonnet, which rose in the air, whirled dangerously over their heads and fell astern into the road with a resounding clang. An old man rushed up to the pair to inform them, somewhat unnecessarily, that they had 'dropped something'.

Norman Birkett enjoyed canvassing in the Liberal cause, and would often travel long distances under difficulty to plead its cause with a mere handful of people. One correspondent, Mr. W. Hardin Osborne, remembers how Birkett and Osborne senior were canvassing and distributing election literature, on behalf of the Liberal candidate Joseph Bliss, for what was then the North Lonsdale Parliamentary Division. The journey was made by horse and trap to Satterthwaite, from whence the pair journeyed on foot to remote villages and farms.

On a very lonely road they stopped to talk to a Council man who was cracking stones. The man said, 'How'd on a bit', and called to a man who was working in the field, 'Hey! There's someone here who can tell thee some sense aboot t'election.' Soon they were joined by four more locals, and for half an hour Norman Birkett answered their questions.

Parallel with his work for George Cadbury junior, Norman Birkett continued his studies, eating the requisite number of dinners each term in the Inner Temple, one of the four Inns of Court—those unique institutions embodying the features of a club, a school, a home, office employers' association and trade union. The lanky, earnest young man loved these dinners, with their pleasant traditional atmosphere, held in the great hall, with its gleaming long tables and tremendous hammer-beam roof, its fine bay window decorated with heraldic glass and, on the panelling round the hall, the coats of arms of treasurers and readers.

The point of the dinners is not purely social, pleasant though they are. This intimate, personal contact with barristers and students is a vital part of legal education; experiences can be exchanged and compared, questions can be asked and answered in an atmosphere of equality and informality, although there is, of course, an underlying discipline such as any stable institution must have. The students wore sleeveless gowns of black stuff and formal dress. Some faces were familiar from University; others, whose friendship he gained during these meetings, were to play a leading part in his life in years to come.

His call to the Bar came in 1913, at the age of thirty; a little later in life than average, although some are called to the Bar at the age of sixty or even later. Not all who are called intend to follow law as a profession. Many find this qualification a useful adjunct in business, politics or journalism.

In Norman Birkett's case, however, his ambition was clear cut; to become a lawyer. His next step was to join the Midland Circuit, which included the Assize towns of Aylesbury, Bedford, Northampton, Peterborough, Leicester, Oakham, Lincoln, Derby, Nottingham, Warwick and Birmingham—in that order. The custom of a judge 'riding the circuit' goes back to the days of Edward I, when it happened only three times a year, with much hardship to prisoners, who were often kept, innocent or not, in noisome dungeons awaiting trial. Some might have to wait for nearly a year and, as Howard pointed out in his exposure of prison conditions, might be so worn down in health by their imprisonment that they did not live to be tried at all.

Birkett first went to work with J. G. Hurst, one of the leading juniors on the Midland Circuit, in his chambers in Temple Row, Birmingham, and a few months later, on November 27th, 1913, himself became a member of the Midland Circuit. Many can remember him to this day, and Arthur Ward, K.C., later Recorder of Coventry, has described in his book *Stuff and Silk* the memorable day when Norman Birkett went with Hurst to the Assize Court in Birmingham. In the robing-room Hurst, in an easy, carefree way, said to the others: 'You fellows, I want you to meet a man who is to be a member of our circuit; he's come into my chambers—Norman Birkett.'

Mr. Ward's first impression of Birkett is interesting as a sidelight on his character:

'. . . he was nervous, and in using the *was* I do not mean at the commencement of his career only—I mean always at the Bar, a nervousness possessed by all artists of sensitive fibre. I have seen him discard his coat and waistcoat in the robing-room after the hearing of a case, and his shirt has been wet from the effects of nervous strain and tension.'

Such nervousness, as all who met him recognised, was not to be equated with weakness; it was the tension of a young man conscientous and earnest in his attitude to his calling, a man who demanded much of himself and desired constantly to improve. The impression he gave others at the time was of a shy, almost self-effacing young man; and yet there was a decision and clarity to his thinking.

His humility was the greatest possible asset to him; a scintillating speaker himself in the Bar Mess, he was also a good and attentive listener with a ready appreciation of and respect for other people's talents.

For a while he helped Hurst in his chambers and observed the ritual and routine of an Assize Court. Each Circuit has four main officials. The Clerk of the Assize has an overall responsibility for the smooth running of the machinery of the law, seeing that indictments are drawn up, summoning the jurors and basing his instructions to them on when to attend on his own shrewd judgement of how long the different cases are likely to take. During trials he reads the indictment to the prisoner, records his plea in the court records and on the indictment itself, informs the prisoner that he is entitled to challenge any juror and gives the prisoner into the jury's charge. It is the Clerk of Assize who asks the momentous question, 'Members of the jury, are you agreed upon your verdict?' and again, 'How say you, do you find the prisoner Guilty or Not Guilty?'

At this time—and, indeed, until 1946—there was a new Clerk of Assize appointed by Mr. Justice Avory known in some quarters as 'the hanging judge'. George Pleydell Bancroft was a remarkable character. His parents were famous on the Victorian stage and in society, and via Eton and Oxford he had entered the Diplomatic Service, learned acting and playwriting while up at Oxford, and later turned to law. There was about Bancroft a presence, dignity and kindly confidence which put everyone (including Norman Birkett) completely at ease; everyone, that is, except prisoners whose consciences were uneasy, but even to them he represented the utter impartiality of the law. In later years Norman Birkett gladly acknowledged his debt to Bancroft, whose friendship was so valuable at the outset of his legal career.

It was Bancroft who gave Norman Birkett one of his first briefs. He had to nominate counsel for the defence under the Poor Prisoners' Defence Act. He met Birkett for the first time in the Bar Mess and engaged him for this important but poorly paid defence 'solely upon the strength of his conversational powers'. From Bancroft, who even as a boy had mixed habitually with famous writers, dramatists and actors, and who was himself an actor and dramatist, this was a compliment indeed. As Bancroft says, in his own account of it:

> 'It was his first Poor Prisoners' Defence, and a murder, mind you. A most ingenious and able defence it was. Mr. Justice Shearman was the judge, and in the opening sentences of his summing up to the jury paid the highest compliment I have ever heard paid to a young counsel. I think I am right in saying that it was the flying start in his successful race.'

The City of Birmingham has always nurtured giants of advocacy, and in the Bar Mess Norman Birkett was to meet some of the greatest names in law. Apart from John Hurst, whose chambers he shared, there were Marston C. Buzzard K.C. ('The Bird'), the leader in 1913, Hugo Young, Henry Maddocks, K.C., and H. H. Joy, K.C., oddly named for all his ability, as he had a most lugubrious manner.

The Bar Mess, with its mellow and friendly atmosphere, appealed greatly to Norman Birkett. It was the ideal place to learn from others about their experiences at the Bar, and to assimilate the many traditions and usages of the profession. Dinners were, of course, characterised by a certain formality. The chair at the head of the table would be occupied by the senior leader or junior present, with the next in seniority on his right. (Sometimes, when there was a guest, perhaps a Judge or visitor from another circuit, he had this place of honour on the right of the chair.)

The member at the head of the table is referred to as 'Mr. Leader' and not by name, while the junior at the far end of the table is called 'Mr. Recorder'. One of Mr. Recorder's important duties was to announce in clear tones: 'Mr. Leader, twenty minutes have elapsed since grace', another way of saying 'everybody is dying for a smoke'.

A character Norman Birkett was to remember all his life—and one known throughout the circuit—was the incomparable, unflappable, infallible John Morris, the circuit butler. He would take newcomers aside and give them useful tips on etiquette and practice at the Bar, and many a junior with an indiscretion on the tip of his tongue while in conversation with a Judge has caught Mr. Morris's warning eye in the nick of time.

Mr. Birkett's first brief, which he kept ever afterwards as a souvenir, was for £1 3s. 6d. Although in the course of his seven years in Birmingham he was to act as junior in some dramatic cases, a great deal of the work was routine. In the earliest days of his practice John Stratford Dugdale was the Recorder of the city, and he had to appear in a case in which he was instructed by the Town Clerk. It dealt with complex food regulations which the Recorder found it difficult to follow; the abstruse legal argument was brought to an end by the Recorder's finding as a fact that 'this meat was substantially a green ham'.

Norman Birkett's impressive appearance—the penetrating blue eyes, sandy, almost reddish hair, and lanky, almost frail aspect, were of obvious advantage to him. He always cheerfully admitted it. 'When I was a lad,' he once declared, 'I worried and was absolutely ashamed because of the colour of my hair. I have been in court and heard people ask, "Who is the man with the red hair?" Well, I have found that it has added to my success, for work has come my way because I have red hair.'

Norman Birkett's reputation, as Pleydell Bancroft noticed even at the commencement of his legal career, grew apace.

According to one member of the Midland Circuit, Birkett's reputation 'had been made' within one year of joining it, and he had acquired a large practice. Such a degree of success, localised though it was, in so short a time was certainly unusual.

During the First World War Norman Birkett was found medically unfit for military service. He continued with his legal practice, combining it with work for Belgian refugees.

During the war years the strain of work was very heavy, and in order to learn as much as he could, Norman Birkett tackled an immense variety of cases, some trivial, others more spectacular.

For the rest of his life Norman Birkett carried a souvenir that came his way as a result of one wartime case. Of all the leaders on the Midland Circuit, Henry Maddocks, K.C., was one of the most amiable, courteous and popular. While working on a case at Leicester Assizes he received the tragic news of his son's death at the front.

By an irony of coincidence, Henry Maddocks later found himself asked to defend his son's batman, who had got into trouble with the police and appeared at Birmingham Assizes. But it is never good for a barrister to be personally involved in or identified with the person in a case, for the same reason that a doctor should not treat his wife. In this instance, seeing the batman would inevitably remind him of his own tragic loss, and as the day neared when he would have to appear, he confessed frankly that he could not undertake it.

He unburdened himself to Norman Birkett, explaining that the young man was poor, that there was no fee attached to the case, but that he felt obliged to help all he could, as his son, were he alive, would certainly have done. Birkett immediately understood, undertook the case, conducted his defence with distinction and secured the man's acquittal. As a gesture of gratitude (the two barristers were the firmest of friends), Henry Maddocks gave Norman Birkett a gold pencil case.

One advantage Birkett did appreciate, of his attachment to the Midland Circuit, was the beauty and diversity of the scenery. His work took him to Aylesbury, the fine old market town in the centre of the Chilterns; Bedford, on the River Ouse, with its beautiful gardens on the site of an old castle, and its associations with one of Birkett's literary heroes, Bunyan, who was born at Elstow, a mile outside the town; Northampton, where the Judges' Lodgings were once so inadequate that their lordships—presumably without their wigs and gowns—all tucked into the same four-poster bed together. The old Roman city of Leicester, now a thriving industrial centre, only a stone's throw from the beautiful Charnwood Forest and the Vale of Belvoir; Lincoln, with its superb cathedral, and where the Assize Courts were held in the castle; Warwick, the ancient town on the River Avon, with its timbered buildings, castle and Collegiate Church. There was often much fatigue involved in travelling from town to town, but there were compensations in the sights and scenery. Both in Birmingham and in the towns he visited, Birkett often found time for preaching in Methodist chapels.

Despite all this work, he found time during the war to help his friend and colleague in chambers, Donald Finnemore (now Mr. Justice Finnemore) with the 1st 'A' Birmingham Company of the Boys' Brigade—a company which Finnemore himself formed in 1913. He frequently presided at its displays and meetings, and often gave talks on a variety of subjects, the pleasure of which is still remembered. He preached frequently at the People's Chapel in Great King Street, Birmingham.

Another activity was his Secretaryship of the Birmingham Liberal Association, and his unsuccessful contesting of the Kings Norton Division as a Liberal in 1918 meant more meetings, speech-making, travelling and late hours. Some time after this he showed signs of severe nervous exhaustion; the cause was overwork, and his medical advisers insisted on him dropping work altogether and taking a protracted rest in Ulverston. It was hard news, just at the point where his practice was prospering so well. His long absence could have meant loss of contacts and continuity. But so high was his prestige at the Bar that, on return, he picked up the strings again easily.

CHAPTER V

The Green Bicycle Case

IN 1920—NORMAN BIRKETT was now nearing forty years of age, and although well known and respected in the Midland Circuit was barely known outside of it—came the chance for which he had worked and waited. The Green Bicycle Case was a *cause célèbre*. Its elements of mystery and drama (plus a touch of the macabre worthy of Edgar Allan Poe at his best or worst) focused the country's attention on the trial of Ronald Light for the murder of Bella Wright on the evening of July 5th, 1919, almost a year earlier.

The Attorney-General, Sir Gordon Hewart (later Lord Hewart, Lord Chief Justice) led for the Crown. Briefed with him were Henry Maddocks, K.C., and Mr. Norman Birkett and Mr. Norman Winning as juniors. They were a formidable team, yet they were no match for the restless, imaginative and temperamental advocate, Sir Edward Marshall Hall, assisted by Mr. Wightman Powers. The trial, before Mr. Justice Horridge, at Leicester Castle, was one of Hall's most spectacular successes. Barristers may not advertise, but it is clearly to their advantage to be frequently in the public eye, to be associated with important cases and, of course, to achieve outstanding successes. If Norman Birkett was not, in this instance, on the winning side, the case did bring him nation-wide publicity and of seeing the great Marshall Hall at work, to watch him tear to shreds the prosecution's case, which, in the early stages of the trial, had seemed unanswerable. The arm of coincidence is long; in this instance, a man charged with murder and faced with an appalling array of circumstantial evidence said in effect: 'I know things look as though I did it; I admit I behaved as though I might have done it; but I *didn't* do it—I was simply frightened that people would say I did, so I told lies and covered up my tracks.' That argument was to nullify the efforts of Birkett and his leaders to secure the conviction of Ronald Light for murder. A quarter of a century later, Norman Birkett, acting this time for the defence, was to save a man's life by this self-same argument.

In a country lane near Little Stretton, Leicestershire, at about half-past nine on the night of July 5th, 1919, a farmer named Cowell found the dead body of a young woman lying near her overturned bicycle. He lifted the body to the grass-bank beside the road, and raced off to find P.C. Hall, the local constable, who in turn got in touch with a Dr. Williams. It was dark when the doctor arrived on the scene, and not unnaturally he concluded that her death was due to accident from falling off her bicycle and striking a stone.

Next day, however, P.C. Hall did some detailed checking of the spot where the body was found and discovered, a few yards away, a bullet partly embedded in the road. He revisited the body, where closer examination revealed a bullet wound about an inch below the left eye and an exit hole near the cranium hitherto concealed by her dense mass of hair.

Bella Wright, aged twenty-one and living with her parents at Stoughton, had been working in St. Mary's Rubber Mills in Leicester, on night shift. She had returned from work at 11 p.m. on Friday, July 4th, 1919, and the following day left her home at half-past six in the evening to cycle to her uncle, a road-man called Mr. Measures, who lived in a cottage in the tiny hamlet of Gaulby.

On the way there she was overtaken and spoken to by a young man on a green bicycle, who accompanied her all the way to the cottage and waited outside for her. Bella Wright told her uncle that the man was a 'perfect stranger' to her. She hung around inside the cottage, hoping that he would be gone by the time she left, but when her uncle and his son-in-law Mr. Evans came to the door to say goodbye to her the stranger was still there. According to them, he said: 'Bella, you *have* been a long time. I thought you had gone the other way.'

They cycled away together, and within three-quarters of an hour Bella lay murdered in the middle of the lonely Gartree Road, an odd route for her to take, as the alternative, the Upper Road, was more direct. The time of her death could be established because of one horrible detail. Shot through the head, she naturally bled profusely. Strange bloody tracks, such as a bird might leave, led from her body to a nearby gate, itself bloodied by similar marks. In the field was found a dead bird, said to be a raven, but more likely a carrion crow. Its claws were blood-stained, and a dissection revealed the nauseating fact that it was gorged with

D

human blood. The ornithologists may argue as they will; there were twelve tracks from the corpse to the gate, six each way. It must have taken the bird at least five minutes to make its sinister journeyings; Bella Wright had, therefore, been dead at least five minutes before Mr. Cowell discovered her.

Who was the stranger on the green bicycle? An hour before Bella had left her home, two small girls were approached on a road nearby by a stranger riding a green bicycle, and being frightened by his manner, they made off on their bicycles back to Leicester.

Police appeals to the public, with an offer of a reward, produced no evidence, despite a detailed description of the man obtained from Mr. Measures and Mr. Evans, from the two frightened girls and two other witnesses who had seen Bella Wright and the stranger riding together towards Gaulby.

The sensation died down. The Green Bicycle Case was forgotten—until, by an odd coincidence, on February 23rd, 1920, a canal boatman, delivering a load of coal to the very factory where the murdered woman had once worked, noticed that the frame of a bicycle had been fished up by his tow-rope; for a few seconds he saw it, before it slipped off and sank, but tempted by the rewards being offered by newspapers for information of the Green Bicycle Murder, he returned, dragged the spot and recovered the cycle frame. It was a B.S.A. model (tallying with the police description) and was enamelled green.

The cycle was not a usual model, but had peculiarities making it easier to track down the dealers to whom such a model would have been supplied. In any case, although the owner had filed away the identification mark, he had missed the number 103,648 on the pillar of the handle-bar bracket.

Further dragging produced a revolver holster containing bullets of the type that had killed Bella Wright and a bicycle wheel.

The bicycle had been sold to a Mr. Ronald Light, a thirty-four-year-old draughtsman who had worked for a railway company, and then fought in France, first as an officer with the Sappers. He gave up his commission to become a gunner with the Honourable Artillery Company, was demobilised in February 1919 and went to live with his mother in Leicester. After Bella Wright's death he had left home to work as a mathematics master in a school at Leicester.

Seen by the police, Light denied ever having had a green bicycle. He repudiated knowing Bella Wright. He declared he had not been near the spot of the murder. Later he admitted to having owned a green bicycle, but declared he had sold it years ago—a demonstrable lie, as he had had the bicycle repaired locally just before the murder. He admitted that he had possessed a revolver in his Service days, and it was established that he had certainly possessed a holster similar to that fished from the canal.

Light was identified as the man seen with Bella Wright in Gaulby. It was found that, after that tragic night when she was found murdered, he had put the green bicycle in a box-room and never rode it again. Light was arrested and charged with murder. . . .

The case for the prosecution, outlined by Sir Gordon Hewart, looked black indeed. There was no question of identity; Mr. Measures, Mr. Evans, the two young girls who were scared of the stranger on the green bicycle, a cycle dealer who repaired the machine and handed it over to a man on the day of the murder—all of them, without hesitation, had picked out Light at identification parades. Why did Light say, '*Bella*, I thought you had gone the other way'—didn't this imply that he knew her? He was the last person to be seen with her alive. He had lied and lied and lied. He had deceived his mother, the family servant, the police.

Mary Elizabeth Webb, who lived with the prisoner and his mother, remembered Ronald Light bringing back the bicycle from the repairers on the night of July 5th, 1919. He went out with it, and although there was to be 'a particular supper' at eight o'clock, he did not return until ten o'clock that night.

Here is a section of the examination-in-chief, planned by Henry Maddocks and Norman Birkett in discussions that stretched far into the night:

Mr. Maddocks: 'Did he look tired?'

Witness: 'He looked tired and dusty, sir.'

'Did you say anything to him about being late?'—'I said to him, "Why are you so late?" and he replied that his bicycle had broken down again and he had had to walk.'

'Did he tell you where the bicycle had broken down?'—'No. He did not tell me anything about the bicycle or where it had broken down, or where he had been.'

'When he got in what did he do?'—'He had his supper and
went to bed.'

'Now, what became of the bicycle?'—'It remained in the back
kitchen for some days, then he took it up into the box-room.'

'Can you tell us when the bicycle was brought down from the
box-room?'—'As well as I remember it was brought down just
before Christmas.'

His Lordship: 'Was it brought down by Mr. Ronald?'

Witness: 'By Mr. Ronald.'

Mr. Maddocks: 'What did he do with it?'—'He took it out.'

His Lordship: 'What time of the day was it?'—'It was in the
evening.'

Mr. Maddocks: 'Did he bring it back or not?'—'No, sir.'

'Did you ask him about the bicycle afterwards?'—'No, I did
not ask him, but he told me some time afterwards that he had
sold it.'

The prosecution team, by a mere glance at the dour, tense jury,
could assume things were going their way. But Marshall Hall
soon tore the prosecution to pieces. Those two young girls of
twelve and fourteen, who had been accosted by the young man
on a bicycle—could they be relied upon to remember *nearly a
year afterwards* on what particular day that had happened? They
had 'talked the matter over and quite made up their minds that
they met this man on July 5th'. As for Light saying: 'Bella',
which would have implied his previous acquaintance with Bella
Wright, he had, Marshall Hall elicited, said *'Hello'*—a very
different matter.

It fell to Norman Birkett, for the prosecution, to question
Muriel Nunney, a fourteen-year-old schoolgirl, living in Leicester,
who was cycling with her friend when they were approached by
a man on a green bicycle. Birkett made the mistake of asking her
whether 'on July 5th' she was cycling with her friend. In a flash
Sir Edward was on his feet requesting learned counsel not to lead
the witness. He did not propose, he revealed, to cross-examine on
the question of identity or the ownership of the bicycle, but proposed to question these girls. In other words, defence would not
dispute Light's ownership of the bicycle, but objected to dates
being suggested to the girls.

Mr. Justice Horridge intervened to address the jury, asking
them to remember that Mr. Birkett had suggested a date to the

girl, and that he must see a date was not mentioned to the next witness. Miss Nunney declared that the man she and her friend had seen that day she had later identified easily and instantly at an identity parade of twelve men. She confirmed the Attorney-General's statement that the man had spoken to them.

In complete silence Norman Birkett looked from the girl towards Ronald Light, and back again before he asked Miss Nunney: 'Do you see that man in court?'

Instantly she pointed to Light and with emphasis said: 'There, sir.'

Within seconds Birkett was to see his point invalidated.

Marshall Hall: 'Did you hear about what was called the Green Bicycle Case?'—'Yes, sir.'

'And I think you saw the photographs?'—'Yes, sir.'

'You knew about this poor girl being found dead in the road?' —'Yes, sir.'

'You read it in the papers, I suppose?'—'Yes, sir.'

'You were asked whether you had seen this particular man on July 5th?'—'Yes.'

'They (the Police) gave you a date?'—'Yes, sir.'

Sir Edward had made his points. Further questioning elicited that although the two girls claimed on July 5th they met this man with the green bicycle, no statements were taken from them until March 9th, 1920, over eight months after the event. After all that time, can one be sure of the particular day on which such a thing happened?

It was in his cross-examination of the doctor and the gunsmith that Marshall Hall began to offset the damnatory evidence adduced by the Crown. The doctor's contention that Bella Wright had been shot from a distance of six or seven feet was belied by the nearness of the bullet when it was found; at such close range the velocity of the bullet would have carried it much farther away. The doctor answered that it could have pierced her head, embedded itself in the soil, ricocheted from a stone and fallen near by. 'That theory,' Hall snapped, 'is tenable only on the supposition that the woman was lying on the ground, or anyway that her head was between the revolver and the ground.'

Norman Birkett listened, fascinated, as Marshall Hall sowed the seeds of further doubts in the jury's mind. Questions to the gunsmith established that the bullet found near the dead woman was of a type which had been made in *thousands of millions* ever since the Boer War. Its similarity, therefore, with bullets found in Light's holster proved nothing; it could have come from his holster—or from hundreds of thousands of other holsters still in existence.

Birkett noted, too, how much 'homework' Marshall Hall had done on the subject of firearms before the case was heard. A mark on the bullet, it seemed, showed that it had been fired from a rifled barrel, which would increase the velocity. Fired from a service revolver, it would have a range of more than a thousand yards. It could have been fired from a rifle as well as a revolver. 'Supposing,' he asked, 'the shot to have been fired some distance away, and that in its flight it came in contact with a fence, tree or something else, and then struck someone on the roadway, would you expect to find that bullet within a few feet of where the person was shot?'

'Yes,' came the reply, 'it is possible.'

Finally, Marshall Hall made the point that, at short range, such a weapon could have blown the woman's head nearly off.

Ronald Light, in the box, gave an admirable impression of being straightforward and at ease. He admitted to having possessed a Webley-Scott revolver in France, and in 1918, passing through a casualty clearing station before being sent to England as a stretcher case (with shell-shock), his revolver being taken away from him with all his other kit. The holster was his. On that fatal Saturday he had collected his bicycle from the repairers and had tea at home, leaving at half-past five.

He had met Bella Wright bending over her bicycle, and she had asked to borrow a spanner, which he could not supply. They had then cycled together to Gaulby. He had waited for her there, and together they rode back as far as the junction of the upper and lower roads, leaving her there about ten minutes after leaving Gaulby. He saw the police notice, was frightened by it and threw the bicycle away.

Despite the care which Maddocks and Birkett gave to their task, they could do little to shake Marshall Hall's defence. That he had got rid of the bicycle having first filed off the identification number, told lies about it and refused to come forward when the police advertised his description was suspicious. But Light told the Judge: 'I did not make up my mind deliberately not to come forward. I was so astounded and frightened at this unexpected thing that I kept on hesitating, and in the end I drifted into doing nothing at all. I had drifted into the policy of concealment, and I had to go on with it.'

Marshall Hall's speech for the defence was one of the finest in his career. He pointed to the absence of motive; the allegation that Light had addressed the dead woman as 'Bella' hardly tallied with her statement to her uncle (at the cottage) that the man waiting outside was 'a perfect stranger' to her. There was no attempt at molestation, no robbery. His eloquence was abruptly halted by the discovery that a photographer in court was about to take a picture. He was brought before the Judge and rebuked, while Hall fretted and fumed at the lost continuity of argument.

He need not have done. After a balanced summing up by the Judge, the jury took three hours to reach its verdict of—Not Guilty. The Green Bicycle Case was not a triumph for Birkett, but by making his name more widely known, it was the open sesame to future triumphs.

CHAPTER VI

Taking the Plunge

NORMAN BIRKETT'S SEVEN years in Birmingham were years of unremitting hard work, uncertain hours, concentration and occasional disappointment. But he had, at least, many friends and no enemies—no mean achievement, for advocates differ widely in their methods and temperaments, and are critical by nature. Many famous judges now knew him by sight. To many firms of solicitors his name was held in increasing regard. He had steered his way through difficult judges, captious clients, demanding solicitors and doughty legal opponents (opponents in court; in the Mess Bar all was harmony again). Unlike Marshall Hall, whose fiery temper sometimes jeopardised his clients' cases, denied him the opportunity of a judgeship and at one time threatened to ruin his career, Norman Birkett had never lost his patience in court.

His social life in Birmingham consisted of lay preaching, visits to Ulverston to stay with his sisters or his cousin and contact with the Cadburys, with whom he remained on the friendliest terms and with whom he frequently stayed as a guest. He read prodigiously, especially Charles Dickens, whom he always considered the greatest of novelists, and whose humanity he so much admired.

It was during his frequent visits to the Cadbury's at Bournville that he met his wife-to-be. Ruth Nilsson, the daughter of Swedish parents, was working as an instructress with the Bournville Girls Athletic Club. They married in 1920, and after discussion, agreed that it was time for Norman Birkett to seek fresh fields in London.

He had felt for some time that despite the goodwill he had established in the Midland Circuit, and the valuable experience he had gained there, he must think of making more money, increasing his influence and taking 'silk'. After all, he was now thirty-seven years old. He did not want to be rising forty before he made some real impact as a barrister. His friend J. G. Hurst, who had been in chambers with him in Birmingham, had gone on to London to work in the chambers of the fabulous Marshall Hall, and was doing very well.

It meant pulling up his roots in Birmingham and, to all intents and purposes, starting afresh. To his great delight, however, A. E. Bowker, Marshall Hall's shrewd and energetic clerk, managed to squeeze him into the great man's chambers at 3 Temple Gardens in the Inner Temple, one of the Inns of Court, where, many years later, Birkett was to become Treasurer.

Marshall Hall was at this time in the hey-day of his career. He was the first and obvious choice for any sensational murder trial. His imposing presence—handsome in looks, over six feet high— immaculate clothing, forceful demeanour and superbly confident air were such that the mere mention of his name would send re- porters scurrying to the courts and the crowds queueing for admit- tance to the public galleries. The mere fact of Birkett being in proximity with Marshall Hall had prestige value, and there was, of course, a good chance that he might be asked to team with him as junior. He had already seen the great advocate at work in the Green Bicycle Case and on other occasions; Marshall Hall, who had initially taken a dislike to Birkett, had later formed a more favourable opinion of him after seeing him in action many times in court.

The beautiful and historic quarter of the Temple, sandwiched between the Victoria Embankment and Fleet Street—between the Thames (which John Burns called 'liquid history') and the head- quarters of Britain's newspapers ('the street of ink')—was an environment exactly suited to Norman Birkett's taste. Its quadrangles of red brick and mellow, grey stone; the rockeries and flowers of Fountain Court; the chambers, with their twisting stone steps and walls crowded with names; the Gothic halls; this combination of the monastic and the scholastic fitted his tempera- ment perfectly.

Here it was that the Knights Templar either ventured forth on crusades or led a monastic life under vows of perpetual chastity, obedience and self-denial. They were known to be established on this site over 700 years ago. Inner Temple Hall, long familiar to Birkett since the days when he was waiting to be called to the Bar and ate his dinners there, stands on the site of the hall used by the original Knights Templar.

Not only was the Temple reminiscent of an ancient university town, but its fascination was enhanced by its literary associations; Crown Office Row, where Charles Lamb was born; Inner Temple

Lane, where Dr. Johnson had his rooms, to which the diligent and faithful Boswell repaired so often, notebook in pocket.

The Birketts took a house in Bigwood Road, Hampstead Garden Suburb. Its countrified atmosphere offset the bustle of London and reminded them of Bournville, the village planned by the Cadburys. Furthermore, it was near to Hampstead Heath, where husband and wife would go to play cricket—Ruth Birkett's enthusiasm for the game was always as great as his—to be joined, before they had been at the game for a few minutes, by children from all over the heath.

In those early days of marriage Norman Birkett worked exceedingly hard. He saved very little money at this stage in his life, and knew that his only hope of success lay in doing as much work as he could, getting to be as well known as possible and giving every single matter, whether the fee was high or low, the careful thought it needed. Often he worked at home far into the night and at week-ends, studying the briefs delivered, often at very short notice, by the solicitors.

His first case in harness with Sir Edward Marshall Hall was on behalf of a blinded ex-soldier who, returning from the battlefields of France, found that his young and attractive wife, whom he had married on Christmas Day, 1916, had lost all affection for him. She was repulsed by his affliction; despite help from St. Dunstan's, the organisation which does so much to mitigate the miseries of the war-blinded, she lacked the *tendresse*, the understanding, the patience and the self-sacrifice implied in having a blinded husband. The cruel and hurtful things she said made his plight, which he had accepted bravely and philosophically, intolerable. A burden he tried stoically to bear was made to seem an incapacity for which he should feel shame and blame.

It was a cruel anti-climax to the years of bitter fighting in France. She left him to lead a life free of responsibility and care, walked out, leaving him, a blind man, with their infant daughter Irene, whom, as best he could, he loved and tended both as a mother and father might, dressing her, feeding her, trying, in his sad, frustrated way, to play and be a good companion to her.

But this sad, broken home could not survive without a mother. The child was too young to guide or help him, much as she loved her father. Leading this lonely, limited life was, he knew, not fair on so young a child, and for her own sake, although it broke his heart, he sent her to a home and groped his way about the silent house, hoping that his young wife would expend her restlessness and be impelled, for the sake of their child, to come home again.

When his wife made one of her infrequent visits to see the child and found her gone she demanded angrily where she was? She insisted that she should have charge of her, although it was she who had deserted her husband—a husband who implored her, even on bended knees, to come home again as his wife. The life she was leading would not provide the background a child needed, and he realised that if he withdrew the child from the home and let her go away with her he would never have contact with either again. 'Irene needs a mother, a father and a home,' he begged, 'please come back!'

Her answer was to return next day and inform him, bluntly, that she was going abroad. 'You can't do that!' he cried, in a panic, 'it's making poor Irene an orphan! She won't see you, she won't be with me—what has the poor girl done to deserve it?' Frantic, he tried to prevent her leaving, and in the process seized her by the throat; she went limp in his arms, but being blind, he could not tell for certain whether she had fainted or not. Back and forwards he kept returning to the room until, in a terrible moment of revelation, he knew she was dead. He tried, unsuccessfully, to kill himself with a razor.

To the strain of constant battle and death in France had been added the curse of blindness, in the flush of youth; next followed the emotional shock and grief of his rejection as a husband; the loss of the companionship of his daughter, whom he loved so dearly, was a further blow; the death of his wife yet another—and now, he stood in the dock of the Old Bailey charged with murder.

Marshall Hall knew that everyone in court, judge, jury and counsel, must feel pity for this brave young man so cruelly treated, but it was on a medical point that he and Norman Birkett defended him. The wife had, as medical evidence confirmed, an enlarged thymus gland, a condition which could make it possible for her to die of excitement; Marshall Hall—having first outlined the tragic background—produced as a witness for the defence a doctor who recalled a patient of his who had a similar complaint and also died of excitement.

It was difficult for Norman Birkett to restrain his own tears as

CHAPTER VII

The Oriental Tyrant

FROM THE VERY day he was called to the Bar Norman Birkett made it a practice to read some literature, probably unrelated to law, before retiring at night. History, biography, poetry, novels, *belle lettres* and, especially, the authorised version of the Bible were always at hand, no matter how much reading he had done in the course of the day in connection with his work.

He believed that a mastery of words, and the most scrupulous attention to choice of words, was a fundamental of sound advocacy. Simplicity of expression was something he always strove to achieve—although one of his juniors remarked to me: 'He could come out with some strange phrases. I have heard him say to a jury: "What boots it, gentlemen, what boots it if..."' Yet there are occasions when incursions into old English are permissible. Only a confident and accomplished orator can decide when the moment has come. In an address to lawyers, Norman Birkett once said: '... there are no fixed standards for forensic oratory, and there are no patterns and types to which the advocate must conform, yet I have found that it is simple speech that makes the most powerful appeal.'

Birkett had studied the techniques of exposition and the forensic styles of the great advocates, such as Rufus Isaacs and Edward Carson. But undoubtedly his sharing of chambers with Marshall Hall was a privilege beyond price. Of course, as Edward Marjoribanks makes clear in his incomparable *The Life of Edward Marshall Hall*, he had his failures as well as triumphs. He had a temper at times ungovernable. He had little tricks, such as the habit of carrying an air cushion with him. If he was dissatisfied with the cross-examination of his client he would put the cushion under his arm and pinch it with thumb and forefinger, making a noise, not loud enough to cause protest, yet (to anyone near) irritating enough to disturb their train of thought.

It was, however, Marshall Hall's oratory that remained as a memory for the rest of Birkett's days. Often he would attend a notable trial in which Marshall Hall appeared, even though he

had no work on it to do himself. In later years Birkett loved to
quote Hall's dramatic quotation from Othello: 'Put out the light,
put out the light', in his successful defence of Harold Greenwood,
at Carmarthen Assizes in 1920. Greenwood, a solicitor, was found
not guilty of the murder by poisoning of his first wife. The
case had aroused enormous interest not simply in Britain but also
throughout Europe and America. It was a trial which Birkett
attended and closely followed.

Mr. and Mrs. Greenwood, together with their four children
and domestic servants, lived at Rumsey House, Kidwelly, Car-
marthenshire. One summer morning in 1919 Mrs. Greenwood
died an agonising death with some of the symptoms of poisoning.
Her medical adviser, a Dr. Griffiths, certified death as being due to
valvular disease of the heart. However, Nurse Jones, who had
been called in two days before Mrs. Greenwood's death to deal
with the diarrhoea and vomiting, was suspicious of what she considered to be Greenwood's casual attitude to his wife's illness.
After the funeral she went around saying that there should have
been a post-mortem. Greenwood, who was not a popular character locally, married again within four months after his wife's
death, the rumours about which became so rife that the police, to
end speculation, told Greenwood that they might decide to
exhume the body. To this Greenwood, almost facetiously,
answered: 'Just the very thing—I am quite agreeable.'

Agreeable or not, the exhumation was carried out, no trace of
valvular or any other disease was found, but the body, still in a
good state of preservation, contained between a quarter and half
a grain of arsenic. A two-day inquest followed, at which the verdict was that Mrs. Greenwood died of arsenical poisoning
administered by her husband.

Sir Edward Marshall Hall concentrated his defence on the in-
consistency of the witnesses for the prosecution. A parlour-maid
swore that Greenwood spent half an hour alone in the china
pantry, something he had never done before, whereas his eldest
daughter declared that at the time stated he was outside cleaning
his car. The same parlourmaid declared that on June 15th, 1919—
the day on which Mrs. Greenwood became fatally ill—Greenwood himself drank whisky, the children water and Mrs. Greenwood burgundy. But her daughter, Irene Greenwood, maintained that she also drank some of the burgundy, not only at lunch

but also at supper. A sad and lugubrious guest at supper claimed that there had been no burgundy on the table. 'Had there been,' declared this female Colonel Chinstrap, 'I should have had some.'

Amidst this welter of confusion and false premise, Marshall Hall used his rhetoric with telling effect; he declared there was little but suspicion, an insubstantial basis for taking a man's life. But as Norman Birkett, listening to Hall's masterly speech, realised, the quotation from Othello and the dramatic appeal that preceded it tilted the scales of justice in Greenwood's favour. 'Your verdict,' he told the jury, 'is final. Science can do a great deal. These men, with their mirrors, multipliers and milligrams, can tell you, to the thousandth or the millionth part of a grain, the constituents of the human body. But science cannot do one thing —that is to find the final spark which converts insensate clay into a human being. . . .'

Sometimes just a few words epitomise what has been said, or summarise the lengths and complex arguments that have gone before. Often a chance happening, a trivial incident, can be used symbolically, as Birkett once observed when his friend Lord Hewart berated, in a few well-chosen words, an unpleasant and unscrupulous Greek witness called Pappinuckulous, who would come in at one court door and leave by the other, and on one occasion pushed his way to the front row of counsel, where the usher straightaway put him out. At the right moment Hewart dealt with the truculent character who, although described as a witness, gave no evidence. 'Members of the jury,' he said, 'then there was the witness, the Greek Pappinuckulous, sometimes coming through that door, sometimes going out through this other door; occasionally trying to push his way into the ranks of counsel, here, there and everywhere. But'—*pointing to the witness box*—'never there, never there.'

One of the finest pieces of cross-examination to impress Norman Birkett was by Edward Carson, whose rolling Irish brogue gave special point or poignancy to some of his terse sayings. 'Do you drink?' he asked one witness, who replied: 'That is my business.' 'Have you any other?' asked Carson politely. And from Marshall Hall, who had described to him some of the main points of the Seddon poison trial in 1912, Birkett had heard of Rufus Isaacs' quiet and effective opening of the cross-examination: 'Seddon, did you like Miss Barrow?' Seddon, puzzled at such an opening, repeated the question: 'Did I like her?' Rufus Isaacs waited, like a fencer sizing up his opponent and watching for his opening: 'That was the question.'

Norman Birkett's court technique was peculiarly his own, for as he often pointed out, there is no one pattern of advocacy. The florid and flamboyant airs of Marshall Hall would never have suited him; come to that, no modern judge and jury would tolerate Marshall Hall's methods either. Even physically, Birkett was differently built, and although capable of firmness and tenacity (as his persistent pursuit of success at the Bar showed only too well) he could not be aggressive. Yet his self-control, prior mastery of the brief (which gave to some of his questions a spurious ring of spontaneity) and quiet, courteous approach to the most hostile or intractable witnesses were infinitely more effective.

Geoffrey Williamson, editor of *John Bull* for many years, including a period when Norman Birkett was on a retainer to Odhams Press, remembers his court manner very clearly: 'He always put on that benevolent, rather silly-ass manner in court; fumbled with his papers, dropped his pencil and allowed his glasses to fall forward on his nose—that sort of thing. He knew the usefulness of being under-estimated. An over-confident opponent tends to neglect his defences. How often have I seen him approach a witness with an air of, "I don't quite understand this yet, but I know you'll make it clear" attitude; as though by inference he would accept uncritically whatever answer was forthcoming. The witness would fall for it; admission would follow admission, the true significance of each being lost on the witness until, like a thrust with a rapier, Birkett would administer the *coup de grâce* with one final, fatal question. . . .'

One of the most famous and unusual murder trials of the 'twenties provided Norman Birkett with yet another opportunity of observing Marshall Hall at his spectacular best.

In the early hours of the morning of July 10th, 1923, a violent storm was raging in London. In the Savoy Hotel, London, most of the guests were asleep. John Beattie, a night-porter, was patrolling the thickly carpeted corridors when, from the open door of one apartment, a young Egyptian came racing towards him, dishevelled and distraught. 'Look at my face!' he screamed, 'look what she has done!'

'She'—a diminutive little Frenchwoman who came racing out after him—babbled incoherently and pointed to her eyes. The night-porter saw, but refused to take sides with either. He muttered something about letting other people sleep and went on his way. The couple returned to their suite. Then the porter stopped dead in his tracks as he heard three shots fired in rapid succession. A woman's screams rent the night air. He raced to the suite from which the quarrelling couple had emerged before, just in time to see Madame Fahmy throw the pistol down. Fahmy Bey, her husband, lay on the floor bleeding from a head wound, and later died in hospital. Mrs. Fahmy was arrested and charged at Bow Street with murder, and at an inquest the jury returned a verdict of wilful murder against her.

Norman Birkett listened fascinated as the story unfolded. Fahmy, a handsome young man with an ungovernable temper alternated by moods of sentimental passion, was the son of an Egyptian engineer, at whose death he had inherited a fortune of £800,000. He maintained several palaces in Egypt, owned several yachts and fast cars, and liked to travel widely and to be both stimulated and solaced by a succession of beautiful women. On a visit to Paris he had fallen in love with a fiery, pocket-sized divorcee and daughter of a cab-driver, Madame Marie Laurent. She did the rounds of European holiday resorts with him, and he returned alone to Egypt, from whence he bombarded her with love letters. 'Your image pursues me,' he wrote. 'If you abandon your journey my life will be aimless.'

Madame Laurent did not abandon her journey. She joined him in Egypt, accepted his proposal of marriage and became a Moslem (it being a condition of Fahmy's legacy from his father that he married into the Moslem faith). With sensible foresight, the niceties of a dowry were arranged by civil contract. The stage was now set for one long, vulgar brawl broken by occasional interludes of mutual affection and periods of uneasy truce.

The trial provided Marshall Hall with magnificent scope for the histrionic role he loved so much. Here he was, the English St. George disguised in black jacket and vicuna trousers, protecting this frail female against the monstrous Oriental dragon.

The trial opened at the Old Bailey before Mr. Justice Rigby Swift on September 10th, 1923. Counsel for the Crown were Mr. Percival Clarke and Mr. Eustace Fulton; for the defence, Sir

E

Edward Marshall Hall, K.C., Sir Henry Curtis Bennett, K.C., and Mr. Roland Oliver. Three barristers, two of them Egyptian, held watching briefs for relatives.

Opening the case for the Crown, Mr. Percival Clarke said that Fahmy Bey was an attaché at the French Legation in Cairo. On a visit to Paris in May last year he had become infatuated with Madame Laurent. They lived together in Deauville and Paris, and later married, but their natures were incompatible. The couple, with their secretary, maid and valet, came to the Savoy Hotel, London, on July 1st, 1923. There had been disagreement between them over the question of an operation which she wished to have in Paris, and which her husband insisted could be performed in London.

On the night of the tragedy they had attended Daly's Theatre with Seid Enani, Bey's secretary, and Madame Fahmy was nervous. Later, dining at the Savoy Hotel, she had snapped at her husband: 'You shut up. I will smash this bottle over your head.' When the band leader asked if she wished any particular tune played, she replied: 'I don't want any music. My husband has threatened to kill me tonight.' Counsel then described how the night-porter heard the shots, of how he took the pistol and put it in the luggage lift, and how Madame Fahmy said to the Manager, who had been summoned to the scene: 'Oh, sir, I have been married six months, which has been torture to me. I have suffered terribly. . . .' At Bow Street Station she told a doctor that her husband had advanced towards her threateningly, and she rushed for her pistol and fired it out of the bedroom window. She hoped this would have frightened him, but he still advanced towards her, and this time, in her unthinking terror, she pointed the pistol at him and pulled the trigger. She was surprised when it went off, as having previously fired it, she thought it was unloaded. She then lost her head and pulled the trigger several times.

In his questioning of Seid Enani, Sir Edward soon destroyed the legend of a loving husband killed by a spitfire of a wife. Fahmy had certainly been infatuated with his wife, as letters produced in court proved. 'Your image,' he wrote, 'pursues me constantly . . . my first thoughts are for you, with your bewitching charm, your exquisite delicacy, the beauty of your heart and your quintessence. Torch of my life. . . .'

Once married to her, however, Fahmy Bey became autocratic,

cruel and inconsiderate. Little by little, the story emerged by skilful cross-examination of the secretary Enani. Sir Edward asked:

'Was he in the habit of beating women?'—'He would dispute with them, but I have never seen him beat them.'

'You have known of his intimacies with many women?'—'Yes.'

'How many wives did Fahmy have when he died?'—'One.'

'He was entitled to have four wives, was he not?'—'Yes.'

Under Moslem law Fahmy could divorce any of his wives at a moment's notice by simply telling her the marriage was ended; but she could not divorce him. At Luxor he locked her in the yacht after smacking her face. Sometimes he fired a pistol over her head. He set powerful guards to watch or restrict her movements, one of them a huge, impassive, muscular Negro unshakeably loyal to his master and unpleasantly reminiscent of Masrur, the monstrous torturer of Flecker's *Hassan*. As for Enani's earlier reply that he had never seen Fahmy beat women, he later admitted to an incident whe Fahmy struck his wife so violent a blow on the chin that he dislocated her jaw. In a letter to Madame Fahmy's sister Fahmy Bey revealed his attitude to his newly acquired Western wife:

'Just now I am engaged in training her. Yesterday, to begin, I did not come in to lunch nor to dinner and I also left her at the theatre. This will teach her, I hope, to respect my wishes. With women one must act with energy and be severe—no bad habits. We still lead the same life of which you are aware—the opera, the theatre, disputes, high words and perverseness.'

Norman Birkett could see the jury's extra awakening of interest as the evidence drew, more and more, a picture of Fahmy Bey as the Oriental despot of romantic fiction. 'Give me details about pretty women who are in the fashion in Paris,' he wrote to his wife's sister. 'If you see . . . tell her my heart, my soul, my sentiments, are at her feet and that I am still in love with her.' And a married man, too!

Once, after a scene on a yacht, Fahmy had taken the Koran and sworn upon it an oath to kill her. And she had received, while staying at the Savoy Hotel, an anonymous letter:

ase permit a friend who has travelled widely among
tals . . . to give you some advice. Don't agree to return
pt for any object or make any journey even to Japan.
abandon fortune than risk your life . . . a journey means
a possible accident, a poison in the flower, a subtle weapon that
is neither seen nor heard. Remain in Paris with those who love
and will protect you.'

Sir Edward's task, despite the character of the dead man and the
mounting evidence of his violent nature, was nevertheless not
easy. For Madame Fahmy had admitted shooting him; furthermore, she had fired not once but *three* times. Cross-examined by
Mr. Clarke, she took the pistol in her hand, pulled the trigger
once or twice and exclaimed, 'I do not know anything about
automatics, I . . .' then, covering her face with her hands, she sank
into a chair.

Mr. Clarke: 'You knew that the pistol contained live cartridges
when you took it up that evening to present it at your husband?'
—'I never looked inside. I felt that when one bullet had gone the
pistol was harmless.' (She claimed to have fired one shot out of
the window to empty it, then pointing it at her husband to
frighten him.)

Madame Fahmy told the court of what had preceded that scene
in the corridor of the Savoy, when each had rushed up to the
night-porter. Her husband had screamed accusations in English
which she could not understand. She had tried to say, in her
babbling, incoherent French, that he had tried to strangle her and
had spat in her face. What had precipitated this scene? She had
told her husband she wished to go to Paris for an operation. He
had dangled money in front of her, offering to give it if she would
accede to his sexual demands, which were not only abnormal and
to her repellent but also, by reason of a physical condition brought
on, possibly (according to one medical witness) by the satisfaction
of his unnatural appetites, intolerably agonising.

Back in their suite after the scene with the night-porter, Fahmy
thumped noisily on her door and, as she opened it, advanced
with eyes blazing and fingers tensed, saying: 'I will kill you!'
Questioned by Sir Edward, she sobbed convulsively as the story
unfolded.

'I had taken the revolver in my hand, and he said: "I will say that you have threatened me." I went out into the corridor in front of the lift. He seized me suddenly and brutally by the throat with his left hand. His thumb was on my windpipe and his fingers were pressing in my neck. I pushed him away, but he crouched to spring on me and said: "I will kill you." I lifted my arm in front of me and, without looking, pulled the trigger. The next moment I saw him on the ground without realising what had happened. I do not know how many times the revolver went off. I did not know what had happened. I saw Fahmy on the floor and I fell on my knees beside him. . . .'

Sir Edward: 'When that pistol went off, had you any idea that it was in a condition to be fired?'—'None. I thought there was no cartridge and that it could not be used.'

She had, in the past, seen her husband pull the breech of a revolver back firmly before removing a cartridge. Resolving to use her revolver to frighten Fahmy should he try to attack her, as he had so often in the past, she tried to draw the breech back at the open window of her apartment. She was not strong enough to do so, and somehow the revolver went off, the bullet spending itself harmlessly into the night air. She thought that the revolver was now unloaded, but in fact the next cartridge was in position, since the revolver was an automatic.

Sir Edward, in his questioning of Madame Fahmy—a petite, pathetic figure between two wardresses—showed that Fahmy had once threatened to horsewhip her. Of Hercules, the burly six-foot Negro who was to all intents and purposes her gaoler, Fahmy had once said that he owed his life to him, and that Hercules would carry out any orders he gave him. Once he said he would instruct Hercules to disfigure her with sand and sulphuric acid. Madame Fahmy's sister testified that she had seen bruises on her sister's face, neck, arms and back and had heard Fahmy threaten to strangle his wife.

An important document, written by Madame Fahmy on January 22nd and deposited with her Egyptian lawyer, only to be opened in the event of her death, was read in court.

'I, Marie Marguerite Alibert, of sound mind and body, formally accuse, in the case of my death by violence or otherwise Ali Bey of having contributed to my disappearance. Yesterday January 21st, he took his Bible or Koran . . . kissed it, put his

hand on it and swore to avenge himself upon me to-morrow, in
eight days, a month, or three months; but I must disappear by
his hand. . . .'

In his final speech Sir Edward was determined to show two
things: that Madame Fahmy knew nothing of revolvers and
genuinely thought the one she wielded against Fahmy Bey to be
unloaded; and that this intention of frightening without hurting
him was fully justified in face of his repeated attempts at violence
in the past and this, his last threatening approach to her. He drew
a lurid picture of this frail, Western, white woman caught in the
evil, licentious toils of an Oriental household. 'This woman,' he
said, with rhetorical flourish, 'made one mistake, she married an
Oriental. I dare say that Egyptian civilisation is, and may be, one
of the oldest and most wonderful civilisations in the world. But
if you strip off the external civilisation of the Oriental you get the
real Oriental underneath.' The *real Oriental*? During his description of the shooting incident, Marshall Hall literally became an
actor, crouching to spring as Fahmy Bey had crouched. Playing
her part, he held the revolver aloft and let the revolver drop from
his hand.

The jury of simple family men and middle-class tradesmen must
have felt a shiver of apprehension down their spines as Marshall
Hall said: 'The curse of this case is the atmosphere we cannot
understand. The Eastern feeling of possession of the woman, the
Turk in his harem, this man who was entitled to have four wives,
if he liked, for chattels, which to us Western people with our ideas
of women is almost unintelligible, something we cannot quite
deal with.'

Well, many Western women have fared not too happily at the
hands of their European spouses—but Marshall Hall gained the
day. When she was found Not Guilty either of murder or manslaughter she gave a faint little gurgling cry and slumped between
the two wardresses. There was a storm of clapping, which was
immediately checked, and as she came outside there were wild
cheers from the waiting crowds. White innocence had prevailed
against the olive-skinned Oriental, thanks to an advocate who
could choose facts with emotional implications and present them
emotionally.

CHAPTER VIII

'The Dustbin Case'

IN 1924 NORMAN BIRKETT had become a familiar figure in the Temple and in the courts. His practice had, with much effort and hard work, been established, and the fees which he was able to earn had increased perceptibly. On the advice of a friend who was a judge, he took 'silk'—became a leading barrister. It remained for him to make some impact as a leader in some outstanding case, and his opportunity came sooner than he might have thought.

The case which made Norman Birkett's name ring with a resounding clang, which established him irrevocably and profitably as an advocate of resource and energy, was what *Punch* described, so truthfully, as 'The Dustbin Case'. This was a protracted, squalid, legal squabble that resolved nothing, tarnished quite a few reputations of the living and the dead, redressed no wrongs, assuaged no grievances and did, in fact, do nothing but make money for the advocates briefed to argue on behalf of their respective clients. Mrs. Dorothy Muriel Dennistoun, who divorced her husband in 1921, claimed from him, Lieut.-Colonel Ian Dennistoun, various sums of money, amounting to £336, which she lent to him before their divorce, the sum of £616 7s., which she claimed to have borrowed at his request to pay his debts, and an order for the performance of an alleged agreement by which, she said, in consideration of not claiming alimony from him, he promised to provide for her as soon as he had the means.

Sir Ellis Hume-Williams, K.C., appeared for the plaintiff, while the defendant was represented by Sir Edward Marshall Hall, K.C., Mr. Norman Birkett, K.C., and Mr. A. H. Davis.

It remains a mystery to this day why Colonel Dennistoun, at the time of this litigation a wealthy man by virtue of his marriage to the Countess of Carnarvon, did not prefer to meet these modest demands rather than bother with the staggering expense of a trial that lasted fourteen days. Of course, he denied all the allegations, as he was entitled to do, since he considered them false; but the denial was an expensive business.

In retrospect, it seems extraordinary that Sir Edward Marshall Hall should have accepted this brief at all. He was very ill, and his handling of the case was at times inept. More important still, he had at one time appeared in court on behalf of the plaintiff, Mrs. Dennistoun, whom he now subjected to much ruthless and humiliating cross-examination; he adduced against her, in this case, information which she entrusted to him in the previous case, when he was her legal advocate. Furthermore, Colonel Dennistoun was a personal friend of Marshall Hall's, and it is never a good thing for a barrister to be personally identified with the fortunes of his client. He cannot be as objective as he should. It is hardly surprising that Hall's appearance in this case caused much criticism in the Temple.

Sir Ellis outlined the story of a very strange marriage. The Dennistouns had married in 1910, each having substantial means; Mrs. Dennistoun brought with her £10,000 to the marriage settlement. Two years later the Colonel's father crashed financially. This had repercussions on the couple's own fortunes. The answer seemed to be a job abroad, so Mrs. Dennistoun interceded with a personal friend, a distinguished General, to use his influence to secure her husband an appointment as Secretary to the Governor of Jamaica. This the General did. The Dennistouns gave up their London home, and to save the furniture being seized by creditors, Captain Dennistoun, as he was then, made the furniture over to his wife.

Captain Dennistoun looked every inch a Grenadier guardsman —tall, imposing and dignified in a rigid way. He dressed at Saville Row and enjoyed the expensive cameraderie of club life. His letters, however, were devoid of all literary merit, being crammed with mawkish sentiment and elephantine humour and even laced on occasions with unsoldierly self-pity:

> 'Darling—I must make all the furniture over to you so that it cannot be touched. Me knows Brownie no sell it, but me wants to sell my watch, please. Good-night, precious. . . .'

Mrs. Dennistoun managed to get £1,000 from her wealthy stepfather, and paid her husband's debts with it. In 1914 they returned from Jamaica, he taking a staff appointment at the War Office and his wife becoming a nurse.

Colonel Dennistoun, Sir Ellis continued, knew that his promotion was due to his wife's friendship with the General, a friendship which, as Mrs. Dennistoun was alleged to have told her husband, was burgeoning into affection and could culminate in only one thing. As Sir Ellis put it: 'Colonel Dennistoun was prepared to accept from his wife that she should pass into a condition of adultery with the General—a relation from which he proposed to profit, as he had done. The jury would find something almost beyond belief in this case. From the correspondence it would be seen that the Colonel was not only encouraging his wife in this adulterous relationship, but was trying to safeguard her in it, giving her hints as to how she should behave lest she should quarrel with the General and lose him:

> 'My own gel . . . Darling heart, take care of yourself. You seemed suddenly such a very tiny little small brown mouse yesterday, and wanting so much care and love, and me felt just like a tiger in a cage behind great big iron bars . . . It does make me so despise myself and everything I do . . . why should you be made a tool? It is the worst fate of all. Darling heart, don't go further than you want . . . great big kiss. TIGER.'

And again:

> 'Now, darling, do not get depressed about the future. All will be well. I feel it. Don't bother with "X"; the less you worry about him the longer you will keep him.'

While, in yet another, he wrote:

> '. . . Me very nearly cried too but just did not. You are such a brave, precious, darling. Me is only a poor mate for you and no one else would have gone through all you have to make Tiger Boy happy. . . .'

In 1916 the Colonel met his wife at the Ritz in Paris, said Counsel, well knowing that the General was coming over to see her. Indeed, it was said in evidence that the Colonel inspected the apartment she was to share. It was at this time, too, that he was sent to Gibraltar and made a Colonel.

After the war Dennistoun was found a job with the Supreme War Council in Paris, but relations between him and his wife were becoming strained. They discussed a divorce; and at the time Colonel Dennistoun wrote:

> 'Darling—You've gone again and I dread just as each other time that it's the last time—I'm not worth waiting for, I know, but you are all that is left of what has been mine. It's not all me. There is some sin I've committed unwillingly and just for that everything goes against what I want most. . . .'

After the Colonel retired from the Army in 1920, honoured by the Royal Victorian Order, the Croix de Guerre and the Legion of Honour, Mrs. Dennistoun obtained a divorce from him in France, where he was then domiciled. When she informed him of this intention he turned bitter and critical, adding: '. . . you loved someone else within a few months of our marriage, and took him to our home when I was away "on guard".' He had forgotten a previous letter in which he declared. 'Don't ever "go off".' Leave that part to me. You've only to say: "Tiger, I want to be free." No more, no details.'

In obtaining her divorce, said Sir Ellis, Mrs. Dennistoun told her husband that she could under French law get alimony; he asked her not to, as he was then without means, but would provide for her as soon as his means permitted.

Because of his desperate financial straits, Dennistoun wrote from the Traveller's Club in 1921, asking her to sell some jewellery: 'I am just busted to the world and I have had to pay a 600-franc doctor's bill for my eye . . . do, if you are in London, sell those silver dishes Boy and Herman gave me. They must be worth a tenner . . . the coat I can get no offer for. . . .' Despite their rift, Mrs. Dennistoun sent him £100 on receipt of this appeal, and he admitted that he 'cried with gratitude'.

Their tangled relationship now took a stranger turn. At one time Mrs. Dennistoun had sent her husband to take some things to a friend of hers, the Countess of Carnarvon. As a result, Dennistoun became friendly with Lord and Lady Carnarvon. Lord Carnarvon, the fifth Earl, was a famous Egyptologist who later died from a mosquito bite received while opening the famous tomb at Luxor in conjunction with Mr. Howard Carter. His death, one of many misfortunes attendant upon this discovery, was commonly said to be 'the curse of Tntankhamen' at work.

That single mosquito bite did, however, affect Colonel Dennistoun's fortunes for the better. For eight months after Lord Carnarvon's death he married the Countess of Carnarvon, who settled on him £100,000. Even a year earlier, however, he had paid £12,752 into his bank account; but at that time it did not occur to him to repay his ex-wife what he owed. He sent her, instead, a sloppily sentimental letter:

'Me walked up Curzon-street and in the window busy packing was Brownmouse. Oh, and I whistled the old call, but I could not more than once as I saw a policeman, so I went on ... Oh, it's all wrong. I had to come that way. Well, take care of yourself, sweetheart. Me just always me, and me there to help all that humanly possible. Some things can never be, that I understand, but some things last for ever. Oh, Gel, it nearly broke my heart tonight.'

The relief from financial worry contingent on his remarriage also mended the Colonel's broken heart, for when Mrs. Dennistoun wrote in 1923 to say that 'things were desperate', the curt reply was that the Colonel did not wish to see her and that all further communications must be made to his solicitor. Thus, the stage was set for one of the most bitter lawsuits in the history of civil law.

Mrs. Dennistoun gave her evidence in a calm, detached way, with only the most infrequent flashes of emotion. She described how her husband's debts had become so chronic that he considered resigning his commission, how she had seen the General and how after several meetings their friendship became affection. Then came his suggestion that if she would be his mistress he might secure for her husband a staff appointment. She told her husband of this, and warned him that this might mean the eventual break-up of their marriage. 'How terrible it will be,' the Colonel was alleged to have said. 'I suppose it must be done.'

The idea was that when her husband returned from his appointment in Gibraltar she was to remain in Paris, where the General would join her at the Ritz Hotel, where rooms had already been booked. Her husband read the General's letter, and helped her inspect the rooms where she was to commit adultery.

There was a deathly silence in court as Sir Ellis asked quietly: 'Did you pay the price?'

For the first time Mrs. Dennistoun's composure deserted her. With trembling lips, she answered: 'Yes.'

This highly sensational allegation sparked off the wildest speculation at the War Office. While he was in the Grenadier Guards, Dennistoun had commanded the King's Company, which in effect was His Majesty's personal bodyguard (hence his M.V.O., a decoration bestowed by the Monarch for personal services to the Royal Household). He had served in South Africa in 1901–2, and in 1916 had become Deputy-Assistant Adjutant and Quartermaster-General, and later Assistant Adjutant. In 1917 he had been Acting Adjutant and Quartermaster-General at Versailles. His rapid promotion had not been thought unusual at the time, but now people asked: 'What sort of a War Office was it, where Generals could offer responsible posts as payment for their illicit sexual adventures?'

So far the General's name had been withheld, but on Mr. Justice McCardie's ruling it was revealed. 'X' was none other than General Sir John Cowans, Quartermaster-General of the Forces during the whole of the First World War. Was this, people asked, why Dennistoun became his second-in-command?

According to Mrs. Dennistoun's story, her husband was a sponger, a willing cuckold and a spendthrift.

In the witness box she was self-possessed, firm in her replies and quick in response. There were moments when her parrying of unflattering suggestions from Sir Edward Marshall Hall aroused obvious sympathy from the jury.

'Mrs. Dennistoun,' he said dramatically, 'did you hear the charge that your late husband had forfeited the right to be called a gentleman and that he was a man who lived on your immoral earnings?'

'I heard what Sir Ellis Hume-Williams said.'

'Do you approve of it?'—'I think that this is an unfair question.'

'How much do you think that a woman who loved her husband would pay to avoid having such a case opened against him?' —'It is a great deal harder for me than for my husband. I am a woman and alone.'

The inference of Sir Edward's questions was that this was a gold-digging action on the part of Mrs. Dennistoun, brought on the assumption that the Colonel, rather than have such unpleasant matters ventilated in court, would prefer to settle for a handsome sum. This, too, she parried with ease. She claimed that when, at the age of twenty-two, she married Dennistoun she was in love with him. During this first cross-examination by Sir Edward— during which he alternated rapidly between harsh accusation and spurious chivalry—Mrs. Dennistoun was under fire continuously for over six hours. She had to appeal to Mr. Justice McCardie for a respite.

The inquisition continued the next day. Private detectives had pried closely into her life, so much so that when Sir Edward asked her details she said: 'You have got the itinerary of my life so wonderfully, I do not keep diaries.'

The essential facts emerging from Sir Edward's cross-examination was that, while having an affair with General Cowans she had also fallen in love with a Mr. Bolin, a Spaniard, by whom she became pregnant following an assignation in an isolated chalet on top of a Swiss mountain.

One witness mentioned by Sir Edward was a Miss Parker, once Mrs. Dennistoun's maid. Many allegations of what she was supposed to have told her maid were put to Mrs. Dennistoun in the form of questions, and the jury became increasingly restive at both the manner and matter of Sir Edward Marshall Hall's cross-examination.

Sir Edward reverted again to his previous meeting with Mrs. Dennistoun, when, at Lady Carnarvon's request, he was acting for her. Mrs. Dennistoun had introduced Mr. Bolin to Sir Edward, saying that they intended to marry. At that time, General Cowans had died, and she had, according to Sir Edward, contemplated suing the executors for the return of a motor-car worth £350; Sir Edward had advised that on the eve of a new marriage it would be impolitic to advertise so widely that one had been the mistress of General Cowans for many years.

One wonders what Norman Birkett's thoughts must have been as, at one point, members of the jury protested openly and loudly at the barrage of imputations to which Mrs. Dennistoun was being subjected. This ambivalent role of protector one moment and attacker the next, this habit of adducing facts against her which had been entrusted to him in the past for quite another purpose did him little credit.

At one point Sir Edward contradicted himself, and as the

imputation he had attempted to make was a highly damaging one, he lost considerable face with the jury, as Mr. Birkett, busily making notes throughout, realised all too well. Mrs. Dennistoun, for example, pointed out that her maid Parker, now being used by the defence to blacken her character, was an unreliable person, for whom she had been asked to give no less than six character references in a very short time. Sir Edward suggested that she had, only the previous day, written to an agency asking for a copy of the reference she had given respecting Miss Parker. This Mrs. Dennistoun indignantly denied, and Sir Edward handed her a letter saying aggressively: 'Is that your handwriting, madam?' 'This is my handwriting,' she said, 'but the letter was written six months ago.' There were murmurs of 'Oh!' from the jury box and all over the court when Sir Edward said he had not suggested the letter was written yesterday.

A curious feature of this case was that the solicitors who had acted respectively for Mrs. and Colonel Dennistoun during their divorce suit were called as witnesses. Sir George Lewis, a distinguished solicitor, confirmed that when acting for Mrs. Dennistoun her husband had promised to support her when he could. That professional relations between solicitor and client should be discussed in the court of a quite separate action introduced yet another distasteful note into this complicated case.

Mrs. Dennistoun refuted allegations of adultery with a Mr. Senhouse, a young soldier subsequently killed in action at Loos. But she admitted to being, simultaneously, both mistress and wife.

'You never loved your husband in a marital way at all?'—'I do not think he has ever had cause for complaint.'

'Since 1916 he has never had relations with you at all?'—'That is absolutely untrue.'

The Judge: 'You had relations with Sir John Cowans and then with your husband?'—'If you put it that way.'

Sir Edward: 'I thought you would welcome the suggestion that after the end of April 1916 there had not been marital relations between you and Colonel Dennistoun?'—'I cannot say what is not true.'

There were bitter exchanges between Sir George Lewis and Sir Edward Marshall Hall, during which Sir Edward lost his temper outright. It was a relief to all when Norman Birkett rose, calm and collected, to state the case for the defence. He had need to be calm. He admitted the obvious, that 'there must be sympathy in the minds of the jury and an alienation of their feelings from the Colonel'. He hastened to pay tribute to the institution of happy, chaste marriage, realising that the opening of the case had put his client in an unchivalrous light. That opening 'was an appeal to the noblest and deepest affection in the mind of men—that a man should cherish and love his wife, that he should protect the sanctity of his home from invaders in any quarter. It has been said that Colonel Dennistoun has betrayed the basest kind of ingratitude ... but if material and vital things have been omitted, and if there appears an unfounded claim for money, the jury might think it right to reserve their judgement until they have heard the full story.'

Mr. Birkett then made several points. There would be a denial of the 'paid the price' story of Mrs. Dennistoun. The story was a 'lie'—not, as some might put it, 'faulty recollection'. A wife said she sold her body to advance her husband's interests, while the husband categorically denied it. Somebody must be lying. Such preferment as Colonel Dennistoun obtained would have been his in the ordinary way of things.

Yet another curious note was introduced by the cross-examination of Colonel Dennistoun's solicitor by Sir Ellis Hume-Williams. Ten witnesses had been brought from abroad, mainly to sustain allegations of immorality against Mrs. Dennistoun, and the suggestion was that this had been done to prevent Mrs. Dennistoun bringing her action at all, since she could not compete with expenditure of that kind herself.

The witnesses were heard. One, a Swiss hotel manager, described how Bolin, the Spaniard she hoped to marry, and Mrs. Dennistoun had stayed at his hotel. The following day a witness described how Mrs. Dennistoun was with Mr. Bolin in her London flat one day when General Cowan's car was seen approaching, and how Mr. Bolin was whisked off to the basement in the nick of time.

The purpose, of course, was to establish that Mrs. Dennistoun was a passionate and impetuous woman who would go her own way in any case, and needed no inducement, by way of the thought that her immorality would help her husband's career, to do so. But the jury must have marvelled at the Colonel's complicated life. At one time, immediately before and even after the Dennistoun divorce, Colonel and Mrs. Dennistoun were living with Lady Carnarvon. The two women were close friends, while Colonel Dennistoun and Lady Carnarvon were becoming closer friends still, until actually engaged.

The Colonel admitted to spending £12,000 on the defence in this action, much of which had gone to proving, as he hoped, immorality on the part of his ex-wife with seven different men. He agreed with Sir Ellis that he was attacking her reputation in every possible way When, however, he admitted that General Sir John Cowans had pushed him into all his appointments, the cross-examination showed him in a less-favourable light.

Sir Ellis took one of his letters to Mrs. Dennistoun: 'Oh, gel, darling, I hate you using that lovely little body of yours as a gift. It is much too good to waste for me.'

'What,' asked Sir Ellis, 'is the meaning of this?'—'The exact meaning of that was that I went to see my wife and she told me she had done this for me.'

'It does make me so despise myself.' 'Why should you despise yourself?' The Colonel answered: 'She had been doing this before. I could not stop her. I never could stop her.'

Later the Colonel said: 'I was in love with her,' and Sir Ellis looked at him with blank incredulity. 'In love with her! And allowing her to commit adultery with the man to whom you owed your promotion?'

'I acknowledge that I was weak,' the Colonel admitted. Further questioning, of both the Colonel and Lady Carnarvon, proved that before Lord Carnarvon died he received about £20,000 from Lady Carnarvon, besides a furnished flat, and that she herself had provided the 'marriage settlement' of £100,000 which he contributed to their marriage, by selling three Gainsboroughs to Sir Joseph Duveen, the famous art dealer. Lady Carnarvon described his condition before she took him, while her husband was still alive, under her wing; he 'looked like death . . . was emaciated . . . his clothes were shiny'.

During this long case the burden had fallen increasingly on Norman Birkett's willing shoulders. For most of the time Sir Edward Marshall Hall was ill and in great pain, making him irritable and clouding his judgement. On the night before the defence's final speech to the jury was to be made he told Birkett that he must hand over this immense responsibility to him. It was a great opportunity for Birkett, for the case had been one of the main topics of conversation for the last two weeks, and the eyes of the country were upon him. It was also a great ordeal. The defence, unlike the plaintiffs, had the advantage of a full shorthand note, which now ran to nearly half a million words. Many points were raised by one side or another at different stages of the trial, so that it was necessary to go backwards and forwards in these notes to get a clear picture. To be asked to prepare the closing speech at the last moment was a well-nigh hopeless task, but throughout the night Birkett worked at his home in Hampstead Garden Suburb, fortified by sandwiches and tea and almost up to his neck in manuscripts. Yet with only a few hours sleep he summarised and clarified the issues (from, of course, the standpoint of his client) and took full advantage of the evidence given by Mrs. Dennistoun's servants. The gravamen of his speech was that there was no agreement between Mrs. Dennistoun and her husband with regard to maintenance, and therefore this non-existent agreement could not be enforced.

The Judge's summing up dealt at length with the story that Mrs. Dennistoun gave her body to General Cowans in return for her husband's promotion in the British Army. Firstly, he did not really think Mrs. Dennistoun a 'little brown mouse', but a masterful, intelligent and entirely confident woman. Perhaps she had aggravated the story to minimise her own dishonour? He pointed to the strange fact that, while in love with Mr. Bolin, she had refused all pleas to visit the dying General Cowans, who was so embittered by her refusal that he sent, from the very edge of the grave, what Mr. Justice McCardie called 'the most terrible telegram ever sent'. Little brown mouse had, clearly, refused to comfort her dying lover in his last moments because she had found another.

After the Judge had addressed a number of questions to the jury they retired and returned with their answers. On the two crucial issues they were agreed; there had, they decided, been a verbal agreement that Colonel Dennistoun would support Mrs. Dennistoun when his means permitted. The sums of money specified were loans, which he should repay. And they awarded damages of £5,000.

Even now, this strange drama was not resolved. Sir Ellis

F

pressed for costs for his client, pointing out that the hearing had been dragged on by the defence's allegations of dishonesty and blackmail and the need to refute them. Mr. Birkett countered by saying that, as the jury had been discharged, he could produce further evidence of the plaintiff's immorality—an offer the Judge declined. The argument continued for another day. Plaintiff's counsel asked for the general costs of the action, while Mr. Birkett, referring to the sums of money Mrs. Dennistoun had passed to her husband, claimed that there was no consideration of a contract and that if one was implied it was too vague to be enforceable. This brought a rebuke from the Judge, who said: 'She helped the defendant readily when in need, and I do not regard with approval any endeavour to escape from these payments.'

But as Mrs. Dennistoun, exhausted after her three weeks' ordeal, heard the judgement, she went pale with grief and disappointment. Mr. Justice McCardie refused to permit the £5,000 which the jury had awarded, on the basis that the jury's finding in this respect was legally untenable. Judgement was given for Mrs. Dennistoun for the sum of £472 18s. 4d., but her claim for £616, which she stated she had borrowed at his request to pay his debts, was dismissed in favour of the Colonel, with the costs represented by that part of the action.

'I am bound,' said Mr. Justice McCardie, giving judgement, 'to apply the rules of the law as I conceive them,' and he added, later, 'I have never known an action fought with greater bitterness and intensity.'

So the story of the strange triangle had reached a new phase. The handsome Grenadier guardsman who married 'little brown mouse' had now found a second wife whose substantial means removed all worries about debt; Mrs. Dennistoun, who did not marry her Spanish lover, and whose other lover, General Cowans, had gone to his grave cursing her name, found herself penniless, and had lost the friendship of her once close companion, the Countess of Carnarvon; the Countess, genuinely in love with Colonel Dennistoun, settled happily to life with her second husband, completely unperturbed by the fact that the whole world knew he was penniless when she married him; the War Office hastily and uneasily forgot the whole matter. Later Mrs. Dennistoun raised enough money to open an antique shop, and three years later married another Colonel—Nicholas Woevodsky, a

Russian nobleman and former air attaché at the Russian Embassy, whose father had been aide-de-camp to the Romanoffs.

What, asked the *Star*, was the use of our much-vaunted system of trial by jury? 'The jury clearly thought that Mrs. Dennistoun should have £5,000 damages. The judge clearly thought not, and what the judge says goes. The judgement may be sound, but why waste seventeen days of the time of the jury?' It also asked who had appointed Dennistoun to the Versailles Council. General Cowans could not have done so, as he lacked the authority; did those who nominated Dennistoun know of his wife's relations with General Cowans?

But for Mr. Birkett the 'Dustbin Case' had been a triumph. The *Daily Mirror* referred to him as 'the youthful silk who is gaining a great reputation from his able support of Sir Edward Marshall Hall in the Dennistoun case'. Said the *Daily Mail*:

> 'A great legal reputation has been made almost at a bound by Mr. Norman Birkett, K.C., . . . the ability shown by Mr. Birkett in this case has won him golden opinions. He is the great legal discovery of the year . . . this case has brought him right into the limelight. At the bar they are prophesying a great future for him.'

The case had, in fact, been sordid and futile, neither side gaining a farthing. But to marshal all his forces, re-read a gigantic mass of evidence and consider not only what he was going to say but also what to omit, to absorb all the details and, after only two hours' sleep, state the case calmly, logically and in sequence as Mr. Birkett did, was truly a great legal achievement.

The case had indeed brought him into the limelight. Nor had it been entirely unprofitable. Norman Birkett's fees amounted to over £3,000.

CHAPTER IX

A Foul Fellow Exposed

IN FEBRUARY 1927 Norman Birkett appeared for the defendant in one of the most sensational and unusual libel suits of all time.

In 1925 Captain Peter Wright, in the course of an essay in a book, *Portraits and Criticisms*, assailed the character of William Ewart Gladstone, the Grand Old Man of Liberalism, in terms which caused grave distress and pain to his two surviving sons, Lord Gladstone and H. N. Gladstone, aged seventy-two and seventy-four respectively.

Of the dead Liberal leader, Peter Wright said: 'He founded the great tradition, since observed by many of his followers and successors with such pious fidelity, in public, to speak the language of the highest and strict principle, and in private to pursue and possess every sort of woman.'

All who achieve greatness in any field have their critics or even enemies, because of obligatory partisanship, genuine difference of opinion or jealousy. Even during his lifetime, as the *Daily Mirror* pointed out, 'many worshipped him as little less than an angel: others regarded him, purely from political prejudice, as a devil incarnate, and were consequently willing to believe any evil of him'. Captain Wright's allegations were only a repetition of vague charges often heard on the lips of gossips during the great statesman's lifetime.

However, those few lines of innuendo, tucked away in the context of an essay on Lord Salisbury, were legal dynamite.

The Press took up the cudgels, mostly on Mr. Gladstone's behalf. 'For my own part,' said a *Daily Mirror* writer, 'I have always believed that the tales of Gladstone's immorality were as well founded as the stories of the Russian army that marched through England in the early days of the war' (with snow on their boots). He added: 'We do know, however, that he left Eton with the reputation of having been a notable influence for good in the college, that he was most happily married to a clever and adoring wife, and that religion played a large part in his life.'

The Nation was one section of the Press that criticised Peter

Wright severely. Wright was a colourful character, dapper, cockily military in manner, quick-witted and monocled. He had achieved a distinguished name as a journalist, had been educated at Harrow and Balliol and throughout the First World War was secretary and interpreter on the Supreme War Council.

Replying to *The Nation*, and determined to make a bad job worse, he wrote: 'I referred to Gladstone's pursuit of women in his own level of life, and I had the best of reasons for doing so. Lord Milner, who was a young and active politician forty-five years ago, told me that Mr. Gladstone was governed by his seraglio.'

Air travel and political necessity have made the British less contemptuous of Eastern life than they were; then, at least, the very word *seraglio* evoked imagery inspired by Victorian artists, of large milky-white ladies lounging around a bathing pool, being fanned by naked Negro boys with peacock feathers.

Now it is not possible to libel the dead, in the accepted legal sense. The social and economic status of a dead person cannot be damaged by any statement, nor can it be proved that it has caused them pain or ostracism. Published epitaphs, and even some on tombstones throughout Britain, are often unflattering in the extreme. The epitaph on Abraham Newland, Chief Cashier of the Bank of England, who died in 1807, is typical:

> Beneath this stone old Abra'm lies
> Nobody laughs and nobody cries
> Where he's gone or how he fares
> Nobody knows and nobody cares.

The descendants of Abraham Newland did not sue anybody for libel, because they couldn't, nor did the relatives of Frederick, Prince of Wales (father of George III), about whom was written the most cruel and sarcastic epitaph imaginable.

Yet clearly a man's immediate descendants have an interest in protecting his good name, both from motives of loyalty to his memory and concern for their own reputations. Time has something to do with it—there is less-vicarious discredit attached to something that happened long ago to something more recent. Tell me that my great, great grandfather was transported to Botany Bay for stealing a bag of corn, and I would not greatly mind. To suggest that my father spent his last days in Dartmoor Prison would be another matter.

Since the Gladstones could not sue Captain Wright for libel, they determined that he should be provoked into suing them, so that the merits and demerits of his allegations could be aired in court. One can almost see the two dignified old gentlemen in the offices of their solicitors, Charles Russell and Co., as the Thesaurus is thumbed for words that would give the greatest offence in the shortest possible wordage. The following letter, signed by both Lord Gladstone and his brother, was then despatched:

> 'Your garbage about Mr. Gladstone in "Portraits and Criticisms" has come to our knowledge. You are a liar. Because you slander a dead man you are a coward. Because you think the public will accept invention from such as you, you are a fool.'

Simultaneously the Gladstones sent copies of this letter to *The Nation* and to Peter Wright's publishers. Wright, in turn, sent a copy of it to the *Daily Mail*, together with his reply, which was intended to add fuel to the flames, and did:

> 'My Lord—I am in receipt of your Lordship's outburst dated July 22nd. I attributed to Mr. Gladstone the character of a hypocrite in matters of sex. I have evidence of his conduct . . . Mr. Gladstone's hypocritical character (which in no way detracts from his merits as a public financier) is the common, though it may not be the official, reputation of him that has descended to us. It was crystallized in Labouchere's famous epigram "that Gladstone might be caught playing with a fifth ace up his sleeve: but he would only explain that God put it there. . . ." '

For good measure, he added that Gladstone had connived at Parnell's misconduct with Mrs. O'Shea, only denouncing it when he found it politically convenient to do so. His Lordship's language, he added, had been picked up in his pantry rather than the House of Lords.

These highly offensive letters Wright wrote on Bath Club notepaper. Accordingly, Lord Gladstone wrote to the Secretary of the Bath Club protesting at the 'foul charge against my father' which had been amplified in the *Daily Mail*, the author 'not daring to face us in court'. In a further letter Gladstone said he was 'so indignant that the fellow was sheltering in my old club, which for my brother, myself and my wife becomes uninhabitable so long as it is polluted by his presence'.

The Committee of the Bath Club expelled Captain Wright without giving him a hearing, an illegal act, for which he obtained an injunction and damages against them.

All these acts by the Gladstones were made, as they intended, in the full blaze of publicity. As one paper put it:

'... the British public will share to the full the indignation of the sons of the late Mr. Gladstone ... it is intolerable that he (Mr. Wright) or anyone else should publish an accusation of this kind against the dead ... the public, as Lord Haldane says ... will form its own judgement if Mr. Peter Wright fails to take action against Mr. Gladstone's sons in a court of law. We shall watch with interest to see whether he ventures to take up the challenge which Lord Gladstone and his son throw out to him. *No man with any pretensions to a sense of honour could, of course, fail to do so.*'

What could 'an officer and a gentleman' do? Mr. Peter Wright sued Lord Gladstone for libel in respect of his first letter to the Bath Club.

The case *Wright* v. *Lord Gladstone* was heard in the High Court of Justice, King's Bench Division, before Mr. Justice Avory, amiably nicknamed 'the hanging judge'. Mr. Frank Boyd Merriman, K.C., appeared for the plaintiff, while Mr. Norman Birkett, K.C., briefed by Charles Russell and Co., solicitors, appeared for the defendant. He was, of course, asked to defend this case because of his standing as an advocate; nevertheless, there is an interesting coincidence in the fact that Gladstone had always been one of Birkett's heroes, that even as a lad he had enthralled his fellow pupils by declaiming a long essay he had written on the subject— and that, having twice unsuccessfully contested a Liberal seat and on a third occasion entered Parliament as Liberal Member of Parliament for East Nottingham, Norman Birkett was well up in the history of the Liberal Party, and Gladstone's life in particular.

There had been several months before the case was called, and during this time Birkett had refreshed his memory on every aspect of Gladstone's life. He relished thoroughly the opportunity of vindicating the memory of the great man, and listened attentively as Mr. Merriman outlined the case for the plaintiff. Merriman recapitulated the circumstances in which Wright had written his book, and the acidulated correspondence which had culminated in the present action.

Merriman instanced a few distinguished people of past centuries whose private life had been the subject of legitimate comment without protest from their descendants. Was there need for diffidence in describing the relationship between King Charles and Nell Gwynne? 'I suppose,' he said, 'that even the family of Lord Nelson are not hurt if reference to Lady Hamilton is coupled with reference to Trafalgar. Coming even nearer to our own time, we were reminded yesterday of the forty-second anniversary of the death of General Gordon, with whose fate Mr. Gladstone was so intimately bound, and in respect of whom and other eminent Victorians not much earlier than Mr. Gladstone a new form of biography had been introduced which made no bones about exposing such human weaknesses as there were without any public reprobation or notorious consequence for the author. . . .'

In discussing the case, said Mr. Merriman, the jury must consider whether the public professions of the dead statesman did not lay him more open after his death to an exposure of the reverse side of the shield if that reverse side is firmly believed in. . . .

No doubt. That there was any basis for analogy between the libidinous King Charles and the God-fearing Gladstone had yet to be established. Captain Wright might well believe in the 'reverse side' of Gladstone's shield, but would have to adduce convincing proof of this moral cupidity if he hoped to show that Viscount Gladstone, former Governor-General of Canada, had been unjust and malicious in writing in the terms he did to the Bath Club. If the looks of Mr. Justice Avory from the Bench were any criteria, Wright had lost his action already. Avory did not even bother to hide his prejudice. Again and again he directed towards Wright bleak and wintry looks, and his interventions were never in the plaintiff's favour.

In view of Captain Wright's temerity in launching so sensational an attack on Gladstone, and his spirited defence of his words, it came as a surprise to the crowded court that he had so insubstantial a basis for his allegations. That the famous Victorian actress Lily ('Jersey Lily') Langtry had been Gladstone's mistress was based on a comment made to him when at Harrow by Mr. James Haslam. Further 'evidence' was a cartoon by Phil May showing a man resembling Gladstone waiting at the stage door with a bunch of primroses—a manifest piece of political satire, as primroses were Disraeli's favourite flower, and Gladstone hated and despised Disraeli.

Dr. Greatorex, whose practice was in the West End of London, had once told Wright that his patients had complained of having been accosted by Gladstone—but Dr. Greatorex was dead and could clearly neither confirm nor deny Wright's story. From an Oxford undergraduate, Wright had heard a story of Gladstone's liaison with Olga Novikoff 'a lovely Russian sent over by the Tsarist Government for the special purpose of fascinating Mr. Gladstone, and she thoroughly succeeded'.

From a friend in Paris, Wright had heard, as a piece of gossip, that Gladstone had had an affair with a French actress called Brassine. Charlie Thompson, an amateur steeplechaser, had told Captain Wright that he learned, from one lady of easy virtue, that Gladstone had tried to get into conversation with her, when he had left her for a moment to fetch something from his flat. From an equally apocryphal source Wright had learned that Laura Bell 'the most famous courtesan of the nineteenth century' had been mistress of the Victorian Prime Minister.

The pattern of the defence was soon obvious during Norman Birkett's questioning of Lord Gladstone. Lord Gladstone said he was the fourth and youngest son of the late William Ewart Gladstone and was seventy-three years old. His brother, Mr. Henry Gladstone, was now seventy-four. The other surviving member of the family was a sister who was aged eighty. His father died in 1898, and up to 1885 he always lived at his father's house at Carlton House Terrace or at Downing Street. Since then he always lived at Hawarden. Living at his father's house, he was brought into the closest personal relationship with him.

Mr. Birkett then asked: 'Having regard to your position as a son, and the position with regard to the offices you have held, what do you say about this passage in Captain Wright's book to which reference has been made?' Lord Gladstone's reply rang throughout the court, and Mr. Justice Avory favoured Captain

Wright with another of his baleful looks. 'It was,' declared Lord Gladstone, 'a revolting passage—a revolting passage which, of course, made me angry to an almost ungovernable degree.'

Mr. Birkett: 'What was the particular cause of your anger?'— 'I knew it was false.'

Lord Gladstone added that when his father died Mr. and Mrs. Gladstone had been married for sixty years. When he referred to 'garbage' in his letter to Wright he had in mind his own knowledge of his father. Until then he had neither spoken nor written to Captain Wright.

Mr. Birkett: 'As a son living at home, I want you to say what was the relationship between your father and mother in the home during all the years you were there?'—'*It was absolutely perfect.*'

Birkett: 'You called it a "foul charge"?'—'Certainly. It was a charge which made out my father to be a foul sensualist and a foul hypocrite. Those were lies, and the charge therefore was a foul one.'

With a significant hitch of his gown, and waving his gold pencil in his hand, Norman Birkett faced the forty-six-year-old Captain. 'Do you regard yourself,' he asked quietly and with a swift look at the jury, 'as a serious journalist?'

'I try,' said Captain Wright quickly, 'not to be dull.'

Quick as lightning the Judge intervened: 'Does that mean all serious people are bores?' The digression was weakening Birkett's opening, and he swiftly changed his phrasing: 'Do you regard yourself as a responsible journalist?'—'Certainly. The newspapers treat me as one, and I conclude that I am one. I speak the truth.'

'Do you agree that the charge you make is about as horrible a charge as can be made?'—'No, because it has been made against innumerable great men.'

'It is a charge that Mr. Gladstone was a gross sensualist?'— 'Yes, I think that that describes him.'

'Is not a charge that a man is a gross sensualist one of the most horrible charges that can be made against him?'—'No, because it has been made against innumerable great men.'

'Is it not a charge which reflects on all the women who honoured Gladstone with their friendship?'—'No, certainly not. He might behave very well at Carlton Gardens, but not elsewhere.'

'Do you agree that it is a very grave charge of hypocrisy?'—

'Oh, yes. That is what this charge is. It is much more a charge of hypocrisy than one of immorality.'

'His religion, you intended to say, was a mockery?'—'No, Gladstone was not like ordinary people.'

'Does it not mean that he was the rankest sort of hypocrite?'—'Yes, but being a wonderful sort of man, he was a wonderful sort of hypocrite.'

Despite his glib confidence, Peter Wright's status in the eyes of the court was ebbing fast; his manner contrasted unpleasantly with the dignified mien of the two brothers whose father had been impugned. Quietly, dispassionately, Birkett continued his deadly inquisition. He read a reference by Lord Rosebery to Gladstone's ideally happy married life: Mrs. Gladstone had 'for sixty years shared all the sorrows and all the joys of Mr. Gladstone's life, received his confidence, shared his triumphs, and cheered him in his defeats.'

Mr. Birkett: 'Is this charge of yours that Mr. Gladstone was faithless to that wife of sixty years?'—'Yes, of course, it is. Men who are very fond of their wives are often faithless to them.'

'Do you regard immorality in a man as an ordinary thing?'—'No. I regard it as culpable.'

'But not horrible?'—'No.'

Wright criticised Lord Gladstone's castigation of him as 'a foul fellow'—a phrase which, he claimed, meant a dissolute person. That, he said, was bad English.

Without a flicker of a smile Norman Birkett threw the ball back into Wright's court. 'If a person made a foul charge against you or your dead father, what would you call him in your beautiful English?'—'I should call him intemperate.'

One stupid—and fatal—thing Wright had done was to allege that the late Lord Gladstone had had an illegitimate son. 'About fourteen years ago,' he had said in evidence, 'I saw at Eastbourne a man named Cecil Gladstone, whose resemblance to the statesman was unmistakable. I was told he was an illegitimate son, but I cannot identify my informant.'

Mr. Birkett: 'How old was Cecil Gladstone when you saw him?'—'I should say in his middle fifties.'

'Will you look at that Certificate of Birth?' He waited while Peter Wright, affecting boredom, glanced at it. 'Does it record the birth of Cecil Thomas Gladstone?'—'It appears to do.'

By question and answer, Birkett established that this Gladstone was born in 1856 in Highgate, his father being William Gladstone, a general merchant and his mother Charlotte Louise Gladstone, formerly Kenrick. Next he handed to plaintiff Cecil Gladstone's marriage certificate.

'Does it,' asked Mr. Birkett, 'record the marriage of Cecil Thomas Gladstone and Norah Heath Curtis on February 11th, 1902?'—'It appears to do.'

'Giving the father of the groom as William Gladstone, deceased merchant?'—'Yes.'

'Do those certificates seem to show that Cecil Gladstone was the son of a William Gladstone, who was a merchant?'—'A general merchant, yes, that's a very large category.'

'Do you think it covers the Prime Minister?'—'I don't know that it does not.'

How long, the court wondered, could Wright's bravado last? He had accepted a piece of hearsay about a man he saw once, and then only from a distance, without any attempt to check his facts and now, faced with tangible evidence of that man's legitimacy, was suggesting that a famous Prime Minister might also be a general merchant.

Mr. Birkett produced the death certificate of Cecil Gladstone. It confirmed the details of the other two. 'Do those documents influence your judgement?' he asked mildly. 'If Gladstone had an illegitimate son,' Wright answered, 'that is the way in which he'd deal with it.'

Casually, Mr. Birkett lifted a volume from the table, opened it and handed it to Wright. 'Will you look at that book? It is *Lodge's Peerage*. Do you know that it contains genealogical tables?'—'I don't study the peerages as intently as some people.'

'Do you know as a fact that Gladstone had a first cousin called William?'—'No.'

'Did you know he was fully dealt with in *Lodge's Peerage*?'— 'No.'

'Then look.'

The eyes of the court were upon Wright. With dissembled boredom, unable to escape Birkett's direction, he read, and saw there official corroboration of the facts on the three certificates.

The Cecil Gladstone he had declared so airily to be the illegitimate son of the Liberal Prime Minister was, beyond question, the legitimate son of Gladstone's first cousin, William.

Mr. Birkett now administered the *coup de grâce*: 'Do you still say Cecil was the illegitimate son of Gladstone?' For the first time Wright's confidence seemed to desert him. 'No,' he said quietly, 'I do not say so now.'

On all his other allegations Wright was so vulnerable that one can only wonder why he should have invited an attack on himself which common sense should have told him was inevitable. As to Lily Langtry, alleged to be Gladstone's mistress, he had never spoken to her; she sent to the court, from her home on the Riviera, an indignant telegram repudiating Wright's accusation—a telegram which Captain Wright's counsel did not challenge as evidence. As to Madame Novikoff, the glamorous Tsarist spy sent to seduce Gladstone, Birkett produced correspondence between the two, extending over years; in none of the letters was there the faintest suggestion of intimacy. The then Lord Gladstone gave evidence that he himself, like his father, had heard of Parnell's affair with Mrs. O'Shea, but to suggest that his father connived at it was manifest nonsense; had this been so, Parnell would surely have made the most of this fact when he attacked Gladstone's reputation later.

What of Gladstone's 'seraglio'—supposedly mentioned by Lord Milner? Mr. T. P. O'Connor, M.P., 'father' of the House of Commons and first Editor of the *Star*, said he wrote the special memoir of Lord Milner in the *Daily Telegraph* of May 11th, 1925, in which he said that whenever Lord Gladstone was mentioned Milner would say that one could never tell what Gladstone was going to do until one knew what his seraglio had decided. Mr. O'Connor said that he had no doubt what Lord Milner meant. 'There were evidences almost every day of the extraordinary solicitude with which Mrs. Gladstone watched the comings and goings' of her husband.

Lord Malmesbury denied having said that Gladstone's detectives had complained of being asked to guard Madame Novikoff's London home for inordinate periods of duty. A surprise witness for the defence was Mr. Charlie Thompson. Having read of the acrimonious correspondence between Gladstone and Wright, he had told Wright of the incident when, walking down Jermyn

Street with a woman of dubious character, he had left her for a moment to fetch a photograph from his flat.

'She said: "See that old gentleman over there?" I said: "Yes, of course, that is Mr. Gladstone." She said: "Is it? He has been trying to get into conversation with me." '

Captain Wright had asked him to write to the Bath Club to that effect, but on consideration Thompson decided against it. He objected to maligning a dead man, and 'in addition the lady who had given me the information was a doubtful character'.

In view of the fact that Gladstone, assisted by his wife, helped with the rescue of fallen women, and that Thompson's companion, by his own admission, might be mistaken for one of them, a conversational approach by Gladstone was not impossible; the inference drawn by Captain Wright, however, had no shred of corroboration or proof.

It might be asked why, in view of the damning refutation adduced by the defence in respect of one or two of Wright's allegations, Mr. Birkett had chosen to deal with and demolish each of Wright's allegations specifically? The answer, I think, lay in Mr. Justice Avory's obvious partiality. If the plaintiff appeared to be labouring under an injustice at the hands of the Judge, members of the jury might be moved to see more merit in his arguments than they might otherwise do—the English jury is predisposed to the underdog. The prejudice could only be neutralised by a barrage of incontrovertible fact.

Making his final speech, Mr. Birkett said that whatever the result of the case might be, the brothers had dignified and exalted the name of sonship. Had they not done what they had they would be unworthy to bear their great name. 'I ask you to give me your verdict for Lord Gladstone on the plea of justification ... there is not a man or woman sitting in the box who will not say that this charge, made against a great figure who died thirty years ago, was a foul charge. It may be that, long after we are gone, the result of this case will be discussed. You will have a great opportunity to strike a resounding blow for the purity of public discussion, to secure that men shall no longer be permitted to traduce or defame the dead on garbage such as has been produced in this case. More than that, I ask you by your verdict, to vindicate the name of a great Englishman.'

Mr. Merriman, for the plaintiff, did his brave best, but after his client's showing in the witness box it was hopeless, as the Judge's summing up made clear enough. 'If history is to be made of the tittle-tattle of the Upper Tooting tea-table,' he said, 'you will no doubt consider whether it would not be better that history should not be made at all.'

'Is not the man who slanders the dead a coward?' asked Mr. Avory, his eyes swivelling, significantly, from the jury to the plaintiff and back again. 'Is not a man who makes a "foul charge" a "foul fellow"?'

After a two and a half hours' retirement the jury returned.

'I understand you are agreed that the gist of the defendant's letter of July 27th is true?' The foreman replied: 'That is so, My Lord.'

The Judge then said that they could, therefore, forget the question of malice, which could only arise if justification had not been proved. 'This is a verdict,' he said, 'for the defendant.'

There was instant applause in court, which Judge Avory sternly silenced. Mr. Birkett thanked the jury for their rider that: 'We are of unanimous opinion that the evidence which has been placed before us has completely vindicated the high moral character of the late Mr. W. E. Gladstone.' People swarmed round the Gladstone brothers to congratulate them on their successful fight.

For Norman Birkett it was one of the happiest days of his life. Professionally, the case was an unqualified triumph for him; and he had cleared the reputation of the hero of his boyhood.

CHAPTER X

Hero and Coward

NORMAN BIRKETT, AFTER the Gladstone Libel Case triumph, had become one of the busiest men at the Bar. The late Lord Hewart, Lord Chief Justice of England, used to say to young barristers: 'Don't despise the small fees; a job done well is never unnoticed in the courts.' When he first took silk, Birkett cheerfully accepted —through his shrewd and capable clerk, Alfred Bowker—fees both adequate and diminutive. As one solicitor put it to me: 'Even though he *had* only recently taken silk, Birkett's name stood very high in the Temple, and I remember the diffidence with which my Chief Clerk approached Bowker on one case we wished Birkett to handle. Cheerfully Bowker said; "He's doing nothing on Monday. Agreed. Five and two." That meant five guineas brief fee and two guineas for a conference, surely the smallest fee ever received by a silk. The case, I remember, was a publisher's dispute with his mother-in-law over some matter of money.'

Yet within three years of taking silk he was reaching into the big-money class.

Soon after the Gladstone case he appeared for the prosecution in two sensational trials, one for attempted murder and the other of murder.

The attempted murder was as dastardly and cowardly an assault on a brave policeman as can possibly be imagined. A Police Constable Dainty, of the Nottinghamshire Constabulary, questioned a man, Edgar Smith, whose car had broken down and, having just been repaired at the roadside, was about to move off. The man corresponded with the description of a suspect, a masked man who had been terrorising local women. When P.C. Dainty tried to take Smith into custody the man shot him twice at close range and made off.

Dainty, bleeding profusely and in great agony, clung tenaciously to the fast-moving car, managed to grab the steering-wheel and directed the car into a wall, falling from the running board at the moment of impact. The assailant fired a third shot

Norman Birkett as a junior barrister

(*Left*)
Mrs. Beatrice Pace, 'the tragic widow', charged with poisoning her husband with arsenic, and acquitted

(*Below*)
The one-time Rector of Stiffkey—the Rev. Harold Davidson—in a lion's cage at Skegness amusement park. In this cage he was mauled to death

at the prostrate policeman, who even then recovered his feet and grappled with Smith in an attempt to arrest him. This, with his numerous wounds, he could not hope to do. The gunman decamped, while P.C. Dainty crawled slowly and painfully to a police box.

There was little defence that Smith could make of violence that had stopped short of murder only by accident. The best excuse he could think of was that he had not intended to kill. 'I could have blown his brains out from the start,' he said, as though anxious for it not to be thought that, had he wished to kill a man, he would have bungled the job. This boastful evasion Birkett countered by a single sentence: 'You poked the revolver into his body near the top of his waistcoat pocket and fired, the bullet coming out of the back of the body. Is not that shooting to kill?'

This savage act incurred a savage sentence—penal servitude for life. For the fearless young constable whose career was cut short by this single act of devotion to duty, there were praises from Mr. Justice Branson and, later, the award of the King's Medal from King George V.

The people of Birmingham were much relieved, too, by Norman Birkett's able and salutary prosecution of the brutal John Joseph Power, a former member of the Birmingham Police Force, from which he had been discharged.

Power was a combination of *voyeur*, blackmailer and sadist—a man without pity and of ungovernable sexual appetite. Although a married man with children, he would sneak away from home and, prowling about by the canal, which was once part of his beat, frighten courting couples by a threat of 'arrest', which he would withdraw if they paid him money.

The diffidence of courting couples in face of this huge, menacing man who claimed to be a policeman is understandable, but it is a pity that he was not denounced more vigorously to the authorities before this last tragedy.

In that quiet, detached way which could be so deadly when he was leading a case for the prosecution, Birkett outlined his case before Mr. Justice Swift and the jury at Birmingham Assizes. The case for the Crown, he said, was that Olive Turner met her death on July 2nd last at the hands of the prisoner Power, and that the chain of circumstances was so complete that the conclusion was irresistible to the ordinary reasonable man.

G

On that day the dead girl, Olive Turner, left the cinema with her sweetheart, Charles Broomhead, at 9.45 p.m., walked a few yards down Winsen Green Road and entered on the towing path. They walked down an arm of the canal known as the Soho Street Branch, and stood together there. As they did so, a powerfully built man passed and repassed them, Broomhead observing his face and clothing at close quarters.

A quarter of an hour later, about 10.45 p.m., the man returned to the girl and Broomhead, who were still standing at the same spot, and said: 'You are trespassing.' Broomhead replied: 'We are not. We are walking down here.' The prisoner said: 'I shall have to take your names and addresses.' The couple gave these details, which Power did not bother to write down, but asked: 'Can you prove they're your right names and addresses?' When they said they could not, Power replied: 'All right then. I shall have to take you.'

The trite dialogue that ensued seems inadequate to the drama of which it was a part. As the three walked along to the main canal the prisoner stopped two or three times to repeat his question about their names and addresses, and, when Broomhead tried to light a cigarette informed him curtly that: 'You are not allowed to smoke while you are in custody.' Broomhead said: 'Take us, then.' Power answered: 'You know you can square me.' They passed another young couple, and poor Olive Turner said: 'Have those two; they're standing.' 'I've got two, that's enough,' said Powers, and when Broomhead appealed to him to 'let the girl go home' he said again: 'You know you can square it. It is up to yourself.'

Alas! Broomhead had only fourpence. 'I have some money, Charlie,' said the girl, now thoroughly frightened and distressed, but the young man could not tolerate such blatant blackmail. 'It's all right, Olive, you go home now,' he said. While the girl cried: 'If you had got a heart you would let me go home, as I have no father or mother.' She started to run back towards Clissold Street, and Power immediately ran after her. Broomhead pursued him and tried to protect the girl against this extraordinary 'policeman', who was physically too powerful an adversary. He seized Broomhead's collar with his left hand and struck him a tremendous blow with his right on the left side of the jaw. Dazed and bleeding, Broomhead fell to the ground and, as he came to, started a frantic search for the girl, but reaching the bridge at the entrance to the arm of the canal, he could not see her. By a bad stroke of fate he then ran to the Winson Green Road end of the canal, reaching there at about 11.30 p.m.

As the girl fled she passed a remark to another couple, Doris Emeny and Edgar Whillock, as she passed, and these two people also ran towards the Clissold Street entrance, reaching the Western Road Bridge. The prisoner, who had followed her, came up and said: 'I want that girl!' pointing to Olive Turner. Whillock asked him what he wanted with her, and he said: 'I am a police officer.' Without further challenge from any quarter, Power put his arm round Olive Turner's waist. She, in a very distressed and exhausted voice cried: 'Oh! Oh!' Her head went back in a half fainting condition, and she was led away by the prisoner, who supported her with his arm, in the direction of the arm of the canal.

'That,' said Mr. Birkett, 'was the last that was seen of the girl alive,' and the time at which the prisoner took away the girl in that condition was about 11.30 p.m. Five minutes later a woman heard the most terrifying screams come from the arm of the canal, and a man who lived near by heard the horrible screams of a woman coming from the same spot. The next morning the dead body of Olive Turner was recovered from the canal. Her watch had stopped at 11.41—eleven minutes after Power was seen to drag the girl away with him.

Positively identified by the three people who had seen him on the towpath—Broomhead and the others—Power tried desperately to fake an alibi. He denied being anywhere near the canal at the time, but admitted in cross-examination by Mr. Birkett that he had worn, on that day, a dark suit, a lighter-coloured cap and a rose buttonhole. One witness said that Power had his cap pulled down over his eyes.

Birkett produced the cap in court. 'Is this cap yours?' he asked.

'Yes,' replied Power sullenly.

'Were you wearing it that night?'—'I may have been.' At this point Birkett asked a warder to hand the cap to Powers, who accepted it with a 'what's-all-this-fuss-about?' look.

'Put the cap on, Power,' Birkett demanded.

Power placed the cap on top of his head and, when told to pull it down over his eyes, made a feeble show of doing so and declared it was too tight to be pulled down. If Power had been speaking the truth, and the cap would *not* go down over his eyes, it would follow that he could not have been the man seen near the canal by that particular witness.

'Warder,' said Birkett, 'pull the cap down over the prisoner's eyes.' It went down easily, and Power's alibi was rejected.

When the jury returned their verdict of 'Guilty' and the Clerk of the Assize asked Power, in accordance with the usual formula, 'Have you anything to say why judgement of death should not be pronounced upon you according to the law?' Power stated that during his five-months' wait in prison for the trial he had been threatened with a poker in the presence of 'the Governor and two officials by a detective-sergeant'. As the Judge pronounced sentence Power repeatedly interrupted with: 'I don't want any sympathy from you!' When Mr. Birkett asked if the prisoner's statement of facts at the conclusion of the trial called for any statement from the Crown the Judge thought not, as they were 'irrelevant to the charge'.

The towpath terror appealed against his sentence, but his appeal was dismissed, and he was duly hanged.

CHAPTER XI

Injured Innocence

THERE WAS LITTLE leisure for Norman Birkett in 1928. When he had any he delighted to read from his ever-growing collection of books, with heavy draughts of poetry, the Bible, history and biography. There were long hours in the Temple, days spent in travelling and a very crowded schedule of civil and criminal cases. Norman Birkett was now a father, and delighted to read to and play cricket with his daughter Linnea. As he continued to do throughout his life, he often visited Ulverston, his home town, and from afar, too, followed its fortunes with the interest of a resident.

In February he found himself in harness with Patrick Hastings, whose practice at the Bar had suffered both from his illness and the pursuit of politics, but who was rapidly coming to the fore again. This was a libel action brought by Mr. Mitchell-Hedges, a colourful journalist who had popularised the *Monomark* (a simple box number for correspondence and a means of identifying the ownership of property) and had a rather profitable arrangement with the *Daily Mail* by which he wrote of his bizarre, exotic and —some thought—unlikely adventures during his travels.

Hastings and Birkett appeared for the plaintiff, who complained that the *Daily Express* had libelled him in a story alleging that a 'hold-up', in the course of which he was waylaid by a gang of hooligans and robbed, was a crude and obvious publicity stunt, and that one of the participants had admitted it. The point was not, of course, whether the 'assault'—in the course of which Mitchell-Hedges and his friend Edgell were bound with ropes and an attaché case stolen—was a hoax on the part of the attackers or not. The allegation of which complaint was made was that Mitchell-Hedges was a party to the whole thing.

Plaintiff came under withering cross-examination from the other two Silks, Mr. William Jowitt, K.C., and Mr. J. B. Melville, K.C. It was by no means clear why a man off for a week-end in Bournemouth should take a few shrunken heads with him, despite his claim that 'they're a sort of mascot. I'm very fond of them'. The missing attaché case, with its unedifying contents, had in any case been returned to him, and he himself had asked the police to call off enquiries, and declined to prosecute. Mr. Bagot Gray, one of the hold-up party, had dinner with a William Shaw, and after dinner the pair of them, with two others, went and held up Mitchell-Hedges' car 'by arrangement'.

Without leaving the jury-box the jury gave a verdict for the defendants. Not even the most skilful cross-examination by Norman Birkett could make the plaintiff's story of what was supposed to happen convincing.

Shortly after this Birkett appeared for the Police before a tribunal known variously as the Hyde Park Enquiry and the Savidge Enquiry.

Early in 1928 two police officers, patrolling Hyde Park, had arrested a well-known author and politician, Sir Leo Chiozza Money and Miss Irene Savidge, who had been sitting beneath a tree. They were charged at Marlborough Street police court the next morning with indecency and appeared again after a week's remand on bail, during which Miss Savidge had been medically examined. The examination revealed nothing that could substantiate the police allegations, nor was there any corroboration of them. Indeed, the two policemen had not even bothered to take down the name and address of a man who had run after Sir Leo, as he was led away, to give him his umbrella, although he must have been very near to the couple at the time of their arrest, and his evidence would have been valuable.

The magistrate dismissed the charge against the couple, and criticised the police for bringing the case.

Questions were subsequently asked in the House of Commons. It was not illegal, it was suggested, to kiss in a park? And when is an embrace chaste or unchaste? There was a suggestion that the police concerned might have committed perjury, and the Home Secretary, reluctantly and only under public pressure, instituted an enquiry. A new and sensational chapter in this strange story then unfolded.

A fast police car, with two policemen and one policewoman, drove up to Miss Savidge's place of work, and under pressure she agreed reluctantly to go with them to Scotland Yard, on a promise that the policewoman would be present. But when they arrived at the Yard the policewoman was dismissed and Miss Savidge found herself interrogated for five hours by Inspector Collins and Sergeant Clarke. She claimed afterwards that the Inspector's attitude was alternately threatening and familiar, that she had been asked questions about the sort of underwear she wore and made to submit to a demonstration of how she and her elderly knight had been sitting in the park. The interview had started, Miss Savidge alleged, by the Inspector saying: 'Look here, Miss Savidge, you have come here to tell us the truth, and if you don't tell us the truth you and Sir Leo Money will suffer severely.' A statement was drawn up which she signed 'just to get away'.

At the official enquiry into these allegations against Scotland Yard, Norman Birkett led for the police and Sir Patrick Hastings for Miss Savidge. On the whole, she got the better of Birkett during cross-examination. Short, slim and dressed discreetly in black, she was 'baby' pretty, with an oval face, fresh complexion, cerulean blue eyes with long fluttering eyelashes, a dimple and a cupid's bow mouth.

No amount of questioning from Birkett would shake her story. She claimed to have been in mortal terror of the police, who arrived unannounced and whisked her off to Scotland Yard without informing her parents or allowing anyone else to accompany her. She did admit, however, that Sir Leo had kissed her—'just a peck at that, there was no passionate kiss'.

By searching questions, Norman Birkett secured certain admissions which he hoped might weaken her complaints against the police. Although she was twenty-two years of age, she was content to be meeting Sir Leo Money and going to cinemas and theatres with him, although he was fifty-eight, married and had a daughter. She had kept this association a secret from her fiancé.

Mr. Birkett, in submitting that the complaints against the police had signally failed, declared that 'a blow struck at the police is a blow struck at the whole fabric of the State'—an argument which would be as equally valid, if one accepted it, in a police State. After all, a blow struck at police *corruption* or *terrorism* would hardly be a blow against the State, assuming that the interests of the State and the freedom of its citizens were equated. Miss Savidge, continued Mr. Birkett, was not a poor girl being bullied by a man, but a girl of a certain independence, perfectly able to look after herself. As he spoke, his adversary Sir Patrick Hastings sketched the people in court, including Mr. Birkett. Hastings, in a brilliant speech, assailed the police, described Scotland Yard as a place of terror and said that the method employed to get the girl there was outrageous.

In the event, the Tribunal cleared the police, but a minority report considered Miss Savidge a more credible witness. There was an unhappy similarity of phrasing between the original statements of the police officers and the wording of Irene Savidge's alleged statement during her detention *incommunicado* at Scotland Yard.

The result of the enquiry was almost a foregone conclusion, as the Home Secretary had only instituted an enquiry reluctantly and under considerable public pressure. In this case, as in others, Norman Birkett had showed that he could use calmness and courtesy as easily to attack as to defend.

CHAPTER XII

The Tragic Widow

As a boy of sixteen, talking to a friend of the Birkett family, Miss Marion Iddon, Norman Birkett once said: 'I'm going to help women who are alone in the world. There are so many who are alone.'

If ever a woman felt alone and helpless in April 1928, that woman was Mrs. Beatrice Pace, 'the tragic widow of Coleford', tried before Mr. Justice Horridge on a charge of murdering her husband, Harry Pace, a sheep-farmer, by administering arsenic to him.

Since their marriage in 1917, the Paces had lived at Fetterhill Farm, Coleford, a lonely spot in the Gloucestershire Hills. Mrs. Pace's life could fairly be called a life of misery. Harry Pace was absorbed with his hundred sheep, but in all other respects was moody, morose, erratic and at times downright brutal.

The catalogue of Harry Pace's outrages against the woman of his choice are surely a testimony to her forbearance and hope that, in the unpredictable future, he might improve; instead, her patience was to put her life in jeopardy by encouraging the suspicion that she had a motive for doing away with him. He had beaten her on the first day of marriage. Just before her second baby was born he had thrashed her unmercifully with a walking-stick. He once soaked the blankets with paraffin, put them on the bed and set them on fire. He had locked his family out so that they had to sleep in the pigsty. He threw Mrs. Pace's pet dog repeatedly against a wall until it died. On one occasion he threatened to shoot his wife, and she sent for the police. He kicked and bit the ears of his sheep and even his dog when he was annoyed with them. He would slap his sides with his hands and crow like a cockerel—so realistically that their cockerel would come over the wall and answer him. Sometimes he would bark like a dog, and often he would keep his household awake—when he hadn't locked them out—by singing all night.

These shortcomings were corroborated by others, and Mrs.

Pace was hardly guilty of exaggeration when she said, in a statement: 'At times for years I have often thought that he was not in his right senses.'

Even so, she was a loyal helpmate, sharing his lonely and rugged existence, helping to tend and dip the sheep and nursing him in sickness.

In July 1927 Harry Pace was taken ill with severe stomach pains and partial paralysis. At Gloucester Infirmary, where he was taken, doctors diagnosed arsenical poisoning, which the doctors thought, though they could not be certain, might have been caused by prolonged and excessive contact with sheep dip.

Although still in need of medical attention, he was discharged from hospital in October, and celebrated Christmas day by attacking his wife with some fire-tongs, smashing the fender and threatening to cut everyone's throat. Two days later his stomach pains returned with renewed violence and on January 10th, 1928, after an agonising illness, he died.

A funeral cortege was about to leave the cottage five days later when police intervened on an order from the Coroner, Mr. Maurice Carter, acting on information received from the dead man's brother, Elton Pace, who had long been hostile to his brother's wife, and suspected foul play.

On January 16th an inquest was held at a local inn. Professor I. Walker Hall of Bristol University had recently examined the dead man's organs and found them to contain 9·42 grains of arsenic.

Then followed an ordeal for Mrs. Pace which aroused the sympathy of the public and, indirectly, caused a change to be made in the future conduct of coroners' inquests. For after the formal opening of the inquest there was an adjournment for two months for a further medical examination of the dead man's remains; incessant hearings and adjournments followed over a period of nineteen weeks and were a never-ending strain. Her health was broken, she had the worry of the publicity and local gossip inspired by Elton Pace's action; she was living in abject poverty and had meantime to care for her two daughters of seventeen and eleven, her two sons, the youngest aged six, and a baby of eleven months, dying from an incurable disease. She had the further burden of meeting the legal expenses of every adjournment, which she could not afford.

Early in March 1928 Scotland Yard appeared on the scene and interviewed everyone who might have knowledge of the circumstances of Harry Pace's death.

Small wonder that the *Daily Mail* declared at the time: 'It is very unsatisfactory and unfair that any citizen should be the victim of such torturing delays', and, on another occasion, called it 'persecution'. In the course of fifteen sittings of the Coroners' Court Mrs. Pace was subject to the most protracted and nerve-racking enquiries.

The inquest, in effect, was a 'trial' without the usual safeguards on the taking and giving of evidence. Mrs. Pace described her unhappy life and gave details of how she had nursed her husband through his illness. In the early part of 1927 she bought two packets of sheep dip, one packet being used to dip some lambs. Her husband was taken ill the same night. He had, she said, threatened to commit suicide while in hospital.

Inspector Alan Bent, of the Coleford police, said that Mrs. Pace admitted to having sheep dip in the house and produced a full packet from the kitchen. In a further search he found a bottle of disinfectant, a quantity of white powder, a small packet of purple crystals and an unlabelled medicine bottle containing a purple mixture.

At the final hearing of the Coroner's Court the jury returned a verdict that 'We find that Harry Pace met his death at Fetter Hill on January 10th by arsenical poisoning administered by some person or persons other than himself. We are agreed that this case calls for further investigation.'

At this point the Coroner, Mr. Carter, told the jury that it was necessary for them to name a person or persons under the Act before they could be committed. 'No person,' he said, 'can be committed by a Coroner's inquisition and so bring about a further enquiry into the case unless some person is named.'

On this queer directive the jury considered the matter again and returned a second and different verdict: 'We find that the deceased Harry Pace met his death at Fetter Hill on January 10th, 1928, by arsenical poisoning administered by Beatrice Annie Pace.'

Mrs. Pace immediately became hysterical, screaming: 'I didn't, I didn't!' Led from the court under arrest to the police-station below, she fainted away and was unconscious for several minutes.

She collapsed as she was guided to the dock of the specially summoned magistrates court, and did not hear that she would be sent for trial at the next Assizes. She was almost insensible as the Clerk read the charge, but Dr. Earengey on her behalf pleaded 'Not Guilty' and reserved his defence. The Chairman then said: 'The accused is committed to the next Gloucester Assizes. . . .' Mrs. Pace, now slightly recovered but still doubled up, muttered something about: 'I am coming home.' Wardresses then lifted her and carried her from court to cries of 'Shame!' from women in the public gallery. Later, accompanied by wardresses and in a closed car, she was whisked away to prison. Several hundred people watched her go, among them Doris Pace, her younger daughter, dangling a doll which a well-wisher had given her.

Truly Norman Birkett could consider Mrs. Pace a lonely woman who needed help. A defence fund of £1,000 was raised by sympathisers (local sympathy was almost entirely in Mrs. Pace's favour), and friends and neighbours rallied to look after her children. Dorothy and the eldest boy went to the care of a widowed aunt. Uncle Fred took six-year-old Teddy. Doris, a charming eleven-year-old daughter whose clear and concise evidence had won praise from both police and jury, on whom the burden of nursing the dying baby had largely fallen, was given a home by kindly hotel proprietors. Mrs. Sayes, who, with her husband, was a close friend of Mrs. Pace, took the sick baby.

The stage was set to find an answer to the question posed with unusual vehemence by the Coroner: 'Is it conceivable that a man is going to dose himself with arsenic from July 1927 down to January 10th, in order to bring about his own death? It must have been agony . . . is it conceivable that this man is going to dose himself in July with sheep dip lotion to see how much he could take or how long he could linger before he killed himself, and then is it conceivable that he is going to take one big dose within a short space of his death?'

The trial of Mrs. Pace opened at the Shire Hall, Gloucester, on July 2nd, 1928. The law's majesty had taken six torturing months to emerge in all its pomp. Now the eyes of the country were on the tragic widow, every hotel in the cathedral city was crowded to capacity; the humble Gloucestershire village had become a place of high drama. I was a junior reporter in Cardiff at this time, and remember distinctly the anguished apprehension in everyone's mind. It seemed intolerable that a woman had been found 'guilty' of murder by a coroner's jury and should then have to stand trial on this capital charge with that pre-supposition noised abroad beforehand. Day after day the newspapers were full of little else but the 'Pace case'—even the family dog was interviewed. 'I tried this afternoon,' wrote one reporter, aflame with missionary zeal, 'to get him to come for a walk, but he would not consider it. He merely came out of his kennel, had a good look at me, and went back again.'

Sir Frank Boyd Merriman, K.C. (Solicitor-General), Mr. St. John Micklethwait and Mr. H. M. Giveen were Counsel for the Crown; Mr. Norman Birkett, K.C., and Dr. W. G. Earengey, who had so ably represented Mrs. Pace during the police-court proceedings, appeared for the defence.

The prosecution's case was that nine and a half grains of arsenic were found in Harry Pace's body, two grains being a fatal dose. Large quantities of arsenic were on hand in the house in which Mr. and Mrs. Pace lived, for it was an ingredient of sheep dip, which had been bought for a perfectly legitimate purpose. The Crown maintained that Harry Pace had been poisoned by arsenic obtained from sheep dip, administered by his wife with intent to murder him.

Sir Frank, however, put the prosecution's case with commendable fairness: 'It almost necessarily follows where poisoning is in question that it has been done secretly and it also follows that, unlike other crimes of violence, you cannot overlook the possibility that it may have been self-administered.

'It follows that proof in any case of poisoning necessarily depends upon drawing the proper inference from circumstantial evidence.' He referred again to 'a plain suggestion, plainly made by the prisoner in a statement . . . that her husband poisoned himself'.

Questions which would need consideration were: (a) the effects of arsenic on the human body; (b) the composition of sheep dip; (c) the disposal of the arsenic found in Pace's body. There were 1,400 fatal doses of arsenic in a packet of sheep dip, which was composed mainly of 21 per cent arsenic, about 65 per cent sulphur and about $6\frac{3}{4}$ per cent soda. When sheep dip was mixed with water the arsenic was easily soluble, but the sulphur was not. That meant that the colourless fluid, containing only arsenic, could be drawn off.

If, continued Sir Frank, sheep dip were taken as sheep dip— arsenic, sulphur and all—Pace's body would have contained three times as much sulphur as arsenic, which it did not. The point about sulphur was not fully pursued during the trial, but Sir Frank Merriman's statement at this point was inaccurate. During the police-court proceedings Professor Walker-Hall, the patho- logist from Bristol University, had said that if sheep dip had been administered to a man he would *not* expect to find traces of sul- phur, as 'it would disappear normally in twenty-four hours'. No sulphur was found in his body. 'One can easily understand anyone seeking to poison a victim with arsenic, taking care not to put him on his guard by giving him something which was in- dicative of sheep dip by the presence of sulphur,' continued Sir Frank. 'On the other hand, it is not so clear why a man minded to administer sheep dip to himself in order to put an end to him- self should take the trouble of getting rid of the sulphur before taking the mixture. An infinitesimal quantity of arsenic was found in the stomach, but four grains were found in the in- testines, over three and a half grains in the liver and over one grain in the kidneys.'

Scientific witnesses would draw from these facts the conclusion that no dose could have been taken within six hours of death, but the presence of over four grains in the intestines indicated that a large dose must have been taken within forty-eight hours of death. Yet forty-eight hours before death, according to medical evidence, Pace was 'practically helpless'. It was almost incredible that he could have got out of bed to search for the arsenical poison, and even more unlikely that in his dying state he could have separated the arsenic and sulphur.

Sir Frank then dealt with motive, the opportunities of ad- ministering arsenic and the means of obtaining it. Motive, he suggested, lay in the couple's unhappy married life.

Crown evidence then established that in June 1927 Pace was taken ill with pains in the stomach, and Dr. Du Pre was called in. On July 22nd Mrs. Pace, at her husband's request, bought two packets of sheep dip. The next day they dipped some lambs, but not using either of the two new packets of dip. That night Pace was taken violently ill and was removed to Gloucester Infirmary, from which, after two months and at his own request, he was returned home. Mrs. Pace tried to get his doctor, Dr. Du Pre, to get him into another hospital.

Before that, however, there was a curious incident. Pace's mother was visiting him at home, and when he asked for some water she pointed to a cup at his bedside. He sipped a little, but put it down saying: 'I can't drink it.' His mother tasted it and found it 'salty and nasty'.

On some occasions Mrs. Pace had been heard to say that she wished she could poison her husband. At about Christmas he had attacked his wife with the fire-tongs, but the fact that he had previously been suffering from partial paralysis implied that he had by then partially recovered from his previous attacks. When Mrs. Pace's brother came, after this trouble, she had said: 'Do you think he has been taking something?' Two months after his death Mrs. Pace handed to the police an empty tin with the comment: 'I remember him saying to me, if you are tired of life, take one of these and you will die.' The empty tin had once contained tablets of three parts sulphur and one of arsenic. He could not have committed suicide in this way, it was alleged, because no sulphur was found.

When ten-year-old Leslie Pace, the son, was lifted into the witness box he described how his father dipped some lambs in a tub before he went into hospital in the summer. His father had taken some powder from a newspaper, but had not used it all, screwing the rest up in a piece of paper which he then put in a box downstairs. Once, when his mother was out and his father ill in bed, the boy was told by his father to fetch the box. He did so, and Harry Pace took out the screwed-up paper. The boy described how he and his sister had protected his mother when Pace came at her with the fire-tongs, of his frequent threats and how once: 'Dad said he was going to shoot us with a gun.' He never hesitated to the questions put to him. He described how, when Pace was dipping the sheep, they kicked and struggled a good deal, so that at the end of the operation his father was 'fairly well wetted'.

Mr. Birkett: 'Has your mum always been very kind to you?'— 'Yes.'

'Do you love your mum?'—'Yes.'

'Has she looked after you well?'—'Yes.'

'And your brothers and sisters?'—'Yes.'

Mrs. Pace wept softly throughout this simple questioning, and there were few who did not feel pity for her, despite the weight of circumstantial evidence.

When Mrs. Porter, the dead man's mother, was called, Mr. Birkett made short work of that sinister anecdote of the cup of water at the bedside, which Pace refused to drink. At the police court she had said that she had not seen her son a month before his illness. She did not know that in July 1926 Mrs. Pace had taken her husband to a doctor in Coleford when he complained of pains in his stomach. And of his later illness, Birkett asked:

'Who was in this little house to do the nursing besides the prisoner?'—'Doris, aged eleven.'

'Yes, eleven *now*. Is it a fact that you, the mother, never rendered one moment's assistance in nursing the son?'—'No, she did not want me.'

'She had had a baby and the baby was sick. That was enough for one woman, was it not?'—'Of course it was.'

'The "salty, nasty taste" of the water, so far as you know, may have been medicine?'—'I cannot say what it was.'

In his cross-examination of Chief Inspector Cornish of Scotland Yard, Norman Birkett showed an asperity which was rare for him: it was Cornish who had taken Mrs. Pace's long statement, and he had done so without telling her that he had previously obtained a statement from her son Leslie.

'You were trying to get admissions from her? You were trying the case?' Birkett said warmly.

Speaking of his second visit to Mrs. Pace, Inspector Cornish admitted that she had given him a letter she had received from Edmund Slinger, who was in hospital at the same time as Pace. In this letter of sympathy to Mrs. Pace on the death of her husband he said: '. . . He told me while in the infirmary that if he was not going to get better quickly he should do himself in, as he could not stick it much longer.'

The Inspector agreed that Mrs. Pace had told him that Dr. Francis had been attending her husband.

Mr. Birkett: 'Dr. Francis was not called before the Coroner, was he?'—'No.'

'Dr. Francis was not called before the Justices?'—'No.'

(*Right*) Alfred Arthur Rouse, who murdered an unknown man in the 'blazing car' case. (*Below*) The Morris Minor saloon car, completely burnt out; note the steering column without wheel

(*Above*) Mr. Norman Birkett (centre) with his clerk, Edgar Bowker (right), photographed at Lewes Assizes during the trial of Mancini for the 'Brighton Trunk Crime No. 2'. (*Left*) Tony Mancini

'Although the doctor's evidence as to the history of previous illnesses was given to you and investigations made?'—'No.'

'Was Edmund Slinger interviewed by Inspector Green?'—'Yes.'

'Edmund Slinger was not called before the Coroner?'—'No.'

'Nor before the Justices?'—'No.'

Mr. Birkett showed that Cornish had spent 'three long days' collecting statements from relatives of the dead man before seeing Mrs. Pace. He dealt with Mrs. Pace's twelve-hours' interrogation by the Inspector, and the methods used. The statement, the Inspector agreed, was elicited by questions.

Mr. Birkett: 'It is clear that this suggestion that he might have killed himself arose with you because Mrs. Pace said she could not explain how the arsenic got into his body?'—'She was nursing him, and I did everything in my power to get from her how the arsenic got into his body.'

'You were trying to eliminate everyone but Mrs. Pace?'—'No, I was trying to get to know from the others as much as from Mrs. Pace how the arsenic got into the body.'

'There was cross-examination?'—'I asked her questions.'

'Did you ask her if she could suggest anyone else who had poisoned him?'—'I asked her to show me how the poison got there.'

'Listen to the question. Did you ask her?'—'No.'

'In the statement this occurs: "I don't think it is possible for any person who has visited him to have given him any poison to take." Do you say you did not ask her?'—'Yes.'

'Where does that phrase come from?'—'I asked her questions, but I do not remember exactly what she said.'

There was some mystery about a little green bottle which Dorothy, one of the daughters, had found in the fender in Pace's room. Mrs. Pace freely told Sergeant Hamblin about this. But another bottle, a blue one, was found, and Hamblin admitted to some confusion about which he had handed to the Inspector.

It was abundantly clear that, despite the mystery of Harry Pace's death, the prosecution had a very weak case against his wife, and it was probably only because of the Coroner's extraordinary action that she was arrested at all. In the course of Mr. Birkett's cross-examination of Dr. Du Pre the jury learned that on Boxing Day Mrs. Pace had trudged through the snow, knee-deep

H

all the way, to his surgery—a distance of three miles—to ask him to visit her husband. The snow was so deep that even the willing doctor could not get through until the next day. He testified to Pace's reluctance to take any medicine that was nasty-tasting (which could account for the 'cup of water' at his bedside) and said that the general improvement in Pace's health before his final illness was due to his wife's devoted nursing.

Mr. Birkett: 'From start to finish of the time that this man was under your care, did the prisoner appear to be a devoted nurse and wife?'—'Yes.'

'And, so far as your directions were concerned, did she appear to do all she could to get him better?'—'Yes.'

Reginald Joseph Martin, a chemist who visited Pace during his illness, described how the daughter had come to him 'all of a shake' after Pace's threat to kill them all with a razor. Martin admitted telling the coroner that Pace was a man 'who would be likely to take his own life'.

Every day, as she was driven from court, Mrs. Pace, looking so diminutive and lost, was cheered by the crowds, while her brother-in-law, Elton Pace, who had stopped the funeral and started the rumours that had culminated in her arrest, was the object of much public hostility. This he tended to make worse by his behaviour in the witness box, for his prejudice against, if not hatred of, Mrs. Pace became all too apparent. With immense patience and self-restraint Norman Birkett allowed Elton Pace to reveal his character in his own words.

Elton Pace declared that he had heard Mrs. Pace say that she wished she could get rid of 'The old ——', and on one occasion she remarked that she could poison him. When he visited his brother in July he had found his sister-in-law stretched across her husband's sick-bed 'a-bellocking' (pretending) and saying: 'Ah, Harry, you be a'dying! We shall not see you much longer.' She was impeding his breath, and he seized her by the back of the neck and pulled her off.

On another occasion Mrs. Pace sent a note saying that a Dr. Nanda would be in the house at one thirty when he was really there at eleven thirty. He (witness) then called Mrs. Pace 'a —— liar', and as a result she ordered him off the premises.

Quietly Mr. Birkett rose, gave his gown a minatory hitch and looked straight at Elton Pace.

'You began your evidence,' he said, 'by saying you were on friendly terms with the deceased and his wife?'—'Yes, sir.'

'Is that true, or is it a lie?'—'True, sir.'

'Four years ago did Mrs. Pace forbid you to come to the house?'—'She told me that very often, sir.'

'Will you deal with this question first. Did she four years ago forbid you to come to the house?'—'I cannot say.'

'When was the first time, and how many years ago?'—'I cannot say.'

'May it have been three years ago?'—'It may have been.'

'Then what do you mean by telling my Lord and the jury that you were on friendly terms when you had been forbidden the house?'—'We made it up fairly often.'

'Did she say you were a bully?'—'She has called me a bully.'

'When was the first time she called you a bully?'—'When Dr. Nanda was there.'

'Was that on the occasion you speak about? When you called her a —— liar, she called you a bully?'—'She did.'

As this cross-examination proceeded, poor Mr. Justice Horridge, who wrote everything down in his laborious longhand, began to suffer from the witness's use of Forest of Dean expressions. 'A-bellocking' had momentarily baffled him. Elton Pace admitted to calling at the Pace home twice a week *after* Mrs. Pace had forbidden him the house, but could not say how many times she had done so. 'I cannot say. I have a lot on my plate.' He explained to the Judge, in reply to his question, that this meant he had a lot of worry.

'I suggest,' continued Mr. Birkett, 'that you never said anything to your brother that he had been called "a mingy old ——".' —'Certainly not. He'd have gone down my neck, he would that.'

'The reason was that the deceased was so fond of the prisoner?' —'He was over-seeing in her.'

'Do you mean he was devoted to her?'—'Yes, he could see no faults in her.'

But in touching on Mrs. Pace's devoted nursing of her sick and irrational husband, Mr. Birkett revealed the depth of animosity which actuated the witness. He said he knew nothing whatever about Mrs. Pace taking her husband to see Dr. Francis at Coleford in 1926, or her calling in Dr. Du Pre.

Mr. Birkett: 'Do you know nothing whatever about the prisoner's efforts to get her husband attended by doctors?'—'No fear.'

'You mean to convey to my Lord and the jury that you do not believe it?'—'No, I don't.'

'And if Dr. Francis or Dr. Du Pre come into that box and swear it, you would not believe it then?'—'No, I should not. I have got my own opinion about them.'

Of the visit to the house where his brother lay dying, Mr. Birkett asked about Mrs. Pace's alleged 'play-acting' ('a-bellocking'): 'Did he say anything?'—'No, he was in far too much pain.'

'And she was play-acting?'—'Yes.'

'You got her by the back of the neck and pulled her off violently?'—'Not violently.'

'I suggest that the whole of that matter is an invention?'—'It is not.'

'Did you say anything to Mrs. Pace?'—'I did not want to talk to such a woman as that.'

'I put it to you plainly that this matter of the alleged false time in the letter is untrue?'—Witness (shouting) 'It is true.'

'Did she seem distressed?'—'Distressed? No, she did not. She can stand more than that.'

'You have just said she had a bad reputation. Do you say that now to injure her while she sits in that dock on her trial for murder?'—'Well, facts are facts.'

At no murder trial in living memory has the public been so moved to sympathy for the accused as in the Pace trial. As it progressed, the arrivals and departures of Mrs. Pace caused dense, good-humoured crowds, including hundreds of village mothers who had come with their perambulators from outlying villages. They cheered, waved handkerchiefs and shouted 'Good luck' and 'Don't worry'. Some of her well-wishers were in tears. She had endured so much. Only five of her ten children had survived, and her baby, because of the cruel beating she had suffered during pregnancy, had been born deaf and dumb. Through the terrible months preceding the trial she had subsisted on parish relief.

The same almost hysterical acclamation was accorded Dorothy and Doris Pace as they waited to be taken to Coleford.

On the fifth day came drama, silently, joyously and unexpectedly. Immediately after the lunch adjournment Mr. Birkett rose and submitted that there was no case to go to the jury. 'I submit,' he said, 'that there is no evidence of administration by the prisoner. The scientific evidence is consistent with administration by Pace equally with any other theory. The fact that there was arsenic in the body, the quantity found, the effect upon the organs, all these are consistent with self-administration. The burden on the Crown is that they must exclude it, and that, in my submission, they have not done.'

As to the Crown asking who else had the opportunity, 'Every wife in the country has opportunity. If it is said that she alone prepared the food, that will not do. There was no one else to prepare the food, and that kind of argument would lead to this—that every innocent thing the ordinary person may do becomes some evidence of guilt.' As to the sheep dip 'the evidence for the Crown showed that precisely similar quantities had been purchased not only in 1927, but in 1922, 1923, 1924, 1925 and 1926. There the mere fact that there were two packets purchased in 1927 proves nothing whatsoever.'

Mr. Justice Horridge sat motionless throughout this speech, a red-robed sphinx, giving not a hint of what was going through his mind. With a quiet earnestness that added drama to this moment, Birkett made point by point, then at the Judge's request exchanged a few whispered words. The Judge pointed out that he could not accept that there was *no* evidence to go to the jury. 'Then,' said Mr. Birkett, 'I submit that there is not sufficient evidence.'

Mr. Justice Horridge turned to the jury and quietly directed them to return a verdict of 'Not Guilty'. Few heard these words, and not until the Clerk asked the jury, 'Are you agreed upon your verdict?' and the Foreman answered, 'Yes sir, Not Guilty' were their full significance realised. The court was silent. Mrs. Pace sat still and motionless, hardly able to realise what had happened until the calm, unruffled Norman Birkett leaned across the railings of the dock and shook hands with her. Then her face flushed and tears of relief welled into her eyes.

Suddenly there was pandemonium such as is seldom seen in an English court. The public in a wild upsurge of joy rose to their feet and cheered and waved. The chorus of heartfelt thanksgiving was taken up by the waiting thousands outside. The Judge hurried off to his lodgings. Mr. Birkett, as he made his way through the crowds, was fêted and cheered. Elton Pace, who had glowered silently through it all, was greeted with boos and protected by mounted police as he made his way to his car.

Mrs. Pace could not be smuggled away. The enormous crowds would not disperse. At last she came—first Doris with her teddy bear, then Mrs. Pace with Dorothy on one arm and Mrs. Sayes, who had cared for her baby, on the other. At last she could smile, and blew kisses to the cheering crowds. Then a brief visit to the house of tragedy, made a shambles by souvenir hunters, where Rover, her dog, went wild with joy at the sight of her, and away to peace and obscurity.

Mrs. Pace's ordeal, and Birkett's masterly handling of his part in the trial, underlined the need for a reform in the law. Here was a woman acquitted of murder by the Assize Court, yet still on record as a murderer by the verdict of the Coroner's jury. Mr. A. A. Purcell, M.P., who promoted the defence fund, wrote to the Prime Minister asking him to compensate Mrs. Pace and institute a public enquiry into the position and powers of coroners.

The Attorney-General, Sir Thomas Inskip, refused to consider compensation, but Mr. Purcell personally raised sufficient funds to ensure Mrs. Pace a life annuity of £3 a week.

One fascinating question remains unsolved to this day. Who *did* poison Harry Pace? Did he absorb arsenic through the mouth and skin, through being slopped over with sheep dip? Was his brain unhinged, and did he choose this long-winded and agonising form of suicide (he had sent his son to fetch the remains of the sheep dip from his box)? Or did Harry Pace, a violent and singular man, tired of life himself, seek a posthumous revenge on his wife by choosing a manner of death which he hoped would throw suspicion upon her?

For Norman Birkett, of course, this was not simply another legal triumph. It was a victory entirely in keeping with popular sentiment. Within four years of taking silk his name was famous. This, however, was no moment for self-satisfaction; many more complicated cases lay immediately ahead.

CHAPTER XIII

The Forbidden Subject

ONE OF NORMAN BIRKETT'S next cases was to be a literary *cause célèbre*. It was also a case which, because of the intellectual climate then prevailing in official quarters, he could not hope to win.

Miss Radclyffe Hall, a novelist and poet of distinction, wrote a novel, *The Well of Loneliness*, whose main theme was homosexuality between women. It was not the only recent novel to deal with the theme of inversion, but unlike the rest, it became the subject of tremendous publicity.

There was no real reason why this should have been so. Rabelais is more impenitently lustful: Bliss Carman's translations of Sappho's poems, most of them extolling the joys of Lesbian love, were freely available; Brantôme's *Lives of Gallant Ladies*, an anthology of libidiny, was on sale, too. And certain passages in the Bible, which were and are most certainly unsuitable for children, are permitted to remain in their context, sombre pieces indeed in a mosaic which, taken as a whole, is considered beautiful.

However, James Douglas, editor of the *Sunday Express*, had either never heard of these books or felt that antiquity had overlaid them with a patina of respectability. But on *The Well of Loneliness* he launched a barrage of moralisation which shook the middle classes from one end of Britain to the other.

'I am well aware [he thundered] that sexual inversion and perversion are horrors which exist amongst us today. They flaunt themselves in public places with increasing effrontery and more insolently provocative bravado. The decadent apostles of the most hideous and loathsome vices no longer conceal their degeneracy and degradation. . . . This novel forces upon our society a disagreeable task which it has hitherto shirked, the task of cleaning itself from the leprosy of these lepers. . . .'

'I would rather [continued this self-appointed guardian of Britain's morals] put a phial of prussic acid in the hands of a healthy boy or girl than the book in question. . . .'

The *Daily News*, although lukewarm about the book's dramatic construction, declared: '*The Well of Loneliness* is not an obscene or indecent book.' Its central figure was an invert, the sort of tomboy who does not take to skirts and frilly things when past adolescence, but strides with masterful tread through paddocks and stables, preferring the pursuits of men and finding in other women her only means of emotional and sexual fulfilment.

Messrs. Jonathan Cape, the publishers, who had had ample opportunity to read and approve this novel before accepting it, now sent a copy to the Home Secretary, Sir William Joynson-Hicks ('Jix') for examination. To the *Daily Express* they also sent a long letter in which they said:

'Publication of this book was not undertaken without very serious thought and consideration. We considered that it should be published, but not as a book for the general and promiscuous reader. To this end we published it in a special and sober format and at the high price of fifteen shillings with a view to keeping it out of the hands of the general novel-reading public. We do not admit by this that any readers will suffer harm if they read the book, but . . .'

The Home Secretary advised the publishers to withdraw the book, which they did. 'Better late than never,' growled the *Daily Express*.

Miss Radclyffe Hall was on the Continent when the storm of controversy broke, and hurried back to face the attacks with dignity and courage. She was, of course, an invert herself—a mere glance at her would confirm that obvious and advertised fact. The firm chin, the severe mannish clothes, complete with shirt and bow-tie, the close-cropped Eton haircut and her monocle—at that time almost a trade mark with female homosexuals—left little room for doubt.

She had, however, the moral courage to live consistent with her own unalterable nature, a form of courage incomprehensible to those who cannot understand these variations on Nature's usual theme. She was a serious writer. The previous year her novel *Adam's Breed* achieved the unusual distinction of winning two coveted literary prizes—the Femina Vie Heureuse Prize and the James Tait Black Memorial Literary Prize and (in America) the Eichelberger Gold Medal. Other works already published included *The Forge*, *The Unlit Lamp* and several volumes of poetry. She was an accomplished linguist, a considerable traveller, a connoisseur of old furniture and an indefatigable firstnighter. She was living with Lady Troubridge at the time, and their house was the Mecca of writers, artists and theatrical personalities.

Radclyffe Hall was too practical a person not to understand the publisher's predicament.

'Two years of incessant work following upon many years of deep study [she declared] have suffered at the hands of wilful ignorance and prejudice amounting to persecution. In *The Well of Loneliness* I have given the public an accurate psychological study of one of the most pressing problems of the day in all its complicated and heartrending aspects. . . . I also claim that far from encouraging depravity, my book is calculated to encourage a mutual understanding between normal persons and the inverted, which can only be beneficial to both and to society at large. . . . I am proud and happy to have taken up my pen in defence of the persecuted.'

The *Daily Herald*, whether from altruistic or political motives I do not know, sprang to her defence. Even before the withdrawal the *Daily Telegraph*, hardly a medium for encouraging depravity, had described *The Well of Loneliness* as:

'a truly remarkable book. It is remarkable in the first place as a work of art finely conceived and finely written . . . it would be a mistake to compliment Miss Hall on her style, on her marvellously just selection of words, and on her burning sincerity, while at the same time condemning her choice of subject and accusing her of lack of restraint. Her book must be accepted as a whole. . . .'

The *Times Literary Supplement* found it 'sincere, courageous, highminded'. George Bernard Shaw, who read it, said that it ought not to be withdrawn.

An enterprising Paris publisher then began printing the books in France and exporting them into England, where, because of the wide publicity initiated by James Douglas, they enjoyed a ready sale. In October the *Daily Express* was able to report, in a flush of moral righteousness, that Her Majesty's Customs, assisted by Scotland Yard officers, had swooped down upon a cargo of the illicit book when it arrived at Dover. Orders for the novel were, meantime, pouring in to Paris from all over the world.

On November 9th the Director of Public Prosecutions applied at Bow Street for a destruction order under Lord Campbell's Act. Eustace Fulton and Vincent Evans appeared for the Crown. Norman Birkett, K.C., and Herbert Metcalfe, appeared for the publishers.

For weeks Norman Birkett had been working on the case, looking at precedents, considering the legal definitions of obscenity and assembling the views of distinguished people in the literary, artistic and social worlds on the merits of *The Well of Loneliness*.

Chief Inspector Prothero, whose literary qualifications were unstated, declared that he had bought a copy of the book, and considered it indecent because its theme was indecent. He found its theme of physical passion offensive. The Inspector's words were a ludicrous over-simplification of the novel's theme, which dealt with the social and psychological implications of a particular sort of personality and not simply with sexual manifestations.

Sir Chartres Biron, the Bow Street magistrate, listened with ill-concealed irritation as Norman Birkett rose to make a logical and considered defence of the book. Homosexuality is a subject which repels and perplexes those untouched by it or bigoted in their monopolistic assumption of virtue; for this reason it is regarded as a merely sexual matter. Norman Birkett tried to draw a distinction, long recognised by doctors, psychiatrists and all who have to deal first-hand with these matters, that there is a positive difference between perversion and inversion. Inverts are persons with inherent tendencies which are an integral part of their mental and physical make-up and personality; emotions and desires which with most people are directed towards the opposite sex are directed, instead, towards their own. It is in their nature to do this, and they often find any thought of intimate relations with the opposite sex repugnant and alien to their deepest feelings. The pervert, on the other hand, is perverting natural instincts; having the capacity to give them normal expression, but by deliberate choice turning to the abnormal.

The book, in brief, was concerned not with perversion but with what is described by medical science as inversion.

To anybody to whom the whole subject was distasteful, however, it seemed a distinction without a difference.

'Do you mean to say,' asked Sir Chartres coldly, 'it does not deal with unnatural offences at all?'

Mr. Birkett: 'I say not. It is a sombre, sad, tragic, artistic revelation of that which is an undoubted fact in the world. It is the result of years of labour by one of the most distinguished novelists alive, and it is a sincere and high-minded effort to make the world more tolerable for those who have to bear the tragic consequences of what they are not to blame for at all.'

A most impressive collection of witnesses had offered themselves for the defence. They included Sir (then Mr.) Hugh Walpole, Laurence Housman, E. M. Forster, Desmond MacCarthy, Miss Rose Macaulay, A. P. Herbert, Storm Jameson and Professor Julian Huxley. But the thirty-nine witnesses, besides including some of the greatest names in contemporary English literature, also included, as Mr. Birkett told the magistrate, '. . . people of every walk of life who desire to go into the witness box and to testify that this book is not obscene and that it is a misuse of words for the prosecution to describe it as such.'

'The test,' said Sir Chartres Biron, 'is whether it is likely to deprave and corrupt those into whose hands it is likely to fall. How can the opinion of a number of people be evidence?'

Fortunately for his clients, Norman Birkett did not possess his late chief's fiery temper. He could have asked how anybody could hope to *prove* that a book would 'corrupt or deprave'—a calculation involving speculation as to the character and susceptibility of the reader, an unspecified reader in the unpredictable future. He could have asked how Chief Inspector Prothero's view that the whole theme of the book was offensive, because it dealt with physical passion, could be considered evidence if the views of erudite, critical and creative people with vastly more experience of the subject was not. Instead, he answered mildly: 'I want to call evidence from every conceivable walk of life which bears on the test whether the tendency of this book was to deprave and corrupt. A more distinguished body of witnesses has never before been called in a court of justice.'

Sir Chartres Biron: 'I have the greatest doubt whether the evidence is admissible.'

Norman Birkett: 'If I am not allowed to call evidence it means that a magistrate is virtually a censor of literature.'

When Mr. Desmond MacCarthy, editor of *Life and Letters,*

entered the witness box and stated that he had read *The Well of Loneliness*, Mr. Birkett's first question was: 'In your view is it obscene?' Immediately the magistrate crushed further evidence along those lines.

'No,' the magistrate insisted, 'I shall disallow that. A book may be a fine piece of literature and yet obscene. Art and Obscenity are not disassociated at all. There is a room at Naples to which visitors are not admitted as a rule, which contains fine bronzes and statues, all admirable works of art, but all grossly obscene. I shall not admit the evidence.' Unfortunately Sir Chartres Biron did not say whether this little digression about Naples was garnered at first-hand or by hearsay. If the latter, it is difficult to understand why he should feel so sure that the objects were 'admirable works of art' or 'obscene'.

Mr. Birkett: 'I formally tender thirty-nine other witnesses. The evidence which a number of them would have given is identical with that of Mr. MacCarthy. In a second category are distinguished authors and authoresses who would have said that they had read the book and in their view it was not obscene. Other witnesses include booksellers, ministers of religion, social workers, magistrates, biologists, including Professor Julian Huxley, educationalists, including the Registrar of Durham University, and representatives of the London libraries.'

Magistrate: 'I reject them all.' Later Norman Birkett asked him to state a case for a higher court on the question of the admissability of the expert evidence which he wished to tender. This request, too, was refused.

After the adjournment Mr. Birkett told the magistrate that he was not in a position to contend further that the book did not relate to unnatural offences between women in every sense of the word. But counsel for both defendants urged that the book in no way outraged decency, that the subject was treated with restraint and that there was nothing which tended to defend these unnatural tendencies, or to their glorification.

There seemed, continued Mr. Birkett, to have been considerable misunderstanding about the meaning of the word 'obscene'. He contended that the book could not be described as obscene, because there were no gross or filthy words in it. Further, that because it was well written, it was to be regarded as a work of literature and not properly the subject of these proceedings.

'I find,' said Sir Chartres, 'that the *Standard Dictionary* describes the word obscene as "offensive to chastity, delicacy or decency" . . . or "offensive to the moral senses as to excite lustful passions".

'With regard to the point that the book is well written and therefore should not be subjected to these proceedings,' Sir Chartres continued, 'that is an entirely untenable position. I agree that the book has some literary merits, but the very fact that the book is well written can be no answer to these proceedings, because otherwise we should be in the preposterous position that the most obscene books should be free from stricture. It must appear to anyone of intelligence that the better an obscene book is written, the greater the public to whom it is likely to appeal. The mere fact that the book deals with unnatural offences between women does not make it obscene. It might even have a strong moral influence. But in the present case there is not one word which suggests that anyone with the horrible tendencies described is in the least blameworthy. All the characters are presented as attractive people and put forward with admiration. What is even more serious is that certain acts are described in alluring terms. . . .'

Sir Chartres then began to over-simplify certain passages relating to ambulance drivers at the front when Miss Radclyffe Hall, who had been listening patiently to this denigration of her work, with its underlying assumption that authors should collaborate with magistrates when touching on emotional and social complexities, was moved to protest.

Sir Chartres: 'I must ask you to be quiet.'

Miss Hall: 'I am the author of this book.'

Sir Chartres: 'If you cannot behave yourself in court I shall have to have you removed.'

Miss Hall: 'Shame!'

He then made an order for the seized copies of the book to be destroyed.

On December 15th an appeal against the order was made at London Sessions, Sir Robert Wallace, K.C., presiding over a Bench of Justices which included two women. It was again held that the book was 'most dangerous and corrupting' and the appeal was dismissed with costs.

Despite the outcry by distinguished writers, publishers and others, the books were burned—as the poems of Sappho of Lesbos, the most famous Lesbian of all time, were burned by order of the Roman Catholic Church—and Miss Radclyffe Hall sold her house and car to pay for her share in the heavy legal expenses.

There is little doubt that the sensational attack in the *Sunday Express* did have its influence on the puritanical Home Secretary Sir William Joynson-Hicks ('Jix'), who was the inspiration of a delightful jingle by P. R. Stephenson:

> *Twinkle, twinkle, little Jix*
> *What a bag of monkey tricks*
> *Up above the clouds so high*
> *Playing pleeceman in the sky.*

What he did was to boost, with this stupendous publicity, a book which might otherwise have enjoyed only a modest sale. Subsequent to the prosecution in London, *The Well of Loneliness* was again published in Paris, translated into eleven languages and enjoyed a steady sale everywhere except in Britain, where it was published again in 1949 without protest from the authorities. The whole public attitude to this contentious topic of homosexuality had in the meantime changed radically. Sales in the United States exceeded a million copies, and when Miss Radclyffe Hall died in 1943 she left a fortune of £116,000.

Norman Birkett had fought hard in *The Well of Loneliness* case, but his eloquence was, for all practical purposes, gagged. How he would have enjoyed the cut-and-thrust of intelligent argument on the pattern and purpose of literature!

CHAPTER XIV

Member of Parliament

ONE OF BIRKETT'S most picturesque clients was Mrs. Kate Merrick, the so-called 'night club queen'. In the 'twenties this little lady persistently broke the drink laws with her numerous clubs. Following a raid by the Flying Squad on the Cecil Club, she was summoned for selling intoxicating liquor without a licence. By that time she had already paid fines of £1,300 on numerous summonses, and was described in court as 'a person who has contrived with considerable resolution to break the law'. As fast as a club was closed it was re-opened under another name; the fines were in no sense a deterrent.

When she appeared before Mr. Fry at Bow Street Mr. Birkett's task was an almost impossible one. Not only had she broken the law incessantly and been fined continually, but had previously served one sentence of six months' imprisonment. The most he could do was to enter a plea of Guilty to the charge of selling liquor without a licence, and to argue that this was not a case for imprisonment. Her heart was bad, and her previous sentence was 'no light thing'. She would, if spared imprisonment, refrain from any further activities in connection with night clubs of that kind.

Mr. Fry, however, was sceptical, and sentenced Mrs. Merrick to six months imprisonment in the second division.

Perhaps Mrs. Merrick felt that, as she was imprisoned despite her promise to stop breaking the law if she were let off with a fine, she was free to pursue her old activities again. At any rate, about a year later her name came even more prominently into the news, this time in connection with the Goddard case, which threw an interesting light on how she had been able to carry on for years without more frequent and effective intervention from the police. With that case, however, Mr. Birkett had nothing to do. It is enough to say that Mrs. Merrick was a colourful and dynamic personality, immensely popular with her customers and possessed of a driving initiative which, in more legal channels, would have been thought highly commendable. Her own view was that the drinking laws were so absurd and unnecessary that they need hardly be taken seriously.

At this time libel actions against newspapers were very popular and profitable. It is possible—and was then—to 'presume' damage in the event of untrue stories being published, there being no onus on the plaintiff to prove damage. Thus, a man of execrably bad character could—and did—sue for libel on the premise that his reputation had suffered!

Such a case was that of William Cooper Hobbs, a former solicitor's clerk, who had been sentenced to two years' imprisonment in 1925 for the part he played in the blackmail of 'Mr. A.'— an Indian Prince (Sir Hari Singh) whose identity was common knowledge—and the extortion from him of £150,000. This sentence was the signal for the publication of lurid accounts of his alleged past misdemeanours, and while some were true, some were not.

Hobbs' exposure as an accessory to blackmail had not inhibited his flair for publicity, or his acquisitive sense. On coming out of prison he bombarded newspapers with libel actions, including the *Liverpool Evening Express* and the *Nottingham Journal*.

The article of which Mr. Hobbs complained was in his view an outspoken one, as he considered himself libelled in it no less than fourteen times. Its allegations included references to Hobbs financing burglaries, running a passport office for criminals, being a receiver of stolen property and of running a gambling den in Paris. Sergeant Sullivan, K.C., appeared for Mr. Hobbs, Norman Birkett, K.C., representing the defendants.

From the very outset of the case Lord Hewart had shown his intense dislike of the plaintiff. He interrupted continually with observations directed mainly against the plaintiff, and for the first time was rather provocative in his attitude to the normally good-humoured Sergeant Sullivan.

Birkett, characteristically, had no wish to profit from this unwelcome tension, and his handling of this somewhat electric situation was admirable. He realised, of course, that it would be a difficult matter to justify every allegation in the article of which complaint was made. He decided to cross-examine the plaintiff 'as to credit' (the point being to show what degree of credence should be accorded to his evidence, having regard to his behaviour in the box).

'Why,' asked Birkett, almost caually, 'have you brought this action?'—'To show the world and my children that the stories which have been told about me are absolute concoctions, and to get damages.'

'I am glad,' replied Mr. Birkett suavely, 'that you added the last words. Have you brought twenty-three actions before this against newspapers?'—'Yes.'

'Is this the first one that has been fought?'—'Yes.'

'Did you issue the writ in this action after you had settled with other newspapers?'—'I could not issue them all at once.'

'Have you more on your waiting list?'—'I think that there are one or two.'

'Do you agree that blackmail is the most horrible crime that a man can commit?'—'I think that it is a wicked thing.'

'Do you agree that a blackmailer is a villain of the deepest dye?' —'I am not in a position to answer that.'

'Do you agree that a man who attempts to blackmail another is a man who has no character?'—'I am not in a condition to answer that.'

'Physically or mentally?'—'Both.'

The Lord Chief Justice, seldom given to gestures of partiality from the bench, intervened:

'Do you mean,' he asked 'that your physical and mental condition is such that you cannot express your opinion of a blackmailer?'—'I think he ought to be shunned.'

'Have you heard,' asked Lord Hewart grimly, 'judges say that morally blackmail is often worse than murder? Do you agree with that?'—'I do.'

On the third day the jury intimated that they had heard enough. Lord Hewart, assured by them that they were prepared to find a verdict for the defendants, plainly hinted to them what damages 'as a matter of law' (since there were allegations in the article which had not been proved) should be awarded: '. . . . your verdict would be for the smallest possible amount?'

The Foreman: 'Yes, my Lord.'

'In other words, a farthing?'—'Yes, my Lord.'

During this interchange Sergeant Sullivan, K.C., was nearing boiling point. Lord Hewart *had* shown prejudice. The jury had not heart Hobbs' rebuttals under re-examination of his own counsel of the damaging allegations bandied about in court.

'Before that result is arrived at,' he told Lord Hewart, 'I should insist on addressing the jury.'

I

An astonishing degree of tension now pervaded the court.

'You would *insist*?' snapped the Lord Chief Justice, 'that is a strange phrase to use.'—'I conceive,' said Sullivan firmly, 'that I am entitled to address the jury.'

'Please do not use the word "insist".'—'Of course, I did not do so against your Lordship.'

'Are you entitled to address the jury when they have said that, on the evidence of the plaintiff himself, they are satisfied that he ought not to recover?'—'I respectfully submit that I am entitled to point out that on the evidence of the plaintiff there is nothing to disentitle him from recovering substantial damages.'

Norman Birkett followed this exchange with misgivings, for personally he liked both of these men; he realised too that Sullivan was being roughly handled. 'What do you say about that, Mr. Birkett?' asked Lord Hewart, but Birkett would not profit from this situation. 'I am loth to be in opposition,' he said, 'my learned friend seems to indicate that he hopes by addressing the jury to persuade them to change their minds. I do not desire in the circumstances to raise any objection. . . .'

Sullivan then addressed the jury, though not without testy interruptions from the Lord Chief Justice, such as: 'Are you addressing the jury as counsel or summing up us a judge?' Unperturbed Sullivan replied: 'I am stating why I consider they were in error in expressing an opinion before hearing the case out.'

The jury, having heard Sullivan, were still of the same mind, and a curious legal situation then arose. As Lord Hewart put it: 'There must be, of course, judgement for the defendants if the law allows . . . another question arises . . . when one is dealing with printed words that are defamatory the law presumes there is some damage. Is that presumption to be rebutted? May the plaintiff appear obviously so worthless a person that it is impossible for him to suffer damage from any libel?'

'I can conceive possibly of such a case,' Birkett told Lord Hewart, 'but in view of the fact that I have paid into court 20 shillings, which is 19s. 11¾d. too much, then even a verdict for plaintiff for one farthing would be, from every practical point of view, a verdict for defendants.'

Judgement was given accordingly, defendants being awarded costs. Sergeant Sullivan rose to object, but was silenced. Next, when Lord Hewart asked if he wished to proceed with the next case, *Hobbs* v. *Nottingham Journal*, Sullivan—realising of course that with the same judge and jury Hobbs would not stand the ghost of a chance—asked for an adjournment. He wanted to empanel another jury. Birkett objected to the adjournment. However, Hewart allowed the case to hold over until the following day, when, being as angry as ever, he was impervious to Sullivan's argument that the papers being full of the previous case, the case against the *Nottingham Journal* should be heard by a new jury. He flatly refused.

Sullivan then asked for leave to appeal. 'I don't think you need apply for liberty to appeal,' said Hewart. 'If you do, I shall not give it to you.' But Sergeant Sullivan, who knew his law, was not going to be pushed about. He took his papers and left the court with his junior and Mr. Hobbs, leaving Birkett with the field to himself.

The situation was now electric, but Birkett looked as calm as ever. He had done nothing to exacerbate the mounting tension between Hewart and Sullivan. Said Lord Hewart, trying hard to dissemble his concern and indignation: 'The usual document is handed to me which purports to show the names of learned counsel who appear for the plaintiff. Two of them who were in court a moment ago appear to be in court no longer.'

Birkett: 'I am not certain whether they left the court to consult with their client or whether it was part of a fixed procedure.' He asked for judgement for the defendants, with costs, and was given it. But Sullivan, meanwhile, had not been idle. He had gone to the Court of Appeal the same day, as a result of which a new trial of both actions was ordered. The Court of Appeal was unanimously of the opinion that there had been a miscarriage of justice. Any satisfaction Norman Birkett may have felt at securing costs against Hobbs and an award to him of a farthing was speedily dispelled. Although the new trials never took place, the various newspapers involved settled the libel actions out of court for sums which have been variously estimated as between £17,000 and £40,000.

Birkett knew that this reversal might not have come about if Lord Hewart had not shown his prejudice, and been openly rude to Sergeant Sullivan. But he had a way of accepting these things philosophically, and he said nothing to add to the disappointment Lord Hewart must have felt at this rather pointed rebuke. Lord

Hewart later recognised his mistake and regretted the estrange-
ment with Sullivan, to whom on the occasion of a chance en-
counter he was generous enough to apologise.

In the summer of 1929 Birkett stood as Liberal candidate for
Nottingham East, Mrs. Birkett accompanying him on his campaign. Claude Westell, who often heard Birkett speak at election
meetings, says that he found it 'a happy assignment, affording as
it did the opportunity of listening to speeches so lucid, with the
points so admirably marshalled and with the ring of sincerity
and humanity shining through the factual political background.
To the reporter such speeches were a gift, and on the rare occasions
when the calls of the domestic circle tempted me to "dodge the
column" and appeal for a dictate, the candidate was willing and
ready with a perfect precis of his speech to the exact length
required.' It was Westell who wrote in the *Nottingham Evening
News* a parody of 'Who is Sylvia' finishing:

> *Then for Birkett let us vote*
> *And do it with good pleasure.*
> *He will never turn his coat,*
> *He'll serve us in good measure.*
> *And to our cause himself devote.*

Reporters noticed that at his election meetings 'women were
very much in evidence'. At a meeting at Victoria Hall Birkett
greatly amused his audience by a reference to Winston Churchill.
'One of the minor problems of the election,' he said, 'is what to
do with Mr. Winston Churchill, because whatever government
gets into power, he will want to be there. If Mr. Baldwin is returned I can see him going to him and saying: "Stanley, some of
them say I am a free trader, but as you know and I know I am a
safe-guarder."'

Birkett was returned as Liberal M.P. on June 1st, 1929, with a
majority of nearly 3,000 votes over Mr. L. H. Gluckstein the
Unionist candidate and more than 4,000 votes over the Labour
candidate, Mr. J. H. Baum. This was a gain for the Liberals, and
Birkett was entitled to feel in high spirits, as it had been a strenuous
campaign for him. Escorted by police and a cheering crowd,
Mr. and Mrs. Birkett went to the Gladstone Liberal Club, where,
from the club windows, he addressed a huge crowd and promised

that ' "irrespective of party" he would further the interests of every man, woman and child in the division'. He repeated this promise in a further speech from the Reform Club.

An incident during one of his meetings he later raised in the House of Commons.

'The matter I desire to raise,' Birkett told the House, 'has to do with a prosecution instituted at Barnsley Petty Sessions. . . .

'As I understand it a boy named Wilfrid Carpenter, of the age of thirteen years, on polling day in the recent election at Barnsley was minded to wear political colours. They happened to be Liberal colours, but I trust that whatever colours they had been I should have raised the matter.

'Two men, one named Hirst and the other named Bradder, pursued the boy, and Bradder caught and held him until the other man arrived. They then desired the boy to discard his colours, which he refused to do. Thereupon Hirst, it is alleged, twisted his arm with such force that the bone was wrenched at the elbow. X-rays showed the arm to be broken.'

The Bench, composed mainly of Labour men, fined Hirst £2 including costs and Bradder £1 including costs. Birkett maintained that the penalty was entirely inadequate to the offence, and referred to 'disquiet in the public mind because the political complexion of the bench was the same as the political complexion of the defendants'.

I have said of Birkett's previous activities in Parliament that some of his speeches were undistinguished; there are few M.P.s of which this could not be said, and few Ministers either. But during Ramsay MacDonald's régime Birkett was certainly very active, and fully honoured his promise to those who elected him to consider the interests of his constituents irrespective of party. His legal knowledge made his interventions both in debate and on Committee of considerable value on occasions, as he could foresee snags as they might affect the private citizen, whereas a layman might consider the wording of the Bill innocuous. The Finance Bill, which so vastly increased the powers of the Inland Revenue authorities, was one in respect of which he felt great uneasiness. Of the proposal to give the Special Commissioners powers to obtain copies of registers of securities he pointed out that the Committee '. . . should realise the great advance in the powers of the Revenue Authorities that this innocent-looking provision involves. The Attorney-General has treated this matter as though it was a slight and necessary extension of the powers which the Commissioners ought to possess. This is altogether misleading . . . under cover of a rather attractive manner of presenting the case the Attorney-General is disguising the fact that a quite revolutionary proposal is being introduced . . . it is a very serious clause, and I hope the Committee will reject it.'

Mr. Winston Churchill, who had been the butt of Birkett's good-humoured opposition in the recent election, paid a warm tribute to the new Liberal Member. 'I have rarely heard a speech more precisely directed to the object under debate, more harmoniously attuned to the character of Committee discussion, than the excellent statement he has just made,' Mr. Churchill declared. 'It seemed to me that there could hardly be a more damaging speech from the point of view of the Attorney-General himself. Not only were his facts traversed, not only was his legal authority impugned and even controverted, but these sharp arrows were planted in his person by his distinguished legal successor in his old primacy on the Liberal benches. He [Mr. Birkett] had been able to answer him in fact and law and leave him, a sprawling, a pitiable object.'

The clause to which Birkett objected was, however, passed.

Norman Birkett's Parliamentary record was very good, allowing for the unpredictable and exacting demands of his busy legal practice. He was especially active with questions touching on welfare, unemployment and social matters, while his acute legal mind seized on any situation where there was the least suggestion of nepotism. He had some awkward questions to ask about public contracts placed privately without competition; he enquired continually about the progress of schemes for increasing employment—unemployment being the great curse of that period—and for making the administration of relief prompt, efficient and as little demeaning to the dignity of the unavoidably idle as could be expected.

One of his longest speeches, excellent in presentation and the cogency of his arguments, was on his favourite subject of the Widows', Orphans and Old Age Pensions Bill. Although he told the House that 'my real task can be discharged almost in a sentence', it took another 6,000 words to make his points. But it was a valuable speech, incidentally making the sensible plea that since the Bill affected the rights of ordinary people, those people might as well be told in plain English just what their rights were under the Act. As a barrister he knew that all too often legal jargon is intelligible only to lawyers.

At about this time Birkett was asked to help in a particularly tragic case. A boy living with his mother, a widow, and his sister in Fulham was charged with manslaughter, the grand jury having previously reduced the charge from one of murder. The dead man, Arthur Thomas Sanderson, a thirty-two-year-old French polisher, a widower with two children who lived with his parents in Fulham, was frequently violent and abusive in drink, and had been on intimate terms with the prisoner's mother.

One night, after quarrelling with her outside a pub, he had called at the house and knocked her down twice. The boy, hearing the disturbance, came downstairs, but knowing the man's violent nature, he brought a knife with him, as the only weapon near at hand he could think of. He came into the hall to protect his mother in the scrimmage that was taking place, and found himself fighting Sanderson, who dealt him a violent blow. In the fighting that followed Sanderson was stabbed and died on the way to hospital. In a statement to the police the boy had said that he did not mean to use the knife, but 'he hit my sister then, so I stabbed him in the back twice'. The police officer who arrived soon after the stabbing found Sanderson bleeding profusely from a wound in the neck.

Told he would be charged with murder the lad had said: 'I can only say he deserved it. He was always causing trouble in our family. When I saw him knocking my mother and sister about, naturally I couldn't stand back, could I?'

In the witness box the boy reiterated his story, and in the simplest possible way Birkett, who defended him, elicited the facts that mattered.

Norman Birkett: 'On that night, May 20th, did you fear for your mother?'—'Yes.'

'Did you fear for her life?'—'Yes.'

'When at the foot of the stairs when he was rushing at you, did you fear anything at that moment?'—'Yes, I thought he would kill me.'

The prisoner added that when he said to the police officer, 'I'm glad I did it', he meant that he was glad he had stopped him from

hitting his mother. He did not know whether the injuries to
Sanderson were serious or not.

The brief examination was a model of simplicity and direct-
ness, and after the prisoner had been cross-examined by Mr.
H. D. Roome, prosecuting, Mr. Justice Swift said that the boy
might have been entitled to resist by violence Sanderson's attempt
to inflict a grievous bodily harm on his mother. Nobody supposed that he intended to kill the man. 'After all,' he told the
jury, 'there are not many of you who would not have done the
same had you seen your mother knocked down twice.'

The jury stopped the case, finding the boy Not Guilty, a verdict
which was greeted by loud applause in court. After thanking Mr.
Birkett in his diffident way, the boy left, pale and unsmiling,
grasping protectively the arm of his wayward mother.

Where does speculation in business end and dishonesty begin?

To those unversed in the intricacies of high finance the distinction or dividing line may appear simple. But all business is
essentially a gamble, the speculation of money in the hope of a
profit. In business the unlikeliest ideas have made fortunes for
their promoters, while ideas at one time sound have, through
some setback, proved disastrous.

In the late 1920s and until the end of 1929 Clarence Hatry was
one of the greatest names in the City of London, having launched
a great number of prosperous companies and having a hand in
many more. In 1929, however, the Stock Exchange suspended
dealings in certain companies, and Hatry, of his own accord and
accompanied by his fellow directors, called on their accountant
Sir Gilbert Garnsey and confessed to irregularities. The extent
and gravity of their admissions left him no course but to recommend that they call on the Director of Public Prosecutions, Sir
Archibald Bodkin.

Hatry and his associates Daniels, Tabor and Dixon were
arrested and held in custody for four months during enquiries,
the magistrates at the Guildhall having on five occasions refused
to grant bail. Application for bail before Mr. Justice Branson in
the King's Bench Division was dismissed, despite Birkett's contention that 'a denial of bail to Mr. Hatry would . . . be a denial
of true justice'. Mr. Justice Branson refused bail, saying he was
not satisfied that when the men went to the Director of Public

Prosecutions they knew what they might be charged with and what the punishment might be. This, I think, was a fallacious argument, as Hatry had ample opportunity, before he himself precipitated the legal action against himself, to leave the country. The prosecution was based entirely on statements he had made himself, and he personally took full responsibility for what was done.

The irregularities were certainly on a huge scale; the liabilities of the companies concerned were nearly £20,000,000, and the shock to the City was immense. The charge, in simple language, was that of issuing forged certificates in respect of Swindon, Wakefield and Gloucester Corporation Stock.

The trial cost £20,000, Mr. Birkett's brief being marked at nearly £1,000, with £100 a day refresher fees, while his junior received £666 with £75 a day. Leaders for the defence of Dixon and Daniels had £300 marked on their briefs, with refreshers. Tabor's counsel received £250 with £75 a day and his junior £169 and £50 a day. These heavy fees, it should be emphasised, did not come entirely from the pockets of the accused men, being subscribed mostly by friends. There were plenty of solid and respectable business men then—as there are now—who believed that Hatry's offence was one quite common in business, that of playing for time, of trying a desperate expedient to bridge a difficult financial gap. Many of his companies were still highly prosperous at the time of his arrest, and it is possible at least that, given time, he might have retrieved the situation.

At the Old Bailey trial before Mr. Justice Avory, Birkett appeared for Hatry, the other defendants also having distinguished counsel. The Attorney-General's indictment was formidable, and Birkett knew that there was little he could do either to prevent a heavy sentence on Hatry or to mitigate it. But on the principle of advocacy that, however black the case against one's client, a lawyer is entitled to stress any facts in his favour, he had studied the mountains of documents night and day; Hatry wanted to go into the witness box, but Birkett warned him that there was little point in his doing so, since he had freely admitted so many defalcations. At first a plea of Not Guilty was entered to the charges, but Birkett advised Hatry to change it, and warned him that he must expect a long sentence, and on the second day of hearing Mr. Birkett rose to address the Judge:

'My client,' he said, 'now wishes to withdraw his plea of "Not

Guilty" ... and to plead "Guilty" to all the counts in the indictment.'

An impressive and seemingly interminable succession of witnesses follow and the dialogue becomes like a dramatised page of a financial journal.

Birkett's one and a half hours' speech was largely an appeal for mercy, spoken with such eloquence that at times Hatry was visibly moved to tears. Hatry, he said, realised the foundations of confidence and security in the commercial world had been gravely injured, but the step was taken to avert a disaster which would involve many thousands of innocent people in loss. Failure could not be envisaged—but now the price was being paid in Hatry's suffering and humiliation. Had not Hatry taken the step he did, a terrible disaster would still have occurred, but he would have been a free man outside the criminal law. Until 1929 Hatry's record was one of honour, successful flotations and confidence. 'If you try to pick out the legal evidence against Hatry,' he said, 'you will find it pretty well non-existent.'

This brought a mild rebuke from the Judge. 'You are straining my credulity with much, Mr. Birkett.' To this Birkett replied: 'I do not stress that point, but, at any rate, the criminal charges were formulated wholly and solely upon the evidence that Mr. Hatry himself gave. Without it the prosecution must have been very long delayed.'

There was little mercy forthcoming from the seventy-nine-year-old Judge. In the final scenes of the great drama, while city men holding their silk hats, smartly dressed women and counsel jostled together, everyone hung on Avory's words.

'Clarence Charles Hatry, you stand convicted of the most appalling frauds that have ever disfigured the commercial reputation of this country—frauds far more serious than any committed upon the public during the last fifty years, in my personal experience.' He mentioned sums of £795,000 and £820,000, and referring to Hatry's confession, which Birkett had tried to suggest was a mitigating circumstance, he said: 'There is not much genuine merit in it, you were merely succumbing to the inevitable.' As to the fact that he hoped to reap a large financial reward from one transaction, it meant, stripped of its rhetorical language, 'Nothing but the plea of every clerk who robs his master and hopes to repay the money by backing a winner.'

'I am,' continued Mr. Justice Avory, 'unable to imagine a worse case . . . under the first indictment you will be detained in penal servitude for fourteen years.' Other sentences were announced on Hatry, to be served concurrently, but the first was savage enough. Daniels was sentenced to seven years, Dixon to five and Tabor to three.

Norman Birkett's subsequent speech before the Court of Criminal Appeal was deeply moving. For an hour he pleaded in vain for Hatry. He stressed again the lack of real evidence, the voluntary nature of Hatry's confession, his refusal to flee the country. 'Fourteen years on a man of Hatry's age [Hatry at the time was forty] is a terrible sentence,' Birkett said. 'His life henceforth must be one of constant grief. The suffering he is undergoing is difficult to conceive and beyond my power to depict.' He quoted the words of Oscar Wilde, who spent two years in Reading Gaol: 'All trials are trials for life. All sentences are sentences of death.'

While the gravity of the offence should not be minimised (the total amount involved in the forgery of Corporation stock was £795,000, and the amount obtained through fictitious certified transfer shares was £400,000), the burden which Mr. Hatry had to bear should not be increased beyond the just amount. Before June 1929 nobody could have made any charge against Hatry. He had put in the whole of his personal fortune of £750,000 to save the loss falling upon innocent people. The motive had not been one of personal gain. The money was intended only to tide him over a few days. 'It is surprising how little direct evidence there is against Hatry,' he added, 'had he not made the voluntary confession.'

But Lord Hewart, Lord Chief Justice, giving his opinion of the court, dismissed the appeal. 'In our view,' he said, 'the sentence is not a day too long.' Even Birkett's request that the sentence should run from the date of his conviction was brushed aside; it must date, the Appeal Court decreed, from the day the appeal was dismissed.

Hatry, after his sentence, generously acknowledged all the efforts Birkett had made for him. He always maintained that, given time, matters would have righted themselves, and his son has written a book in an attempt to vindicate his father from the allegations of fraud confirmed by the sentence at the Old Bailey and the dismissal of Hatry's appeal.

CHAPTER XV

Millions for the Asking

IN THE COURSE of his busy life as an advocate, Mr. Norman Birkett was to know many spectacular successes. He was also to experience some notable failures.

This is only to be expected. During his legal career he never believed that an advocate should only undertake tasks for which he felt, sentimentally, intellectually or politically, any personal preference.

The Portuguese bank-note case of 1931 was one in which he failed to win for his clients a single concession or point—except, of course, the point that their integrity was not in question. It was a case unique in the history of banking, and a classic of human audacity and credulity.

The story really starts on December 4th, 1924, when a well-dressed, cultivated and charming gentleman of Dutch extraction, bearing the name of K. Marang van Yssleveere called on Waterlow and Sons Ltd., who were and are one of the most famous, capable and respected printing firms in Europe. His copper-plated visiting card described him as 'Consul General de Perse', and when he asked to see the highly respected chairman of the Company, Sir William A. Waterlow, K.B.E., a former Lord Mayor of London, he was admitted immediately to the sanctum sanctorum.

Under a pledge of secrecy he unfolded to the conservative and sympathetic Sir William a most unusual story.

Angola's finances, he said, were in a state of chaos. He was a member of a Dutch syndicate which had been requested by the Portuguese Government to do what it could to put Angola's finances in order. Angola, it should be added, is a Portuguese colony on the West Coast of Africa, about half a million square miles in extent, with a population, at that time, of about 2,500,000. The syndicate did not propose to finance hydro-electric schemes, build railways or construct vast housing settlements; its remedy was to introduce more money into the country —to increase the circulation of working capital.

Mr. Marang, as we will call him for short, presented a letter of introduction from one of the most prominent firms of printers in Holland. It was to the effect that Mr. Marang had approached the Dutch firm with an order for the printing of Portuguese bank-notes, but felt that—

> 'the work is more in your line and so we advised Mr. Marang to discuss the matter with you. We think it would be possible the order in question will be executed by your firm and the delivery of the notes will take place by the intermedium of our firm.'

Waterlows knew the Dutch firm well, and as Marang produced a diplomatic document signed by Signor Antonio Bandeira, the Portuguese Minister at The Hague, it is scarcely surprising that his bona fides were accepted. The world of finance is a queer one, in which one man may be refused an overdraft of a pound despite an impressive bundle of documents, while another can raise a million pounds by a mere telephone call. According to Senor Bandeira, Mr. Marang was a carrier of despatches for the Portuguese Government.

Now Messrs. Waterlow and Sons Ltd. had, in 1923–24, printed for the Bank of Portugal—under contract—600,000 notes of the value of 500 escudos each, roughly equivalent in value to the English £5 notes. They bore a portrait of Vasco da Gama, circumnavigator of the Cape of Good Hope in 1497. Waterlows had not printed any bank-notes for the Bank of Portugal before 1923 or since, but they still had, locked away, the plates from which these Vasco da Gama notes were printed.

Mr. Marang's proposition, in brief, was that Messrs. Waterlow should print for a Dutch syndicate of which he was a member 500-escudos notes to the value of £3,000,000 for circulation in Angola, where they would be over-printed with the word 'Angola'. It was, however, essential that the matter should be treated as highly confidential, because another bank—the Banco Ultramarino—normally printed Portuguese notes for the colonies.

Now the Bank of Portugal had issued 1,000- and 500-escudos notes printed by another commercial house, of a different design —known as 'poet' notes, because these bore the portraits of famous Portuguese poets. It was these which Mr. Marang at first suggested should be printed, but as Sir William pointed out,

Waterlows had only the Vasco da Gama plates. Marang said that they would do.

Sir William said that as the plates were the property of the Bank of Portugal, he would need that bank's authority. Waterlows had a representative in Lisbon, a Mr. Romer, who could soon clear that formality up.

Mr. Marang, member of an audacious gang of confidence tricksters, kept his nerve. 'Of course,' he said, 'and by a happy chance my secretary Mr. Jose Bandeira (he is the brother of Mr. Antonio Bandeira, Portuguese Minister at The Hague) is going to Lisbon. He could see your Mr. Romer, and they could deal with that matter between themselves.' Sir William gave Mr. Marang a letter of introduction for Mr. Bandeira, and himself wrote direct to Mr. Romer, telling him to expect Mr. Bandeira.

After several days Mr. Romer's visitor had not appeared and, disliking the whole business, he telegraphed his superiors in London: 'Bank of Portugal have nothing to do with the matter. Bank Ultramarino is the bank dealing with Portuguese colonies. Telegraph what I am to do.' A curt reply from London told him to 'do nothing, say nothing, wait call of gentleman'. Still nothing happened, and Mr. Romer warned London again:

'I cannot help thinking that the Bank of Portugal would never consent to their plates being utilised for the purpose of making a new emission of notes for a Portuguese colony whose finances apparently appear to be in a state of absolute chaos.'

On December 16th Marang telegraphed Sir William that he had received the bank's authority to print the notes, and would be calling. The following day he appeared with impressive contracts, one between the Government of Angola and Mr. Reis, an engineer, and another between the Bank of Portugal and the Government of Angola, authorising it to manufacture up to 200,000 notes of 500 escudos and up to 100,000 notes of the value of 1,000 escudos.

These forged documents, therefore, purported to be an authority by the Bank of Portugal, vested in Angola and delegated to Mr. Reis.

Now came a moment which must have caused Mr. Marang's heart to miss a beat. Excellent, said Sir William. It now remained for Messrs. Waterlow to get specific authority from the Governor of the Bank of Portugal to use the plates in the firm's keeping. He would write to him!

Quick as a flash Marang had the answer. By a 'happy co-incidence' his secretary, Mr. Jose Bandeira, was leaving for Lisbon that evening, and could deliver the letter to the Governor of the Bank of Portugal. The letter, of course, was never delivered. In due course Marang reappeared in London with a faked authorisation from I. Camacho Rodrigues, Chairman of the Banco de Portugal. The work of printing the notes was put in hand.

Because of the alleged need for secrecy, Sir William had hitherto not been in direct communication with the Bank of Portugal, but at this stage sent to the Governor a letter, by ordinary post, acknowledging 'your confidential letter of December 23rd. . . .' Had that letter ever reached the Governor, the whole plot would have been exposed. But he never received it.

Sir William was a business man of the old school, combining commercial assiduity with old-time courtesy. He even arranged, at Marang's request, the purchase of the seven trunks which were to contain the notes, which were delivered to Mr. Marang on February 10th, February 25th and March 12th, 1925. The trunks were deposited in the left-luggage office of Liverpool Street Station, where Marang enthused at the economic charge: 'Fancy all this for 1s. 6d.!'

The fabulous fortune remained at the station until Marang, armed with a diplomatic passport issued to him by the crooked diplomat Bandeira, took them out of the country. The passport, of course, gave him immunity from Customs inspection.

But what to do with £3,000,000 of forged notes? With incredible impudence the gang decided to open their own bank in Portugal! Their first application was refused by the authorities, as there seemed no need for another bank, and except for Reis, a Dutch engineer, the other sponsors did not seem of sufficient consequence. On May 23rd another application was made, with Reis still among the sponsors, but with some names dropped and others added. This application was approved by the Banking Council under the Presidency of the Governor of the Bank of Portugal.

'The Bank of Angola e Metropole' was an admirable blind for the disposal of the forged notes, but in due course the appearance of such a flood of new notes aroused suspicion; the bank was raided and seized, and its chief officials arrested. But the Bank of Portugal was in a quandary. Being printed from the original plates, the forged notes were indistinguishable from the genuine. To repudiate Vasco da Gama notes would victimise holders of the genuine and shake confidence in the Bank. So the Bank took instead the bold course of withdrawing the whole issue, genuine and forged alike, each holder of a Vasco da Gama note being given another note of equal value and different design.

In all, 795,556 notes were exchanged, some 200,000 more than the original issue.

There was tremendous excitement in Lisbon over this colossal fraud. Tempers mounted so high that the Governor and Deputy-Governor of the Bank of Portugal were for a short time actually under arrest.

On December 9th Colonel Lucas of the Portuguese Embassy in London called on Sir William Waterlow, was told of the negotiations with Marang, and shown the contracts, which he at once declared bogus. Reeling under this terrible shock, Sir William, with two of his experts, arrived in Lisbon to place all the information in his possession before the authorities there. Such was the hostility awaiting them there, that Sir William and his two companions had to come away under false names.

When the situation cleared, the Bank of Portugal claimed from Messrs. Waterlow and Sons Ltd. the sum of £1,106,691—representing the value of the notes they had paid out in exchange for the unauthorised notes.

The claim against Waterlows, heard in the King's Bench Division, was based on the allegation that in printing and delivering the notes to Mr. Marang without the authority of the Bank, Messrs. Waterlow and Sons had committed a breach of contract and been guilty of negligence. Being obliged to withdraw the entire issue of Vasco da Gama from circulation, it had issued notes to the value of 104,859,000 escudos; the Bank of Portugal, having received nothing in exchange, considered itself entitled to the entire face value of these issued notes, at current sterling value.

Mr. Norman Birkett, who represented Messrs. Waterlow and was assisted by Mr. H. Bensley Wells and Mr. Theodore Turner, worked for weeks on end familiarising himself with the complexities of banking practice in Portugal and the underlying economics of banking in general. The defence was a denial of breach of contract or negligence. It maintained that the withdrawal of the Vasco da Gama issue was a voluntary act on the part of the Bank, and an unnecessary one, as many of the unauthorised notes were distinguishable from the authorised. More important, perhaps, was the contention that the Bank of Portugal had *not* suffered great financial loss; it had exchanged paper for paper, its only expense being the printing of the new notes and the expense of distributing them.

Mr. Stuart Bevan, K.C., Mr. C. T. le Quesne, K.C., Mr. D. B. Somervell, K.C., and the Hon. H. L. Parker appeared for the Bank of Portugal.

Then Dr. da Matta, Professor of Law at Lisbon University, and Legal Adviser to the Bank of Portugal, said that the Bank was liable to pay out on the Vasco da Gama even after the date of withdrawal had passed, and could not cancel its liability in respect of any of the notes.

In cross-examination by Mr. Birkett, Dr. da Matta did not agree that it was considered patriotic of Portuguese lawyers to refuse to help Messrs. Waterlow and Sons in their defence. (Obviously the company needed advice and help from the standpoint of the law as it applied in Portugal, as well as in Britain.) In view, however, of the exceptional frauds that had been committed and the great alarm which had been caused among the public in Portugal, it did not seem strange that Portuguese lawyers should be reluctant to help Messrs. Waterlow and Sons.

Mr. Birkett: 'Do you know how many Portuguese lawyers have been approached by Messrs. Waterlow and Sons?'—'I do not know.'

'None of those who have been asked have spoken to you?'—'No.'

Mr. Justice Wright: 'In this country during the war we constantly appeared for enemy aliens in the Prize Court. I did so on many occasions.'

Mr. Birkett: 'I should have thought that the spirit of law was international.'

The witness said that some 2,500 persons had written to the Bank after the Vasco da Gama notes had been withdrawn asking for the exchange of about 8,000 notes.

Mr. Birkett: 'Have you advised the Bank not to pay them?'—

K

'I have not given an opinion. The Directors of the Bank decided not to pay.'

'If the Bank fails in this action, will it pay the notes?'—'Yes.'

'All that the holder of a Bank of Portugal note can get in exchange for it at the Bank is another note?'—'Yes.'

'It may be many years before the Bank redeems that other note save by another piece of paper?'—'Yes, unfortunately this happens in other countries. It is not common to Portugal.'

'The only difficulty that the Bank has experienced up to now is that it has put a number of notes into circulation to replace Marang's note?'—'Yes.'

Opening the case for Messrs. Waterlow and Sons, Mr. Birkett claimed that the allegations 'constituted a very highly coloured picture. Throughout Sir William Waterlow and those associated with him were not careless or negligent in the smallest particular.' It had been said that this ought to have been observed or done, or that ought to have been observed or done, but it was easy to be wise after the event. The test that should be applied was: what was the state of Messrs. Waterlows' knowledge in 1924? What ought reasonable and prudent men to have done in the circumstances?

Sir William Waterlow and his colleagues should not be judged by the accumulated knowledge of five years. In 1924 nobody in the world would have guessed, when Marang entered the office of Waterlow and Sons, that he was the innocent tool of a gang of swindlers or that he was a principal of a gang. Between 1914 and the present time the firm had printed 5,000 million notes of our own currency. The Governor of the Bank of Portugal had admitted that if the swindle had been described to anyone in 1924 it would have appeared to be inconceivable.

Birkett then outlined the circumstances of Marang's visit. His credentials were impressive and appeared genuine. Of Mr. Romer's letter to Sir William, Mr. Birkett suggested that this was a warning that there might be difficulty in getting paid for the printing, and not a warning of a fraud.

Of Marang's second visit, when he brought two contracts with him, Sir William Waterlow asked him to leave the documents with him, and Marang agreed to do so—that did not look like a fraud either. The documents were submitted to a solicitor. 'Wherever you touch this case,' said Mr. Birkett, 'you find that

so far from there being lack of care, every step was marked by
vigilance, forethought and prudence. Although everything appeared in order, the solicitor had advised the sending of a letter to
the Governor of the Bank of Portugal. It had been suggested that
Sir William had been negligent in handing that letter to Marang
for conveyance to the Governor instead of sending it by post. But
Marang had been vouched for by persons in the highest position.'

The answer to the letter was received through the Portuguese
Minister to The Hague. How was Sir William Waterlow to
know that the Minister was dealing wholesale in forged documents? All the documents on which the acceptance of Marang's
order was based had been sent to Waterlow's solicitors, who pronounced them satisfactory.

Mr. Birkett mentioned Sir William's letter, written on the day
the contract for the printing of the notes was signed, to the
Governor of the Bank of Portugal and sent by ordinary post,
acknowledging receipt of the Governor's letter. Although not
received, the letter sent would have averted a gigantic fraud if it
had reached its destination. That action alone acquitted Sir
William Waterlow of having been guilty of any negligence.

Mr. Justice Wright found, in his judgement delivered in the
King's Bench Division on December 22nd, 1930, and January
12th, 1931, under the terms of their contract dated November
27th, 1922, the company undertook to 'exercise all reasonable
precaution and supervision so as to prevent the misuse or theft of
the plates or of the finished or partly finished notes . . .' and that
the company 'will keep the plates when same are not required for
working with all possible care in their strong rooms'. In this
matter, he found, the company fell short of that standard of care,
but hastened to add that: 'No one suggests for a minute a word
of reflection on the honour and good faith of Messrs. Waterlow
or any of the Directors. It is merely one of those unfortunate circumstances . . . in which the wiles of the swindlers distract the
minds of those concerned from the clear sense of what they ought
to do in duty to those who have placed confidence in them.' He
gave judgement against Waterlows for £567,421, which the
Court of Appeal reduced on March 26th, 1931, to £300,000. At
this appeal Norman Birkett appeared for Waterlows in team with
Sir John Simon, K.C., Mr. James Wylie and Mr. Bensley Wells.

The Bank of Portugal, however, took the case to the House of

Lords, where it was heard before the Lord Chancellor, Lord Warrington, Lord Atkin, Lord Russell of Killowen and Lord Macmillan. Mr. Birkett again appeared for Waterlows, this time in team with Mr. Gavin T. Simonds, K.C., Mr. Wylie and Mr. Wells.

Mr. Birkett's assertion that the Bank of Portugal had simply exchanged paper for paper and lost nothing of intrinsic value was rejected, Lord Macmillan remarking:

'. . . the fact that a sum of nearly half a million pounds has been recovered by the Bank from the conspirators gives occasion for comment on the leading contention of Messrs. Waterlow and Sons that the Bank lost nothing by issuing its good notes in exchange for spurious ones. The conspirators constituted themselves an illegal bank of issue for the spurious notes, which cost them nothing but the cost of paper and printing, yet they seem to have made half a million sterling, and, probably, much more. Why should it be said . . . that the bank would not equally have received value in return if it had issued a corresponding number of genuine notes in ordinary course and that it has been deprived of nothing by having had to issue them gratuitously?'

They then gave judgement for £610,392 against Messrs. Waterlow and Sons.

In retrospect, it does seem odd that nothing suspicious was seen in the whole transaction. On one of the signed contracts the date was different from that given by the notary who was supposed to have witnessed the signatures. It must have been strange to be asked to print notes and not to communicate directly with the owners of the plates. On the other hand, no ordinary person would expect that the Ambassador of Britain's oldest ally was an out-and-out crook, cheerfully swindling both parties to the Alliance.

Opinions still differ among economists as to the precise degree of loss which the Bank of Portugal really suffered. The late Sir Cecil Kisch, the distinguished authority on banking, held to the view that Mr. Norman Birkett's argument was right—Sir Cecil points out, in a fascinating study of the whole case, that since 1891 Portugal had been on an 'inconvertible' currency, so that the popular idea of 'cashing' notes could be misleading; 'the practical obligation on the Bank was to exchange a note of one denomination for others of equivalent amount'.

In other words, said Sir Cecil, it was a matter of paper for paper, a thesis put forward by Mr. Birkett, and which the Law Lords did not accept.

Ironically, one factor helped Marang in twisting Sir William Waterlow with his golden tongue. Remember that he throughout emphasised the need for secrecy. 'Private', 'confidential' and 'secret' were the Dutchman's favourite words. In his lifetime Sir William had kept some very unlikely secrets—he had at one time been a member of the British Secret Service. The cloak-and-dagger atmosphere of this strange financial transaction may have had a special, and fatal, appeal to him; a sense of soldiering on.

CHAPTER XVI

The 'Blazing Car' Trial

ONE OF THE most famous murder trials in which Norman Birkett appeared was also to prove one of the most notorious in criminal history. It is still known as 'The Blazing Car Murder', which was committed in the early hours of the morning on November 6th, 1930. The culprit was a thirty-six-year-old commercial traveller, Alfred Arthur Rouse, whose sexual appetite (he was credited with affairs with eighty women in the course of his travels, and with being the father of many illegitimate children) might be thought excessive.

Rouse had served in the First World War, and was injured in the head, which may or may not have effected a mental change which was to have for him a disastrous sequel. He had married in 1914, and at the time of the murder was still living with his long-suffering wife and had even taken one illegitimate son into their home. Yet another illegitimate child was due to be born, not to a domestic servant whom he had bigamously married, but to his latest conquest, Ivy Jenkins, who fondly believed that the lecherous gentleman with the Morris Minor saloon car was just counting the days before taking her off to a beautiful house in Kingston.

Financially and emotionally—perhaps even physically—Rouse was finding these amorous complexities too much for him. He found a macabre answer to his problem, and but for his own stupidity and lack of foresight, might have passed off the murder as an accident.

At 2 a.m. on November 6th, 1930, William Bailey and Alfred Brown were going home from a Bonfire Night dance when, walking down Hardingstone Lane, a turning off the main Northampton to London road, they saw something blazing by the side of the road about fifty yards away. A man appeared to climb out of a ditch near by and remarked as he passed them: 'It looks as if someone has had a bonfire.'

Inspecting the scene closer, Bailey and Brown found the Morris Minor ablaze, the flames leaping as high as fifteen feet in the air. They called the police, and as the fire died down a charred body was seen slumped face downwards across the front seats. The car, of course, was traced through its undamaged number-plate to Rouse, and when his wife was contacted she said she last saw him at 1 a.m. that morning. She was, in fact, mistaken as to time: it was 6 a.m. She went that day to Northampton and, shown pieces of clothing retrieved from the car, thought they might be her husband's. She was not shown the corpse, which was burnt beyond recognition.

The police, of course, were told of the man who appeared near the scene of this tragedy, and as it had been a clear moonlight night, they had also the advantage of a good description, which they issued, noting that this tallied with their description of Rouse, owner of the car.

Rouse, whose motives for the murder were supposedly a desire to be written off as dead so that he could start a new life under another name and be free of vexatious marital and quasi-marital obligations, then went to Gelligaer, Glamorganshire, to see Ivy Jenkins, who was ill. While there, her father produced a paper with a report of the discovery of the car. Rouse set off next morning for London, and was arrested at Hammersmith Bus Terminus.

Rouse told the police that he had picked up a hitch-hiker on the Great North Road 'just this side of St. Albans', had stopped the car in order to relieve himself and while doing so had asked the stranger to fill the car with petrol. Then, looking round, he saw the car was on fire. Before he had left the car there had been talk of having a smoke (odd that so experienced a motorist as Rouse would allow a total stranger to tinker with petrol and matches at the same time). According to his first statement: 'I saw the man was inside and I tried to open the door, but could not, as the car was then a mass of flames. . . . I did not know what to do. . . . I saw the two men. . . . I lost my head.'

But if the car had caught fire while the man was filling the petrol tank, how did his body come to be slumped over the front seats? Why had Rouse lied to the two strangers, instead of saying: 'Come quick! My car's caught fire and there's a man inside.' Why did he not hasten to the nearest police station and tell them what had happened? Had he done this, his diabolical scheme might have succeeded, for both actions would have pointed to his innocence. It is usual enough to give hitch-hikers lifts, and car accidents of all types are a common occurrence.

Rouse's scheme for disappearing was well thought out, but it was bad luck for him that Bailey and Brown, on their way home from a dance, should have passed that lonely spot, at an hour when most people are abed, just a few seconds after Rouse had lit the fatal match. It was clever of him to choose Guy Fawkes Night as the occasion of his crime, since with so many bonfires being lit, a blazing car would attract less attention than normally. It was less clever not to have noticed that it was a bright moonlight night, and that if he were seen his build and features and clothing could be easily remembered and his pretence of disappearance made useless. It was strange not to have remained concealed in the ditch as the two men passed. . . .

He was charged with murder, and in his statements to the police, which, of course, figured in the preliminary police-court proceedings, spoke at length of his amatory adventures. These were reported at length in the Press, and the problem of his defence by Donald Finnemore greatly aggravated—it is no advantage to be on trial for one's life under a cloud of severe moral approbrium.

Coming of respectable middle-class people, he was educated at a council school and worked as a youth in an estate agent's office and a soft-furnishing-goods house. He was a keen Anglican, liked music, singing and athletics, and was both good-looking and popular. Following his injuries in France, however, he developed a flair for phantasy easy to indulge because of his glib tongue and good looks. Private Rouse, to his inamoratas, was always a Major. His family had been distinguished, he said; he had been educated at Eton and Cambridge; these fanciful yarns, told with conviction to shop assistants, servants, office-workers and the scores of women he met on his rounds in his Morris Minor proved the open sesame to their tenderest affections. One illegitimate child, as I have said, was being raised by Rouse's tolerant wife. In respect of another, by a charming seventeen-year-old girl, Miss Nellie Tucker, he was already paying one maintenance order when, a few days before the crime, she gave birth to another—at a time when Ivy Jenkins was lying, desperately ill in labour, in Glamorganshire.

Payments on his house, on his car, on maintenance orders, and the complications of maintaining his extensive *ménage* were too much for him. Long before the trial began, his motives for attempting to stage a disappearance were transparent.

The stage was set, on Monday, January 26th, 1931, for one of the most dramatic murder trials ever held in Britain. Mr. Norman Birkett and Mr. Richard Elwes (junior) were Counsel for the Crown, while Mr. Donald Finnemore and Mr. A. P. Marshall were Counsel for the Defence. Mr. Sidney R. Campion held a watching brief on behalf of Helen Campbell, one of Rouse's many women friends. Campion, who was once a newspaper-seller in Leicester, was then a reporter on the *Daily News*, had recently been called to the Bar at Gray's Inn. Although the unfolding drama of the trial had kept Birkett hard at work day and night, he yet had time to greet this forty-year-old journalist who had the temerity to be called to the Bar at so late an age.

Mr. Campion formally met all engaged in the case. 'There had been some gossip published about the lawyers engaged in the case,' he told me, 'and attempts were made to romanticise my appearance—you know, "Newspaper Seller to Barrister"—so it was not surprising that Norman Birkett was curious about me. He took my arm and led me aside for a private chat, saying that he was interested in me coming to the Bar so late in life, although he knew two others who had made a success of it even later. Did I, he asked, intend forsaking Fleet Street? Or would I run in double harness? If so, was it a wise move? It might be if I were in the twenties, but in the forties, ah! that was another matter. Unless I had private resources I would find it terribly difficult to make a living during the first few years. . . .'

Campion still speaks of Birkett's 'eagerness to help'—'to single me out for personal attention, an elderly man, emphasised his warm humanity. He was cordial without being effusive, friendly without being patronising. Every morning he greeted me with a smile and encouraging words.'

In his opening speech for the prosecution Birkett displayed from the outset his sense of exposition—leading inexorably from one point to another, in proper continuity, using the clearest and most unambiguous of phrases. He retold the facts about the car blazing, the men passing and Rouse's absurd remark: 'It looks as though someone is having a bonfire up there.' Birkett let that fact sink in. 'No appeal for help! No call for assistance! Nothing! And then—"It looks as though someone is having a bonfire up there."'

The prisoner had walked a few yards towards the main road,

changed direction twice, then stood still. That was the last the two young men saw of him. Bailey, when he and his friend saw the car blazing, went to fetch his father, who was the village policeman. Brown went and fetched P.C. Copping of the Northamptonshire Constabulary. The four went as near to the inferno as they dared, and Copping could just discern a human body in the enveloping flames.

When the flames died down the body was found lying face downwards, the face upon the driver's seat and the trunk on the left-hand seat next to it. The right arm, extended and uplifted, was burned off at the elbow, the left arm destroyed entirely. The position of the corpse was of crucial importance in the case.

Near the wreckage of the car was found a charred boot or shoe, and—of immense importance—a petrol can, empty and burst in one of its seams, with handle and screw cap missing. Fourteen yards in front of the car Sergeant Harris had found a wooden mallet, with human hairs adhering to the dirt. As to the fire, a Colonel Buckle would say, from his considerable experience (he was a fire assessor), that it was designed and not accidental.

The sustained intensity of the fire, Birkett continued, should be noticed; that fire had been fed. The union at the tank end of the petrol pipe was so loose that the pipe could easily be moved; the nut was one whole turn slack. That, and the damaged petrol can, were the sources of the fire. Fires, of course, can occur by many means, but more demanded that the engine should be running. This engine was stopped. The heat was so intense that the brass windscreen frame had been melted—which would demand a heat of 1,850 degrees Fahrenheit.

From that loose joint, as Colonel Buckle would tell them, there was a petrol flow from which half a tumbler could be filled in just over a minute. Such a flow could not possibly escape detection. All the evidence would show that the petrol pipe had been loosened deliberately.

Medical evidence from Sir Bernard Spilsbury and Dr. Eric Shaw, pathologist to Northampton General Hospital, would say that the body was that of a young man of about thirty, either a miner or someone who had worked in a dust-laden atmosphere. His name, his parentage, where he lived, his circle of friends, acquaintances and workmates were all unknown. The unknown man was alive when the fire started—carbon deposits in the air passages showed that he had continued to breathe as the fire consumed him.

Mr. Birkett described how at six-thirty on the morning of the crime Rouse, in seeking a lift to Wales, had approached a porter, lied about having had his car stolen and, as the manager of the transport company (to whom the porter introduced Rouse) would say, was 'jovial and talkative'—the inference being that this was an unusual state of mind for one whose unknown companion had a few hours ago been burned to death. In fact, such excessive cheerfulness is consistent with shock.

That evening, Rouse called at Primrose Villa, Gelligaer, where Ivy, his girl-friend, was ill. Again he said something about his car having been stolen—and as he had been in the habit of visiting Ivy Jenkins from Thursday to Monday in his Morris Minor, Mr. Jenkins, the girl's father, knew the sort of car he used. A Mr. Reakes, who called at the Jenkins' home, showed Rouse a newspaper with a picture of the burned-out car and said: 'Is this your car? If so, you will see it no more.' Rouse said it was not. Phyllis Jenkins, another daughter, showed Rouse another paper with the picture of the burned-out car, its registration number and his name printed underneath it. That report said that the Northamptonshire Police wished to interview a man seen near the car at the time. Rouse put the paper in his pocket.

A Mr. Brownhill gave him a lift to the bus terminus in Cardiff, and on the way asked Rouse if he had reported the loss of his car to the police and the insurance company. He said he had—another lie. When they arrived at the bus station Rouse said he did not like that service, and they went instead to another; the first bus station was uncomfortably near to the police station, only forty yards away. Rouse was arrested, on his arrival, at Hammersmith.

Birkett read verbatim Rouse's long statement to the police, describing how he had given a lift to a stranger, how the engine had begun to splutter and how he had asked the stranger to fill the tank while he went to minister to his personal comfort—thoughtfully taking his case with him.

A long succession of witnesses followed. Alfred T. Brown, one of the two men who came upon the blaze and who saw Rouse near it, thought it strange that Rouse should have shouted his comment back to them from a distance of fifteen to twenty yards.

After cross-examination by Mr. Finnemore, Birkett asked Brown:

'You told my learned friend that you were impressed by the fact that the man you saw was respectably dressed. In what way were you impressed by that fact?'—'When you go home at that time in the morning you do not usually see well-dressed men getting out of the ditch.'

Rouse's calmness immediately after the event was to tell heavily against him. But since his defence was that he had panicked, Mr. Finnemore, in his cross-examination of the other man, William Bailey, who had been with Brown, tried to establish that Rouse had lost his head.

Mr. Finnemore: 'And apart from what he shouted, the way he shouted struck you as being strange?'—'Yes, it did.'

'... did he sound hysterical?'—'I thought he did at the time, but since hearing his voice I think it was his natural voice.'

Mr. Birkett, in his examination of Bailey, made the point that, lying in the ditch, Rouse would be hidden, and that, when he passed the two men, he could have stopped and spoken to them.

Evidence for the prosecution was also given by P.C. Copping, P.C. Valentine, Inspector James Lawrence of Northamptonshire Constabulary and others, but it was the evidence of Colonel Cuthbert Buckle, a well-known fire-loss assessor, which held the closest attention of the court, for on his evidence rested, to a great extent, the question of whether this fire was accidental or deliberate.

In his twenty-six years of experience he had investigated over 10,000 cases of fire—eighty-three of these during the previous four years being of burned-out cars.

Colonel Buckle listed the various causes of fires in cars, and Norman Birkett, during a long examination, established that none of these familiar causes could account for this particular fire. Much of it was technical, but the thoroughness was essential if the jury were to be convinced, for a man's life hung in the balance. The fire, Buckle insisted, was deliberate; there had been a fire *underneath* the car as well, which was most unusual, because flames go upwards. The fire was sustained. The petrol leakage could not have gone unnoticed by those in the car, because the fumes would be insufferable—'you would have an explosive atmosphere'.

A great deal was to depend upon that loose union joint.

Mr. Birkett: 'Could the union joint come a whole turn loose accidentally, in your opinion?'—'I do not think so.'

Buckle followed with a great deal of technical information to sustain his point.

Cross-examined by Mr. Finnemore, Colonel Buckle thought that the fire underneath the car was due to flowing petrol spilling between the joints of the floorboards, and not by the floorboards and upholstery falling through and continuing to burn. Norman Birkett's questions to him, after a very long and inevitably tedious disquisition on the structure of the car and its engine, the behaviour of its various parts and the scientific facts underlying the fire, were typical of the immense pains he always took with detail:

Birkett: 'If the fire had started in the space under the bonnet where the engine is, could the passenger have got out of the body?'—'Oh, yes.'

'If the fire had started there, would you have expected to see the passenger foremost in the driver's seat?'—'I should have expected to see him on the road trying to put the fire out.'

As to the petrol can in the car, the absence of a cap and the rent in it pointed to an explosion, which would have required 'considerable heat'. But the real cause was sustained fire.

Birkett: 'If you got an explosion, I understand you to say the car would be blown to bits?'—'Very violently—blown to bits, and all the neighbourhood would hear it for miles around. . . . Bailey and Brown on walking up from Northampton . . . would be able to hear an explosion walking up the road, and so would the whole village of Hardingstone.'

Back to that loose petrol pipe. Could it happen accidentally? Had it been loosened by the idle knocking of a foot, or by vibration? Buckle was certain it had not. He had tried with his foot and found it impossible, even with a partially loosened nut. The nauseating smell of leaking petrol, so near to the foot of the driver, could not possibly have gone undetected.

The evidence and cross-examination of Dr. Eric H. Shaw concerned the pitiful remains of the unknown man. A petrol-soaked rag was found in the fork of the left leg. As to whether the hairs on the mallet were human, as these were broken off without their roots, one could surmise, but not be certain, that they could be human. Death was caused by shock from burns. Regarding the position of the body (on which much verbal evidence was given by witnesses), the police had not made notes about this at the time, and he could not speculate as to the position of a 'corpse which has been wrapped up in sacking and bundled about'.

The evidence of Sir Bernard Spilsbury, on the third day of trial, confirmed Dr. Shaw's findings, adding 'he was clearly alive when the fire started' (there were signs of inhalation of poison gases), that there were no signs of injuries caused during life.

Mr. Finnemore stressed that most of the evidence was circumstantial, that theories as to how the fire started must remain theories. Having regard to the fact that the victim was unknown, there should be 'an even greater onus than usual, if one may use that expression, upon the prosecution to prove beyond all doubt that there was, first of all, a crime, and secondly, that the accused committed it'. He pointed to 'the complete absence of motive' and suggested that there was insufficient evidence to be considered by the jury. Mr. Justice Talbot did not uphold him in this, and Mr. Finnemore opened his defence.

The mallet, said Mr. Finnemore, proved nothing; of the one hair which seemed fairly certain to be human, no real proof was forthcoming, and anyway, nobody knew whose hair it was or how it got there. There was no blood, tissue or skin on the mallet, which could have been handled by the public during the time the wrecked car was left unattended.

Two hours before the tragedy the car had been stopped by a policeman, who had seen two men in it (the car's lights were out). From that moment Rouse, to whom was attributed the plan to murder the man, would know his chances of anonymity had disappeared; he had been seen with the missing man. The prosecution's thesis of murder as a prelude to disappearance was, therefore, untenable. Cars, said Mr. Finnemore, could catch fire in many ways, even when the engine was not running. As to the union joint whose nut was loose by one turn, what more preposterous way of setting a car on fire by a man who not only had his tank but also a separate can of petrol? Why only turn the nut once—why not three or four times so that the petrol might come through quickly and the fire be more rapid and fierce?

He proposed, he said, to call the prisoner to tell his own story. . . .

Rouse, over-confident, brash, glib, told on oath of his activities that fatal night. He had picked up the stranger near Barnet; he smelt of drink. The man, region indeterminate—'he might have come from the south'—was rather fidgety when they pulled up to have a short nap at Markygate, about thirty-seven miles from the scene of the crime. It was there that the policeman told Rouse about his lights. He 'woke up properly then' and continued his journey.

Of the fire, he described how he ran towards it: 'Of course, I was a bit panic-stricken. I went as near the car as I could. . . . I do not remember what my thoughts were. I know I said something, "My God, My God!" I know I did not know what to do.' And of the two men who came up then: 'My first thoughts were to get help from them. If I were going to speak to them I do not know. Anyhow, I ran past them; thoughts must have struck me. Well, I do not know. I cannot account why I did not speak to them. . . .'

He then got a lift to London on a lorry.

There was a certain unwholesome jauntiness about Rouse's replies which did not go down well. Asked about being picked up, he said: '. . . I do not remember what I said, to be quite frank I asked for a lift.' And again, asked: 'Did you go direct to the [Thames] Embankment?' he answered: 'To be honest, no . . .' He had paid a brief visit to his home before getting a lift to Wales. He admitted telling lies about what had happened before his visit to Wales, but claimed that he went to Cardiff in order to get a connection to London, where he intended to visit Scotland Yard.

During all this Norman Birkett was busy jotting down points with his silver pencil. Rouse had, so far, had an easy passage in the box, but when Birkett rose to question him, to quote Sidney Campion's recollections of that moment: 'Rouse's demeanour underwent a change, very obvious to those of us who were able to study him at close range. The buoyant self-confidence suddenly evaporated; it was as though he had blown up and was now deflated. Yet he had tried his utmost to present himself as an innocent man, and was taken unawares by the quiet voice and gentle gestures and probably wondered whether he was as meek as he appeared to be, or was he playing a quiet game, and might suddenly reveal the strength of his hand?'

Birkett started with the lies. 'Rouse, when you told my learned friend that the lies you had told in Wales were unfortunate, what did you mean?'—'Well, I think that it is always best—I have always been noted for telling the truth, the whole of my life; I am not used to telling lies. At the time, I thought it was the best thing to do.'

'Why? Why was lying better than telling the truth?'—'Because there were many members of the family, for one thing, and I should have to tell the story over and over again, and I did not like to tell it with ladies present.'

'Why tell it at all, if you told a lie?'—'I was asked where my car was.'

'You think it was unfortunate that you should tell lies in Wales?'—'It turned out to be subsequently, now, against me.'

'What do you mean when you say that it has turned out against you?'—'People seemed to think that I did tell lies, and I admit I did tell lies. My name has been clear up to now of lies.'

'Do you think an innocent man might have told the truth?—'Yes, no doubt, to your way of thinking.'

'No, I merely want the fact?'—'I think I did the best possible thing under the circumstances. . . .'

With deadly logic, Birkett led up to that moment when Rouse told the police who arrested him at the coach station: 'I am glad it is all over.'

Birkett: 'You had abundant opportunities to get it over at Cardiff at the police station twelve hours before?'—'You mean going to the police station?'

'There was a police station forty-one yards from you, facing you?'—'You think I know Cardiff, but I did not. If I had seen it, I should not have gone in. My reason is that I have very little confidence in local police stations.'

'Of course you knew that in a place like Cardiff there was a police headquarters?'—'No, I did not, and I do not think there are. There is one policeman only in the village.'

'In Cardiff, I put to you?'—'I do not know about Cardiff.'

'You are not saying to the jury that you did not know that in a place like Cardiff there would be a big police station?'—'I wanted to get to London. That is all. . . .'

'But you would not have gone to the provincial police because you do not trust the provincial police?'—'If you want my candid opinion, I have not much faith in them. I was going to the fountain head.' He added, as though giving Norman Birkett advice which might help him in later years, 'One usually goes to the fountain head if one wants things done properly.'

What, asked Mr. Birkett, did he mean by telling the police: 'I am glad it is all over, I am responsible?'

'Thinking it over,' said Rouse, 'I will tell you. I handed the man a cigar. I asked him to fill up my car with petrol. I did not know whether he was capable of doing that, filling it with petrol.'

'Why did you let him do it?'—'I asked him because I thought he could do something. He had been riding in the car all the time ... and I thought he might do something in return. Quite frankly, he volunteered himself; I think quite frankly he did; I am not certain.'

In a previous statement to Detective-Sergeant Skelly, Rouse had said: 'I saw the man was inside and tried to open the door.' In another statement he had said: 'I could not see inside the car for the flames; the doors were both shut.'

The two statements were contradictory. Birket asked: 'Which was true?'—'The latter one, naturally, because it was true. No one could see through a mass of flames seventeen feet high, at least, as far as I know, you could not.'

More and more Rouse entangled himself in a mesh of improbability.

Birkett: 'It is quite clear that the evidence that you desire to put to the jury is that you did nothing to help the man because you were unable to help him?'—'Exactly.'

'Is that quite clear?'—'Exactly.'

'So you did not see the position of the body in the car?'—'No.'

'You heard it described here the other day?'—'Yes.'

'You now say you did not see the man inside?'—'No.'

'This was a horror?'—'Yes, exactly. In any case, I am certain that I did not see the man inside.'

'The recollections of the horror, when you tried to give the narrative this morning, made you rather break down?'—'Exactly.'

'It was the recollection of the horror?'—'Exactly.'

'Imprinted on your mind so that it would never go away?'—'Yes.'

'Do you say that you cannot tell the members of the jury whether upon that dreadful night you saw whether the man was inside the car or not?'—'I did not see the man at all.'

L

Then followed a masterly piece of cross-examination, consisting of the simplest questions about the dead man.

'But let me ask you a question or two about this man. His name you do not know?'—'No, I do not know now.'

'You never asked it?'—'No. One does not ask a passenger's name and address and all that sort of thing.'

'You did not ask him?'—'No.'

'Where he lived?'—'No.'

And so it continued until nearly fifty penetrating yet mildly worded questions established that he had no luggage, his destination was unstated, he appeared rootless, down on his luck. . . .

'Did you not gather that, as far as you could judge from the conversation with him, he did not seem to have any connection with anybody else; he was a homeless drifter?'—'I dare say he had connections; I do not know whether he had connections.'

'Judging from what you said and from what he said, was he the type of man whose disappearance would not cause much stir in the world?'—'I was not to know that.'

Later a witness for the defence, described as an expert on car fires, declared categorically that the loose union joint (which the prosecution claimed must have been loosened deliberately) could have been caused by heat. Linked with another defence witness's claim that leaking petrol from the joint would not—as was alleged by the prosecution—have caused a puddle, but would have seeped between the cracks, causing a build-up of fumes which would be highly explosive, it began to look as though the possibility of an accidental fire might be accepted by the jury. One witness for the defence had said that sparks are easily caused when wire insulation gets worn, and that a spark could have started an explosion.

When, however, Norman Birkett rose to cross-examine this witness, who claimed that a nut a whole turn loose 'is invariably found at all fires that have been intense', he decided to come to grips immediately with the man's qualifications for saying dogmatic things about the effect of heat on metals.

'What,' said Mr. Birkett, 'is the coefficient of the expansion of brass?'—'I am afraid I cannot answer that question off-hand.'

'If you do not know, say so. What do I mean by the term?'—'You want to know what is the expansion of the metal under heat?'

'I asked you what is the coefficient of the expansion of brass?

Do you know what it means?'—'Put that way, probably I do not.'

'You are an engineer?'—'I dare say I am. I am not a doctor, nor a crime investigator, nor an amateur detective. I am an engineer.'

'What is the coefficient of the expansion of brass? You do not know?'—'No, not put that way.'

Scores more questions followed, but that one question literally put a noose around Rouse's neck; for a moment, it seemed doubt had been thrown on the prosecution's claim that the loose nut could not have been accidental, and that it had been loosened in order to permit a steady flow of petrol, feeding a sustained fire. But doubt had now been thrown on the witness's knowledge of these matters.

Over the years Birkett's questions have been quoted and re-quoted as an example of brilliant questioning. Some, however, consider it a trick question that ought not to have been put. All those who have studied highly technical subjects learn much which they cannot instantly remember, but can find if given time. In 1953 *Glim*, the journal of the Inns of Court, published an article entitled *Brass*, which quoted that famous question. The author was a barrister-at-law of the Middle Temple and also a qualified engineer, and ventured 'humbly to assert that if the President of one of the great engineering societies had been asked the same question he would have said, "I don't know" as did the "expert" witness'.

Birkett decided to ask that question while the witness was giving his evidence in chief, taking the fact from an engineer's diary loaned to him by Colonel Buckle. Said the author of the *Glim* article: 'Had the witness been asked what was meant by the expression "coefficient of expansion" quite apart from the numerical value of any given coefficient, his reputation might have been saved.' What would Birkett have done if the witness had given the answer alleged to be correct—0·0000189? He said, years afterwards, that he would have gone on to copper, then to aluminium, so that if he knew the first answers, Birkett could leave the subject as being of no special importance and switch to some other subject.

Rouse was found guilty on January 31st, 1931, his appeal was rejected on March 4th and he was executed on March 10th.

Rouse's web of lies and deceit, his behaviour during and after the fire, his absurd pretence that he did not know a man was in that fire and—as emphasised by Birkett's deadly barrage of questions— his calm and callous demeanour when the police were looking for him sealed his doom.

Outside of the court, and during the case, Birkett 'divested himself of the mantle of the successful King's Counsel and became a man of wide reading . . . he held the general attention not because he forced himself upon us, but because we were all eager and willing to listen,' says Campion, recalling their lunches together. 'I remember a fascinating conversation about Thomas Hardy—he discussed the main characters, Tess of the D'Urbervilles, Eustacia Vye, Jude and the Mayor of Casterbridge, and dwelt upon the fate that overtook them, a sort of blind mechanistic fate and relentless Sophoclean doom, and how puny the characters appeared against the enormous background of creative life forces. I think he had in mind at the time—I certainly had—Rouse at that moment eating his meal in the police cell and the unknown man who had been Rouse's victim. In the case of Rouse, an uncontrollable sexual appetite had brought him inexorably to the gallows; the unknown man was bludgeoned into unconsciousness and then set on fire. Thomas Hardy characters in a new setting!'

An aspect of the trial which impressed Campion was that despite the immense weight of work, Birkett travelled at least twice to the House of Commons to attend to his Parliamentary duties; laden with Parliamentary papers he would set off by a fast train after the day's proceedings had ended in court, studying the papers *en route*. He would return to Northampton by the midnight train from Euston or an early train next morning, this time studying the papers concerned with the trial and planning the course his work was to take. It was typical of how he would drive himself to the limits, yet appear fresh and clear-headed.

After Rouse's execution some wondered whether the evidence had been conclusive enough to warrant a capital sentence. Birkett himself, however, had no doubt whatsoever of Rouse's guilt; he was, he told a friend, a cold-blooded murderer who fully merited his punishment. Before he died, Rouse confessed. He had strangled his victim, whom he had met several times before in the Swan and Pyramid public-house in Whetstone High Road, soaked him with petrol (opening the can with the mallet), loosened the petrol union joint, laid a petrol trail to the car and lit the end of it. When this confession was published, Rouse's devoted and heroic wife, who had fought to the last ditch to save his life, admitted that before his appeal Rouse confessed to her that 'the jury's verdict was the correct one'.

CHAPTER XVII

The 'Poisoned' Sandwich

DURING THE ROUSE trial and for many weeks before, Birkett had been acting as chairman of a committee set up by the Liberals to investigate the provisions of the Trades Disputes Bill, which the Labour Party was anxious—during the administration by a National Government under Mr. Ramsay MacDonald—should undo some of the vexatious legal restrictions imposed after the General Strike of 1926.

Birkett's long speech in the House during a debate on the Bill was a masterpiece of common sense and sage humour which had all parties laughing, at each other and at themselves. He dealt skilfully with the issues involved, making it clear that nobody wanted a general strike again, whether it was legal or illegal, but that in defining the sphere of legality and illegality in industrial disputes, care had to be taken that the hard-won rights of trade unions were not whittled away.

Political partisanship was something Birkett found impossible. He had as many friends among Conservatives and Labourites as among Liberals. When, during this debate, the Attorney-General pointed out that a Liberal Party pamphlet had stated only three years earlier that 'contracting-in' was 'wrong in principle, futile in practice and dangerous in effect'—for Birkett was now defending contracting-in—Birkett said he could now appreciate the feelings of a witness in the box when confronted with a letter he had written a long time ago and had forgotten all about. There were roars of laughter. There was more laughter when he added that it could be said: 'Look how inconsistent you were; look what a false prophet you were; look what a time-server you were.' But experience had shown that contracting-in had not been dangerous in effect or futile in practice, and the Liberals proposed to stand by it. Of the closed shop, he thought it an 'invasion of the elementary right of freedom'.

Birkett was now in the big-money class. One considerable source of income was libel actions, which he was frequently called upon to defend on behalf of the newspaper (although, as in the famous Mountbatten case, he sometimes appeared for the plaintiffs). Odhams Press, which had formerly paid a retainer to Sir Edward Marshall Hall, retained Mr. Birkett on a similar basis, although later there was a disagreement as to fees and the arrangement was dropped. But in the meantime he appeared on numerous occasions for that firm, particularly on behalf of *John Bull*, which, with its editorial policy of exposing individuals and organisations which it thought dishonest or mischievous, was especially vulnerable to this sort of action.

In such cases Birkett's fees were often considerable. His brief in the Jonescu libel case, when he appeared for the *Evening Standard*, was marked at 1,500 guineas and, allowing for daily refreshers in a case that lasted thirteen days, his own fees were between £3,000 and £4,000 for less than a fortnight's work. Looking, for example, at the number of big cases he handled in a single year—in 1928, for instance—it seems amazing that his vitality could stand such an incessant burden of work. But as all who met and worked with him know, his heart was in advocacy. He enjoyed it. He thoroughly believed in the worthwhile role of the advocate; it was not, he always said, a barrister's job to be a judge. The law provided that an accused man could defend himself, and he was entitled to employ one skilled in law to present his case for him. The law also ensured that the State could prosecute those who broke its laws, or the citizen could seek redress for wrongs in the civil courts. And so it was that his rhetoric would be used one day to send a man to the gallows and on some other occasion to save a man from that fate. But the lawyer, of course, is neutral. It is for the Judge and jury to decide the merits of a case; the advocate's job is to present it for either party, to the best of his ability. Thus he would defend Odhams Press with every artifice he possessed, and attack them with equal zest when Lady Louis Mountbatten sued one of their newspapers, the *People*.

By the early 'thirties Birkett was earning between £25,000 and £35,000 a year, at a time when money was worth at least three times what it is today; an equivalent income today would be at least £100,000 a year. Income tax was far less onerous then, and Norman Birkett, prudent by nature since his childhood, had few extravagant tastes, except to buy books and employ servants at

home, such as a nursemaid for the children (Linnea had been followed by Michael, born in 1930) and housemaids.

The need to make hay while the sun shone is understandable in
one who started his professional life so late. It takes time to make
an impact in the legal profession, and a few lost years make an
immense difference. By 1930 Birkett was forty-seven—though
he certainly didn't look it, and even when he died over thirty
years later, people were surprised because he always looked so
much younger than he was.

One secret was plenty of physical exercise—not dull exercises,
but golf and swimming, cricket and curling. He was an able
golfer and captained Harewood Downs Club. In winter he would
pay flying visits to Switzerland, sometimes to Murren, where he
could play at curling.

Most of the supervision of his children, as he frankly admitted
later, he left to his wife, for although his home was his greatest
pleasure, the constant absences at courts all over the country,
the frequent conferences and consultations, attendance at his
chambers, all made great inroads on his time. His success did not
come as a gift, but as a reward for hard and unremitting work.

It is not surprising that Birkett became the most sought-after
defence counsel in Britain. Of the dozens of murder cases which
he defended, he secured a verdict of Not Guilty in all but three;
an almost incredible record. I have told how in the trial of Mrs.
Pace he turned an original supposition of guilt into a declaration
of innocence. The same thing happened in the strange case of
Mrs. Annie Hearn, who was tried on June 15th, 1931, at Bodmin
Assizes before Mr. Justice Roche with the double murder of her
sister, Lydia ('Minnie') Everard, and Mrs. Alice Thomas.

Mrs. Hearn, a woman in her middle forties, had since 1925 been
living with her sister, Miss Everard, in the Cornish village of
Lewannick, near Launceston. Her sister died of a stomach complaint in 1930 after complaining to a friend that her medicine was
'too strong'.

Mrs. Hearn was friendly with a farmer, William Henry
Thomas, and his wife. They had been in the habit of visiting each
other and performing the simple friendly offices of good neighbours. When Minnie Everard died, of course, Mrs. Hearn was
lonely, and tended to see more of the Thomas's than she did

before. She was also very poor, and had borrowed sums of money amounting to £38 from Mr. Thomas, with his wife's knowledge and consent.

On October 18th, 1930, Mr. and Mrs. Thomas, who were going to drive to Bude in their car, invited Mrs. Hearn to come with them. She accepted with pleasure, and the three had a pleasant trip, with an interval for tea and cakes at Littlejohn's Café on Bellevue Hill. Mrs. Hearn thoughtfully supplemented the meal by some tinned-salmon sandwiches, which they all ate. On the car journey home Mrs. Thomas became violently ill with stomach pains and vomiting. Mrs. Hearn stayed at the farm and helped to nurse her.

The doctor who attended her from that day, apart from noting the patient's depressed mental condition ('she appeared to be agitated and worried'), thought it was a stomach upset until two weeks later, when he suspected arsenical poisoning and called in a consultant from Plymouth City Hospital, who confirmed the diagnosis and ordered her removal to hospital, where she died on November 4th.

By the time of the burial at Lewannick Church on November 8th the whole village was alive with sinister rumours. Everybody, it seemed, knew that arsenical poisoning had been diagnosed, that Mrs. Hearn had made some sandwiches, that certain organs taken from the body of Mrs. Thomas were being examined by the County Analyst.

Between Mr. Thomas and Mrs. Hearn had developed a certain coolness, and he pressed her for a return of the £38 she owed on the very day of the funeral. Many villagers suspected one or the other, and the dead woman's brother was outspoken with his suspicions at the funeral—'Tis that woman!' he said.

The next day Mrs. Hearn fled the district and sent Mr. Thomas what read like a suicide note: '. . . Goodbye. I am going out if I can. I cannot forget that awful man and the things he said. I am innocent, innocent, but she is dead, and it was my lunch she ate. I cannot bear it. When I am dead they will be sure I am guilty, and you at least will be clear. . . .'

A nation-wide hue-and-cry followed, but for the moment Mrs. Hearn had completely disappeared. An inquest was held at Plymouth on Mrs. Thomas, and the jury returned a verdict of death by arsenical poisoning. The bodies of Miss Mary Everard and

Miss Lydia ('Minnie') Everard, aunt and sister of Mrs. Hearn respectively, were exhumed.

Miss Lydia Everard's body was found to contain three-quarters of a grain of arsenic. The *Daily Mail* found that Miss Mary Everard had left all her estate to Mrs. Hearn in her will, and offered a reward of £500 to anyone who could confirm her death or give information which would enable the police to interview her.

Mrs. Hearn's black-and-white coat was found on the cliffs at Looe, and many assumed that, as her letter to Mr. Thomas implied, she had committed suicide. A shoe was washed up by the sea, and the *Daily Herald* reporter declared that the police had given her up for dead.

Meanwhile, Mrs. Hearn, using an assumed name, had obtained a post as cook to Mr. Cecil Powell, a Torquay architect, who had followed the Hearn case with interest but only identified her when her photograph was published in his newspaper. He straightway lost his appetite and reported her to the police. But he behaved towards her with commendable generosity and humanity. Having collected the *Daily Mail* reward of £500, he handed it over to a Grimsby solicitor, Mr. Walter West, as a contribution towards the cost of her defence. Thus it was that Mrs. Hearn was defended by the finest defence lawyer in the country—Mr. Norman Birkett. He had, of course, heard of the case, which had been making headlines for weeks.

Birkett knew that this was bound to prove a most difficult case. It would be impossible to summon any jury whose members had not read, somewhere, items of news to Mrs. Hearn's detriment. Her mysterious flight from the Cornish village, her faked suicide, her working under a false name, the exhumation of Mrs. Hearn's aunt, and sister, the fact that Mrs. Thomas had died after eating sandwiches which Mrs. Hearn had made; these cumulative facts made the supposition of her guilt appear overwhelming. In the intervening weeks Birkett refreshed his memory on the medical details of arsenical poisoning (which had been a feature of the trial of Mrs. Pace) and enlisted the help of Sidney Smith, Professor of Forensic Medicine at Edinburgh University. He also studied closely the voluminous evidence given before the magistrates at Launceston, concerning the death not only of Mrs. Thomas but also of Mrs. Hearn's sister, Miss Everard. On that occasion Mr.

Devlin, for the Director of Public Prosecutions, had closely questioned the doctor who had attended Miss Minnie Everard and had given as the cause of her death 'chronic gastric catarrh and colitis'. Miss Everard had kept a diary, one passage of which read: 'Very faint, hands and arms all prickles. Then began to feel stiff. No proper use of them. Then got it in the legs, pain in the stomach, and all over.' The passage ended: 'Oh, I was awfully bad, *and seemed as if I was poisoned.*'

Mr. H. du Parcq, K.C., assisted by Mr. Patrick Devlin (who had appeared in the earlier proceedings) conducted the case for the prosecution, while Mr. Birkett, defending, was assisted by Mr. Dingle Foot.

Mr. du Parcq, re-stating the circumstances in which the sandwich was eaten, and of Mrs. Thomas's illness and death, claimed that the sandwich eaten on October 18th contained arsenic, and that a further dose of arsenic was administered to her before October 29th, which was the day Mrs. Parsons, Mrs. Thomas's mother, came to stay with her, and took charge. He referred to a conversation between Mr. Thomas and Mrs. Hearn when the former told her: 'They are going to send some organs for analysis, and they will find out what it is. They will blame one of us. The blame will come heavier on you than me. People are saying so, and a detective may be here at any moment.' He described the funeral scene when Mr. Parsons, the dead woman's brother, had asked who made the sandwiches, Mrs. Hearn's flight to Torquay and her elaborate efforts at concealment, calling herself Mrs. Ferguson at one hotel and Mrs. Faithfull at her lodgings.

Of Mrs. Hearn's sister, Minnie Everard, Mr. du Parcq maintained that Mrs. Hearn had been giving her arsenic over a period of seven months. Those two women had lived alone in their house, Mrs. Hearn doing all the nursing and cooking. Mrs. Hearn was known to have bought weed-killer, which contains arsenic, in 1926. Nobody, he suggested, would commit suicide by giving herself an agonising death over a period of seven months.

By cross-examination of Mr. Thomas, Norman Birkett conjured up for the jury a picture of Mrs. Hearn harrassed and frightened by village gossip.

Birkett: 'Is it true, then, that Mrs. Hearn said people were blaming her?'—'I might have said people were talking about the poison in the sandwiches.'

With a swift look at the jury, as though to confirm that they were following this vital point, Birkett said, sternly: 'Poison, sir! Did you use the word *poison* to her?'

Mr. Thomas hastily retracted. 'No,' he said.

Mr. Birkett got back to that tea in the café at Bude, when Mrs. Hearn produced the sandwiches. 'There was no pushing of the plate, or juggling with them?' he asked.

'No,' Mr. Thomas agreed, 'there was no juggling at all.' He denied saying that 'the blame will come heavier on you than on me'. Mr. Birkett had made his point that there was no palming-off of the sandwiches to Mrs. Thomas. He then dealt with her letter.

Birkett: 'When Mrs. Hearn wrote "cannot forget that awful man and the things he said", did you know she meant Parsons?' (the man who had voiced suspicion on the day of the funeral).— 'Yes.'

'"I am innocent—innocent." Were those two words underlined?'—'Yes.'

In preparation for Mr. Birkett's cross-examination of Dr. Roche Lynche, the Home Office Analyst, the Defence had actually bought a tin of salmon of the identical brand used by Mrs. Hearn, made sandwiches of them and tried putting fourteen grains of weed-killer in one of them. The result is what Professor Sydney Smith told Birkett ought to happen—combining with the moisture of the salmon, the sandwich went bright blue, both at top and bottom. It is inconceivable that anyone offered such a sandwich would want to eat it.

Hence Birkett's question to Dr. Lynche: 'If you put fourteen grains of blue weed-killer on a sandwich and carried it for hours, I suggest it would be blue?'—'I have not tried it, but my opinion, for what it is worth, is that it would not be.'

'But you have not tried it. On the theory of the prosecution it was a most terrible risk to run?'—'Personally, I don't think so.'

'If you have sandwiches in two piles of three each—assume for the moment that the topmost sandwich in one of those piles alone contains arsenic—am I right in assuming that the sandwich with the blue weed-killer would stain downwards?'—'Yes.'

'The white bread ... would make the stains instantly discernible?'—'I agree ... the blue would come through in spots or stains.'

'I am much obliged. And would not the stains also go upwards?'—'Yes.'

Mr. Birkett had made a vital point based, as usual, on his characteristically thorough research into the technicalities of the problem. Dr. Lynche had earlier declared that two grains of weedkiller added to Bengers Food would turn it blue. Seven times that amount would, obviously, produce so violent a discoloration that surely Mrs. Thomas or Mr. Thomas would have noticed it.

The assumption that Mrs. Thomas's vomiting and illness on the car journey back from Bude must have been due to poisoning was challenged by Birkett. Might it not have been ordinary food poisoning? His questions to a food chemist revealed that there are cases of food poisoning in which one person has been affected although others have eaten the same food.

But there remained the sinister evidence of the arsenic found in the exhumed body of Mrs. Hearn's sister. Most people have some arsenic in their bodies, in a proportion of 1·5 parts in 1,000,000. The proportion of arsenic found in the remains of Miss Everard, however, was to a proportion of *16 parts* per 1,000,000, suggesting a steady absorption over the last seven months of her life.

Norman Birkett, while respectful of experts, was never dominated or overawed by them. On what basis was the proportion of arsenic in Miss Everard's body arrived at? Both in his cross-examination of Dr. Roche Lynche and Dr. Eric Wordley, Birkett went very carefully into the criteria by which they reached their conclusions.

Dr. Wordley, describing how the post morten on Miss Everard had been conducted, revealed that the amount of arsenic in the soil over her grave was unusually great—as much as 125 parts in 1,000,000, while the amount below the coffin was 62 parts in 1,000,000. There is a good deal of tin in the Cornish soil—there were tin-mines in Cornwall under the Romans, and arsenic is usually present where tin is to be found.

Mr. Birkett: 'Didn't a little snow fall while you were actually doing the post mortem?'—'I don't know. There might have been.'

'How long did the post mortem take?'—'About an hour.'

'There were nine jam-jars into which you put the organs. Where were those jars?'—'The post mortem was done on trestles some little way away from the grave. My impression is that there was another sheet of galvanised iron upon which the jars were put.'

'Unstoppered?'—'There was no cover on them at the time.'

'So that minute particles of dust in the atmosphere might have got in?'—'Yes, microscopic dust.'

Minute particles of soil, he agreed, might have entered the jars.

Birkett: 'Am I right in saying that a piece of soil so small that you could hold it between your fingers dropped on to this body would make every calculation wrong?'—'Yes.'

Norman Birkett's intention was plain. The infinitesimal quantities of arsenic found might, he believed, have seeped into the coffin from the surrounding soil. Falling dust, the tiniest clod of earth falling accidentally on the body from the uneven and hastily dug walls of the opened grave, a policeman's dirty finger thrust into an open jar—all these might have altered the calculations.

The shroud that enveloped the corpse was stained, but it was not analysed. No chippings were taken from the coffin to see if the wood had become impregnated with arsenic from the surrounding soil.

Statistics, it is said, can prove anything. Dr. Lynche had taken a sample of muscle weight one-eighth of an ounce and found in it one-6,400th of a grain of arsenic. Muscles usually constitute four-tenths of a person's total weight, and as Minnie Everard weighed eighty pounds, Dr. Lynche assumed that Miss Everard's muscles must have weighed thirty-two pounds. Because the tiny sample of muscle contained one-6,400th of a grain, he assumed that in all of the muscles there must be a total of three-quarters of a grain. Putting it another way, he was taking less than one-10,000th part of the dead person's muscle tissue and assuming that what applied to that tiny sample applied to all the rest.

Birkett pointed out two main fallacies in this argument. Even assuming that multiplying the results from that tiny sample was a valid method, Minnie Everard was so sick as to be wasted away, and would not have anything like the weight of muscle tissue attributed to her.

Birkett's penetrating cross-examination of the medical witnesses shook the whole basis of the prosecution's case. Until then, things had looked sinister, for Dr. H. A. Galbraith, partner of Dr. Gibson, gave evidence that when he called on Minnie Everard she complained of the medicine and told him she was being poisoned. He had a look at the medicine, recognised it as having been prescribed by Dr. Gibson and knew that there could not have been any poison in it. He did not think to take away a sample of the medicine for analysis, in case anything had been added to the mixture as dispensed.

Addressing the Judge, Mr. Birkett submitted that: 'In the case of Mrs. Thomas, which is the case we are trying at the moment, . . . there is no evidence to go to the jury. I will be brief advisedly, because if your Lordship has already formed a view on the matter it would be a waste of time. . . .' The Judge had. 'I think,' he said, 'that there is ample evidence to go to the jury.' Norman Birkett thereupon called Mrs. Hearn, a quietly dressed, timorous lady of forty-six, whose evidence was given in a straightforward manner. Explaining her flight from Lewannick after Mrs. Thomas's death she said: 'There were people in the dining-room, including Mr. Parsons. Mrs. Thomas, senior, was not there then. They were having lunch, and I had been preparing some things that had been taken in. There were a good many people there, but practically all strangers to me. Mr. Parsons was sitting on the opposite side of the table . . . when I came in I was facing him. Some of the women were discussing Mrs. Thomas's illness and naturally looked to me for information. Of course, I said the doctor thought it was food poisoning and something we had eaten in Bude. I do not know whether I mentioned sandwiches first or someone else did. That was before Mr. Parsons had spoken about it. Then he said: "Oh, sandwiches? Who took them?" I said, "I did" and he said, "Where did you get them?" "Were they taken from here?" . . . questions like that. . . .'

Birkett: 'In what kind of tone was he speaking?'—'In an enquiring tone, but when I said about the sandwiches he stood up, and the rest of his conversation was, I can only say, shouted.'

On the question of her own marriage, Mrs. Hearn was certainly vague. Before her arrest newspapers had searched in vain at Somerset House for her marriage certificate. A photograph of her husband which she gave relatives was published in one newspaper, and proved to be one of Lieutenant Charles Hewart Vane-Tempest, great-grandson of the third Marquis of Londonderry. She had bought the photograph in 1919, the year of the reported marriage. In fact, Lieutenant Vane-Tempest was killed in action in 1917.

Mr. du Parcq, however, did not go into that story. Mrs. Hearn told him she was married in 1919 at a register office not far from Bedford Square in London. Her husband was Leonard William Hearn, but she lived with him only a few days, and six days after marriage read in a Harrogate newspaper that he had died. She was living at the time with her aunt and nursing her sister, and could not think of anyone else who saw her husband. She could not mention any living person who had seen him.

However strange that sounded to the jury, the real issue was: did Mrs. Hearn kill Mrs. Thomas? The prosecution had suggested that Mrs. Hearn's motive was that, with Mrs. Thomas out of the way, Mr. Thomas might marry her. She was poor, and therefore implied the prosecution, she killed her. But nobody had proved that any affection existed between Mr. Thomas and Mrs. Hearn. When arrested, Mrs. Hearn is supposed to have said that Mr. Thomas often brought a paper to the house 'but it was a blind'. What she really said, declared Mr. Birkett, was '. . . he was very kind'.

The case for the Crown, Birkett continued, rested on the blue weed-killer bought in 1926, but there was no evidence of it ever being taken to Trenhorne Farm, the Thomas's home. No evidence had been called to carry that matter beyond 1926, but from October 18th to November 10th, 1930, there were in the house Cooper's worm tablets, which contained not only arsenic but also what Mrs. Hearn's weed-killer did not contain, copper. 'And,' said Mr. Birkett slowly and dramatically, 'in the organs of Mrs. Thomas there was found copper.'

Mrs. Thomas, said Mr. Birkett, contracted food poisoning on October 18th and arsenical poisoning on November 2nd. Other people had equal opportunity with Mrs. Hearn to give poison after October 18th. He quoted Mr. Thomas's words to Mrs. Hearn after the funeral: 'They will blame one of us. The blame will come heavier on you. People are saying so. A detective might be here at any time.' 'What language,' exclaimed Mr. Birkett, a ring of indignation in his voice, 'is this for a distraught, innocent, unsuspecting husband?' His speech finished, Birkett, bathed in perspiration from the nervous tension, turned to Dingle Foot and said: 'You know, cases like this take years off a man's life.'

'Perhaps,' replied Foot, 'but they add years to the client's.'

Mrs. Hearn was found Not Guilty, but Mr. Birkett was not in court to witness that final emotional scene. Outside the court thousands waited, clamouring for a sight of Mrs. Hearn, but she could not face them. After hours of waiting in a private room at the Assize Court, she changed clothing with her sister, Mrs. Poskitt, and was smuggled away unnoticed, the crowd cheering Mrs. Poskitt when she first appeared, until they realised they had been tricked.

There is little doubt that Mrs. Thomas *was* murdered, perhaps by her husband, who had the poison and the opportunity; after her death he lived in lonely solitude in his remote farm, where he died in 1949. Birkett himself never had the slightest doubts of Mrs. Hearn's innocence; and in a moving letter of thanks which she sent to him after the trial it was clear she knew that she owed her life to him.

M

CHAPTER XVIII

A Cruel Libel

THE ERA OF prosperity in which Birkett now found himself did little to alter his essential way of life. Plentiful money meant servants and a good standard of living for his family, and it enabled him to buy a large house in Chalfont St. Giles with a fine panoramic view of the surrounding countryside. Later he acquired a sheep farm in the Lake District, and so was able to follow his country pursuits to offset the strain and perpetual rush of a busy and growing practice.

Some solicitors thought Birkett's fees too harsh, but though they might say this, they nevertheless clamoured and competed for his services. On one occasion a brief was marked at 1,500 guineas, but the case was disposed of before Birkett could get there—it was simply dismissed. But he was paid his fee just the same.

Birkett's tremendous self-control, his inability to grumble and his tremendous application made him a boon indeed to clients. Equally remarkable was his quick grasp of totally unfamiliar subjects—in 1932, for instance, he switched happily from the financial intricacies of the trial of Arthur Jack Klein at the Old Bailey to the mysteries of a murder; from murder he turned his attention to the doings of an errant Church of England clergyman, the Reverend Harold Davidson; from the Church to the squashing of an infamous rumour concerning Edwina, Lady Mountbatten; from that gross libel to the nether-world of spirits and spooks and ectoplasm galore in the libel case of *Louisa Ann Meurig* v. *Associated Newspapers*; and from spiritualism to the mysterious murder of a humble grocer's assistant in a Birmingham street—this gives only a slight idea of the range of his work. In that year, as in those that followed, there were innumerable other cases, often with no break whatsoever between them. For example, he left the Hearn trial as soon as he had finished his speech to the jury, and did not reappear the next day to hear the acquittal; instead, he was in another court, defending another case.

Birkett often had less success in cases involving finance than those of murder, possibly because the former involved more argument on fact and offered less scope for eloquence. In the case of Arthur Jack Klein, the son of a rabbi who was charged with receiving over £250,000 which had been obtained by fraud, Birkett's efforts on his behalf could only mitigate, and not prevent, sentence. Klein was sent to prison for twenty-one months, Mr. Justice Finlay remarking that the case, from the cruelty and magnitude of the fraud, was 'of the most appalling gravity'.

Klein had come under the influence of Jacob Factor, a swindling financier, whom the Judge no doubt had in mind when he said there was force in the statement by Birkett that Klein 'came under the influence of a stronger and it may well be a wickeder man'. Klein had a power of attorney to sign cheques on the account of H. Wise and the Broad Street Press Ltd., and was found guilty of betraying that trust. The trial lasted eleven days, in the course of which Norman Birkett perused and memorised mountains of financial statements and documents.

February 1932 found Birkett at Hereford Assizes for the defence of Mrs. Edith May Dampier for the murder of George Benjamin Parry, whom she had employed as a handyman and who was found shot in the kitchen of her house, Hunter's Hall, Lea, near Ross-on-Wye.

The trial was heard before Mr. Justice Roche.

It was a terribly story that Birkett unfolded; of stark tragedy, of unmitigated horror. Mrs. Dampier was suffering from the general paralysis of the insane as the result of venereal disease. Before the murder she had threatened to drown herself and shoot her nine-year-old son, who had lost the sight of his left eye owing to his mother having communicated the disease to him.

A doctor testified that the knowledge that her son had lost the sight of an eye had a terrible effect on the mother; she frequently told him she intended to commit suicide, and on one occasion the boy telephoned for him. When he arrived the boy was in a state of utter terror; his mother had threatened to cut out his blind eye with a pair of scissors. From the mother the doctor learned that there were two men in her life, one her 'new husband' and another who casually visited her and was, she hinted, responsible for her disease. Dr. Dunlop was convinced Mrs. Dampier was insane when she shot Parry, who was not one of the two men concerned. The Birmingham prison doctor agreed that she was insane.

Birkett told the court that her son's blindness was the most dreadful thing that a mother could have to bear, and her mind and reason might well have been overthrown by the thought: 'Through my sin he will go through life without the sight of an eye.'

This eloquent appeal was lost on Mrs. Dampier, who sat in the dock for five hours totally without movement, like a waxworks figure from Tussaud's. She was a slightly built woman with sharp features, thin lips and sallow complexion, and stared fixedly down at the floor, taking no interest whatsoever in the proceedings.

Mr. Justice Roche, in summing up, said it was a miserable story of a woman suffering from the two forms of a dread disease, one of which caused general paralysis of the insane. The jury, without leaving the box, returned a verdict of Guilty but Insane, and the Judge ordered her to be detained during His Majesty's pleasure. Docile and indifferent, she walked down the steps to her cell.

It was said at this time that Norman Birkett was to play a leading part—as defence lawyer—in one of the most sensational trials in church history. It concerned the Rector of Stiffkey, Norfolk (population 300), who, when the scandal began to break, told newspaper reporters that Mr. Norman Birkett would conduct his case, which was to be heard before the Consistory Court at Church House, Westminster. Birkett did not, in fact, do so, and no further announcement ever explained why; but he did represent Odhams Press at the enquiry.

The Reverend Harold Davidson, an actor and comedian in his youth, had saved his earnings and studied for the Anglican Church, in which he had, for years, a highly successful career. He settled in Stiffkey and raised a large family.

Gradually, however, it was noticed that except for Sundays he seemed to be hardly ever in his parish. Rumours said that he was 'a ladies' man' and was picking up girls in London and having gay week-ends in Paris. In fact, he had permission to pursue his rescue work in London. The Bishop of Norwich instituted an enquiry and he was ordered to face charges of 'habitual association with women of loose character ... annoying and making improper suggestions to young women ... taking girls to Paris and theatre schools ... the habitual accosting and molesting and importuning of young girls.'

Hardly the sort of thing expected of an Anglican parson in a village where tradition has held sway ever since William the Conqueror was Lord of the Manor. Davidson was fundamentally a kind-hearted man. He would empty his pockets for a tramp and keep open house for anyone with nowhere to sleep. Rootless, shiftless people found him a good friend. His heart must have been in the Church, because he gave up the stage to become an ill-paid curate. His father had been a clergyman and so had twenty-seven relatives.

Most of Davidson's time was spent in saving 'unfortunate' girls in London. The charge was that he was not seeking to rescue them from a life of sin, but meeting them for the purposes of self-indulgence. 'We believe,' the court declared, 'that the Reverend Harold Davidson had a right and duty to rescue maidens from a life of sin.'

Such crusading fervour did not, however, in the court's view, justify the rector in kissing and hugging one woman in a Chinese restaurant in Bloomsbury, allowing a seventeen-year-old girl to sleep in his bed, pay room rent for a dozen girls with whom he had unclerical relations or embracing an actress while she was clad only in her nightdress. With one prostitute, it was alleged, he had maintained a continuous and intimate association for over eleven years, although his original pretext for picking her up in Leicester Square was to rescue her.

Much of the evidence against Davidson had been collected by private detectives, who had interviewed about forty women. The prostitute with whom it was alleged Davidson had been intimate for many years had been seen by a reporter from the *Daily Herald*. In the course of the interview she claimed that the statements alleging an association between her and the rector had been obtained by bribery and were false charges.

Such a story, published before the trial, constituted a very serious libel on those instituting the enquiry, and Mr. Birkett said that his clients desired to express their profound regret to the court, and to 'apologise humbly both to that court and to the Consistory Court at Norwich', and nothing which he (counsel) might say was in any way intended to detract from that apology. Birkett then read affidavits from Julius Elias (later Lord Southwood), Managing Director of Odhams Press Ltd., and William H. Stephenson, editor of the *Daily Herald*.

Davidson was found guilty and unfrocked by the Bishop of Norwich before the High Altar in Norwich Cathedral, where he was 'removed, deposed and degraded from all clerical offices of priest'.

Moral or not, the deposed rector had great courage. Penniless and discredited, he faced life afresh with a cheerful and adventurous spirit. Since entertainment was the only profession he knew outside of the Church, he offered himself as an exhibit in a barrel, and drew crowds at Blackpool's 'golden mile' by undergoing a protracted fast. This method of earning money brought him much hostile criticism. However, his end was as unexpected and dramatic as most events in his strange life. While working with a lion-taming act with a travelling fair at Skegness he accidentally trod on one of the lionesses. In a second another lion had sprung on the rector, grabbing him and stalking round the cage with him in its mouth, shaking him as a cat shakes a mouse. As the watching crowd screamed and fainted a sixteen-year-old lion tamer bravely went into the cage and managed to drag him free. But the Rector of Stiffkey, still remembered by many residents as 'the best preacher we ever had', was dead.

There is a delightful neutrality about being a successful lawyer. At one moment you are drawing large fees from a client to protect his interests, and the next you may be hired by somebody else to attack him. Within weeks of appearing for Odhams in the Consistory Court, Birkett had to conduct the plaintiff's case in a libel action against them.

The 'atrocious libel', as Norman Birkett described it before the Lord Chief Justice in the King's Bench Division, appeared in a Sunday newspaper and concerned Lady Louis Mountbatten, formerly Miss Edwina Ashley, granddaughter of Sir Ernest Cassell, the millionaire friend of King Edward VII, who was her godfather.

Lady Mountbatten had returned from a tour of the West Indies and Mexico to find London alive with a most damaging and hurtful rumour. Mr. Birkett unfolded the story, sequence by sequence.

At the very outset Birkett announced the settlement of the action. Defendants had submitted to every demand made upon them by Lady Louis Mountbatten, and after the statements which would be made in court he would ask that the record be withdrawn on terms which he would state.

Plaintiff was the wife of Lord Louis Mountbatten, a naval officer attached to the Mediterranean Fleet. In August 1931 he was ordered with his ship to Malta for an appointment which in the ordinary way would be two years. As was only natural and right, Lady Louis decided to go with him, taking her children with her. She intended to make her home in Malta for the period of her husband's service.

The inevitable and natural desire on her part to be with her husband gave rise to 'the most atrocious and most abominable of rumours'. Lady Louis Mountbatten took a prominent part in the social life of London, and her departure 'gave the opportunity for the malignant, poisonous and lying tongues of scandal to wag'.

'It is,' continued Mr. Birkett, 'always a matter of difficulty to ascertain the actual carrier of a dastardly rumour, and even now, although the most rigorous steps are being taken to track these rumours to their source, I desire to state publicly that if the author or, indeed, the repeater, of these rumours is discovered, no mercy will be shown. . . .

'The practice on these occasions,' continued Birkett, 'is not to read the libel to avoid giving further publicity to it, but after careful consideration and, indeed, at the personal request of Lady Louis Mountbatten, I propose to read it. I will do that in order that its full enormity may be known and every fact in this case plainly, completely and publicly stated without concealment of any kind, so that the whole world may know that these foul and lying rumours have been brought out of the region of hints into the light of publicity and by these proceedings wholly destroyed.'

Mr. Birkett then read the article:

'I am able to reveal today the sequel to a scandal which has shaken society to its very depths. It concerns one of the leading hostesses in the country—a woman highly connected and immensely rich. Her associations with a coloured man became so marked that they were the talk of the West End. Then one day the couple were caught in compromising circumstances.

'The sequel is that the society woman has been given hints to clear out of England for a couple of years to let the affair blow over and the hint comes from a quarter which cannot be ignored.'

The item appeared under a nom-de-plume, and Birkett did not spare the newspaper or the writer. This was 'a contemptible feature' of the libel—that short of naming Lady Louis everything was done to identify her, while everything 'is done to conceal the identity of the loathsome person who wrote it. That concealment was made in the expectation, I suppose, that this foul defamer might escape.'

Many witnesses were present, willing to testify that, having read the paragraph, they believed it pointed unmistakably to Lady Mountbatten. She was a famous hostess; she was one of the leading hostesses of society; she was highly connected; she was immensely rich; and she had to go to Malta for two years. Friends had informed her of the identity of the coloured man supposed to be referred to in the article. She had never met him or had anything to do with him whatsoever.

Lady Louis desired to go into the witness box to 'deny upon oath these poisonous allegations'. Defendants had never sought to defend the action. They had given to Lady Louis the fullest indemnity for the costs and expenses. But although a jury would certainly have awarded very heavy damages, and the defendants were willing to pay damages, 'to accept one penny would be in the highest degree distasteful'. What Lady Louis did desire was that she should have a speedy and public vindication of her name.

In the box, Lady Mountbatten refuted on oath the allegations in the article. Then Sir Patrick Hastings, for the defendants, expressed their regrets for the 'grievous wrong'. He agreed that if damages had been asked for they must have been extremely heavy, and that the only reason she was not asking for them was that in her view damages would have been wholly inadequate to right such a wrong.

Lord Hewart agreed: 'I should be very astonished if she had accepted them, because there are some libels which are crimes on the part of everybody concerned.' He agreed to Birkett's request that the record should be withdrawn on the terms stated, 'with considerable reluctance', and ordered that a copy of the offending newspaper should remain in the custody of the court. The record was then withdrawn.

There was general sympathy in her plight, and admiration for the courageous way she had grasped the nettle of scandal and crushed it. But such is the mischief of these things, once started,

that new mischief is often spawned. *Time*, the American magazine, for example, wrote: '. . . Lady Louis Mountbatten, wife of
King George's first cousin once removed, stood before Lord Chief
Justice Baron Hewart and heard herself exonerated on a charge of
consorting with a negro.' Put like that, with the word 'charge'
(when *Time* meant the published libel) read as though it was a
'charge' in the legal sense. Readers abroad would imagine that it
was illegal to consort with a Negro, whereas Lady Mountbatten
had never met or had anything whatsoever to do with him.

CHAPTER XIX

The Punctual Spirits

AN ENTERPRISING REPORTER'S refusal to be overawed by an assembly of spirits who chose a Mrs. Meurig Morris as their mouthpiece brought Norman Birkett one of his most interesting, least sordid and most amusing assignments.

Mrs. Morris, daughter of a market gardener in Worcestershire, was born in 1899, attended a village school, married in her teens and later moved to Newton Abbott, where she became interested in spiritualism, and started preaching under the influence, she said, of a spirit known as 'Power'. She did not go in for spectacular phenomena, such as floating, luminous trumpets or levitated tables, but would go into a trance and then hold forth on anything and everything.

Later she converted to her cause Mr. Laurence Cowen, a dramatist with a sense of showmanship, and thereafter he became her organiser and business manager. Through her mediumship he contacted many people in the netherworld, including Israel Zangwill, the Jewish lecturer, novelist and playwright, who had died in 1926 and his own brother, who dictated an entire play from the other side; its dramatic merits are unknown, as it has never been produced.

Cowen brought a brisk commercial touch to her life. Photographs and gramophone records were made of 'Power' at work through her privileged mind and body, and the climax of showmanship came with the presentation of Mrs. Morris in a series of Sunday spiritualistic services at the Fortune Theatre in London. When a spirit from beyond the veil addresses whole audiences it is not surprising that newspapers should be interested. Charles Sutton, then a *Daily Mail* reporter, attended services there, watched Movietone News make a film of 'Power' in action and even interviewed the 'spirit' as well as Mrs. Morris; in other words, he talked with Mrs. Morris both when she was in and out of trances.

The *Daily Mail* from then on had some really unusual headlines for its readers. 'WOMAN'S AMAZING SERMON IN A TRANCE: ON A

THEATRE STAGE: SOPRANO THAT CHANGED TO BARITONE' it announced on January 12th, 1931, and Sutton described the 'small, slim young woman in a voluminous gown of amethyst velvet' who walked nervously on to the stage and sat in a chair among Lady Conan Doyle, her son and Mr. Cowen. Hymns, addresses, invocations and music followed; then Mrs. Morris sat bolt upright, and delivered a sermon in a ringing baritone voice.

Such odd happenings were a tremendous draw, and crowds started queueing for admission hours beforehand. The next issue of the *Daily Mail* carried Sutton's interview with Mrs. Morris, while the following day the paper printed the interview with 'Power'. The next instalment in this odd drama was the making of the film, when Mrs. Morris went into a trance before cameras and Kleig lights, the microphones falling inexplicable during the performance. When this film was shown, Sutton wrote of it that Cowen seemed to be hypnotising Mrs. Morris—which Cowen vehemently denied.

The articles on Mrs. Morris, which were started on a more or less uncritical basis, became increasingly sceptical in tone. Whatever the 'control', declared Sutton, Mrs. Morris said more or less the same things and phrases. 'To the sceptic, the agnostic, and even to tens of thousands of people with open minds,' he said, 'Mrs. Morris is an extremely clever woman. But her spiritualism is unconvincing.'

Later the *Daily Mail* spoke their mind outright. A poster announced: TRANCE MEDIUM FOUND OUT, while the article was headed 'Power's Sermon Jargon'; 'One Talk for All Texts'.

A libel action followed. The *Daily Mail* pleaded fair comment on a matter of public interest, and that what they had written was true. The trial was heard before Mr. Justice McCardie and a special jury at the Law Courts, Sergeant Sullivan, K.C., appearing for Mrs. Morris and Birkett for Associated Newspapers Ltd., proprietors of the *Daily Mail*.

For the next few days Norman Birkett kept strange company; he had to familiarise himself with the temperament and doings of denizens of the spirit world for whom Mrs. Morris was their chosen amplifier.

Mrs. Morris claimed that the placard implied that she was a deliberate fraud. In her examination in chief by Sergeant Sullivan she told the remarkable story of her life and supposed psychic gifts. Describing how she felt when 'Power', her principal 'control' approached, she said, 'I first of all see a great yellow light, which is like a searchlight, and it comes right over me. Then I seem to grow tall and my neck begins to get big. . . .' Once she lost consciousness, in the trance, she was not aware of what happened. In the eight years of 'Power's' visitations she had not studied spiritualism, comparative religion or anything of the sort, or read books of philosophy.

'In the course of your life,' asked Sergeant Sullivan, 'have you ever had access to the information that apparently may be given in your sermons?'—'No.'

The cross-examinations were seemingly endless, and Mr. Justice McCardie had a struggle to keep the proceedings on a sane and legal level. Cohorts of invisible spirits rallied round Mrs. Meurig Morris in court, and Mr. Birkett expressed understandable curiosity about them, particularly her 'controls', 'Little Sunshine', for example, and 'Father O'Keefe', whose comments from the other side were frequently interspersed with 'Sure and begorra'. There was 'Sister Magdalene', 'Selina' and a 'Red Indian Squaw': Mr. Birkett made conscientious efforts to visualise this multi-linguial Indian, who, said Mrs. Morris, 'had a band round her head, and it looked like a feather'.

'The typical squaw of fiction?' asked Birkett politely.

'I have never read any fiction about squaws,' said Mrs. Morris, 'so I do not know.' Mr. Justice McCardie asked about business organisation in the spirit world. 'Do these Controls,' he enquired, 'come when you call for them, or do they come unexpectedly?'

'No; I do not have them just when I want them. They come when they have a message or some purpose to come for, not otherwise.'

'"Power",' said Birkett, 'comes every Sunday night at the starting of the hymn, does he not?'—'I know that he does, but that is his mission, to work with me.'

'Absolutely like clockwork?'—'Yes.'

'He has never failed?'—'He never failed.'

'He preaches for forty-five minutes and goes away for a week?' —'He does not go away for a week.'

'Unless you have an engagement in the country?'—'I feel his presence, yes.'

'He will go to Brighton, to Birmingham or to Nottingham, as

long as Mr. Cowen has advertised that he will be there; is not that right?'—'It is nothing to do with the advertising at all.'

Birkett was throughout courteous and quiet in his questioning of Mrs. Morris; the point of his cross-examination was, however, to discredit her. Of the talks given by 'Power' Birkett asked: 'There is nothing in that which has not been said a million times, is there?' To which she replied: 'Mr. Birkett, there is no new truth in the world.'

The presence of spirits in court was of interest to Birkett. 'Sister Magdalene', a French nun who spoke (rather usefully) broken English, was in court with Mrs. Morris.

'Is she here now?' asked the Judge.

'She is here, and that is why I have been trying to get as near to her as possible.'

Had she come to stay? Birkett asked: 'Is she still here?' With a pitying look at the unregenerate Birkett, Mrs. Morris pointed a minatory finger at nothing—'She is here—there!' she said dramatically.

Mr. Birkett's eyebrows went up just perceptibly. 'She has never moved from there?' he asked. Another you-are-beyond-redemption look from the witness. 'She stands and watches me,' she explained.

The enquiry was resumed, after the Judge had asked if the invisible 'Sister Magdalene' was speaking to her then and was told that she was not.

Birkett: 'If "Sister Magdalene" spoke to me I could not hear it?'—'No, I have what they call a clairvoyant power.'

'When she speaks to you she uses her own vocal chords?'—'I am able to hear it because I have the power.'

'But she uses her own vocal chords when she speaks to you?'—'I suppose that she has vocal chords in the body that she has got. She is bound to have.'

'I want to pursue this matter. She is in this court now?'—'Yes, she is just *here*. I wish that you could see her.'

'An ethereal shape?'—'Yes.'

'How is she dressed?'—'In very deep purple.'

'Velvet?'—'It is flimsy. I cannot describe it. She has been standing here, and she is standing now.'

'Is she stationary?'—'Yes, she is stationary, watching me.'

The point of this questioning had yet to emerge. In her own

words, Mrs. Morris was being led on to reveal her own incon-
sistencies.

Back they came to the invisible nun.

'Is she still there?'—'Yes, she is.'

'You can tell, can you, that her frame looks like a physical
frame—it is the same outline?'—'Yes, it is the same type of body
as ours, but it is more ethereal. I cannot understand it at all.'

'Subject to that, it is a human form wearing a purple gown?'—
'Yes, it is clothed in purple. It looks like a human form, yes.'

Mr. Justice McCardie intervened: 'Can you see the face?'—
'Yes.'

'You can see the face, the eyes and the lips?'—'Absolutely like
I am looking at you.'

'That is what I meant,' said Birkett, 'with your ordinary physical eyes you can see the form?'—'Yes.'

'You can see the form of "Sister Magdalene" in a purple
gown?'—'I have a clairvoyant power and I am able to see it.'

At this point Birkett read from one of 'Power's' sermons. 'If
you had the greater vision you would find, not a physical body,
nor a body that you term the astral body, but you would see the
body was likened just to a streak of light, a streak of light which
would come like a streak of lightning.' Mildly he asked her: 'A
streak of light could not wear a purple gown, could it?'—'You
are muddling. My vision only enables me to see the next world.
I have not got the greater vision that "Power" is speaking of.'

Suddenly in the course of questioning Mrs. Morris turned very
pale and stared ahead with strange, glassy eyes. Something was
amiss, and Birkett asked kindly: 'Shall I stop for a moment, Mrs.
Morris, while you rest?' From the back of the court voices cried:
'Don't touch her! Leave her alone!' Mrs. Morris became more
tense, clenched her fists and cried out: '*The Christ!*' Ushers, on
the Judge's orders, closed in but did not touch her. She recovered,
while Norman Birkett asked if she would like a doctor. She burst
into tears. 'It was only a vision,' she sobbed, 'the Christ came.'

The court was adjourned, and on another day was regaled with
gramophone records of 'Power's' sermons and a showing of the
film.

One witness described how he had conversed in French with
Lumière, the French pioneer of photography, who had given him
a formula for the development of psychic photographs. Birkett

asked his occupation. 'I am a Customs and Excise Officer,' the witness said. 'Testing spirits?' Birkett asked. 'Yes,' said the officer, 'but not the spirits which we are speaking of now.'

A doctor maintained that Mrs. Morris was genuine, in that there was no deliberate pretence on her part. He had found that, in a trance, Mrs. Morris became insensible to pin pricks, that her pulse raced and that one side of her face became clammy and cold. He thought Mrs. Morris was an hysteric.

Some of the witnesses were odd people. One told Birkett that she could see the aura of his 'etheric body' and that the pineal gland at the top of his head was a vestigial remnant of a third eye.

Lady Conan Doyle and Sir Oliver Lodge gave evidence in support of spiritualist beliefs, and the court was crowded with spiritualists. A charwoman, however, gave evidence that she once heard Mr. Cowen and Mrs. Morris rehearsing. She heard a little child's voice saying, 'I so happy', and Mr. Cowen saying, 'I would like that a little louder, my dear.' Employees at the Fortune Theatre had also heard what they thought was rehearsing for Mrs. Morris's demonstrations. A throat specialist said that her throat was quite normal and that to speak as 'Power' spoke she had only to speak with greater volume.

Charles Sutton, who wrote the article complained of, asked whether he considered Mrs. Morris a fraud replied: 'I do! I think she is not what she claims to be.'

In addressing the jury, Birkett said that the issue was what view the jury formed of the plaintiff. Was she genuine or not? He remarked unfavourably on the fact that Mr. Cowen had not given evidence. It had been stated that this was to be the greatest trial in the history of Spiritualism. 'I ask you, members of the jury, to put that thought aside. You are not trying the future of spiritualism, and your verdict will not affect the march of events in spiritualism. Your verdict may have a powerful and beneficial effect if it does something to put a check to the kind of matters which are broadcast and which delude innocent and suffering people.' Of Sir Oliver Lodge, who fervently believed in Spiritualism, Birkett said he would not be the first distinguished man who in his own sphere was supreme, but outside it was a mere child.

'A great scientist,' said Birkett, 'can weigh the atom and the star, he can tell all about the nature of light and the vibrations of the ether, projecting his mind into space and making a most fruitful suggestion, yet it would not be the first time that such a great mind had gone completely wrong when stepping outside that sphere.' Nor, he added, would it be the first time that 'a frail, petite, emotional woman' had deceived people.

Mr. Justice McCardie began an admirable summing-up, when Mrs. Morris rose to her feet and, assuming a declamatory attitude, thundered in the deep, resonant voice of 'Power': 'Thou who art a brother judge, hearken unto my voice. . . .'

The Judge's patience was badly strained. Had he chosen, he could have declared her conduct contempt of court. 'This really must be stopped,' he snapped. 'Tell her to stop. She knows better. Let her stop!'

'Power', or Mrs. Morris's subconscious mind, was not intimidated. 'I will say this . . .' he began, but Justice McCardie ordered her to leave the court. 'Do not touch her till I have left the body,' thundered her spirit, solicitous and protective to the last. 'The jury will see,' said the Judge, 'why I say advisedly that I dislike every minute of the case. As long as I remain a Judge I care not for all the incarnate or discarnate spirits in the world . . . you have got to find out what the truth of the matter is here . . . you have got to give your verdict.'

The jury found for the *Daily Mail* on their claim of fair comment on a matter of public interest, adding 'we do not consider that any allegations of fraud or dishonesty have been proved'. The Judge gave judgement accordingly, and it was upheld subsequently by the Court of Appeal and the House of Lords. Lord Justice Greer, however, did remark, sensibly, in the Court of Appeal that a court competent to decide questions of libel and slander would not necessarily be competent to decide on the mystery of life and death.

CHAPTER XX

An Unsolved Murder

A BIRMINGHAM MURDER WHICH remains, to this day, an unsolved mystery was to prove for Norman Birkett yet another legal triumph, for which he received the sum of fifteen guineas instead of the 200 to 500 guineas usually marked on his briefs. In this instance, he accepted the defence of two girls, Marjorie Kathleen Yellow, aged nineteen, and her sister Emily Eleanor Thay, aged sixteen, under the Poor Prisoners regulations.

It is not often that two sisters of such tender years are jointly charged with murder, and the case aroused tremendous interest when it was heard in December 1932, before Mr. Justice Humphreys.

One night in October two people passing a house in Willows Crescent, Cannon Hill, Birmingham, were startled by a woman's cry: 'Murder! Murder! Fetch the police.' Mr. Thompson, a gun-smith, went immediately to investigate. Emily Thay rushed out of the house, followed closely by Marjorie Yellow, who called out: 'Come here and get this strange man out of the house!'

Thompson asked, 'Who is he?' and Marjorie replied, 'I've never seen him in my life before.'

In the vestibule, leaning against a wall, Thompson found a young man, whom he took by the wrist. Murmuring, 'I've done nothing, I've done nothing', the man slumped to the ground, dead.

'He's only shamming,' said Marjorie, 'he's done that before.' He had been stabbed in the chest just below the collar-bone, and the blade of the knife was found in his overcoat pocket, while the handle was found near by.

At the proceedings in the police court Mr. M. P. Pugh, a solicitor representing the Director of Public Prosecutions, said that when Sidney Marston went to the house 'some sort of trouble occurred'; there was a quarrel, a violent struggle, in the course of which Marston was stabbed with a sharp, thin-bladed table knife and died from the wound. No one was in the house except the

N

two sisters. Various statements made by the girls after the tragedy were read.

Marjorie Yellow denied that she had ever known or seen the dead man. Later she said she had met him and given him the name of Miss Marjorie Gwinn, and the address at Willows Crescent. These details were written in the dead man's pocket-book.

Marjorie Yellow was living in the house under the protection of a man called Herbert Gwinnell. Medical evidence from a Professor of Birmingham University and Sir Bernard Spilsbury would show that the wound could not have been self-inflicted, and that there were signs of a struggle, bruises on the young man's face and head, tears and cuts in his clothing.

On the floor of the house was found a woman's belt and in the kitchen a broken string of beads, suggesting that the death struggle between the girls and Marston had taken place there. Normally, continued Mr. Pugh, it was unnecessary for the prosecution to impute motive, but in this instance there was a clear motive; Marjorie said after the death of this young man: 'He hit me in the mouth. There was a ten-shilling note on the table and it has gone now.' A loose ten-shilling note was found in the waistcoat pocket of the dead man; it was his habit always to keep his money in a wallet.

At the subsequent trial at Birmingham Assizes the ineptitude with which the Birmingham Police had handled the matter made an acquittal inevitable. For the two sisters were charged jointly with murder, whereas although there was some sort of evidence against Marjorie Yellow, there was not a shred of evidence against her young sister Emily.

P.C. Davey said that when he called on the girls on October 9th he heard Marjorie say to her sister: 'You don't say anything. You were only trying to shield me.' Later, Marjorie said to him, 'They do not hang women, do they?' and, when he did not reply: 'You've only got to die once. Women go to prison for life, don't they?'

Under cross-examination from Norman Birkett, this constable was soon feeling a little uncomfortable.

'Did you tell the girls,' he asked, 'that your girl was waiting for you out in the cold?'—'Yes.'

'Did you tell them that it was your birthday?'—'Yes.'

'Did you try to cheer them up?'—'No.'

'Did you not say: "Cheer up, they don't hang women"?'—'No.'

Davey said that he made notes in the kitchen, writing them in pencil and 'afterwards in ink'.

'Let me see the book,' said Mr. Birkett. He turned the leaves quickly, read, then handed it back to Davey.

'Just look,' said Birkett dramatically, 'at your entry of the words "Don't say anything. You are only trying to shield me." Is that in pencil?'

'No,' replied Davey.

'Why not?'—'I added it at the police station afterwards.'

'Why didn't you make a note of it at the time?'—'I thought that they were watching me.'

Detective-Inspector Vince, who later committed suicide because of the criticism which his conduct of the police investigations brought upon his head, said that when he took a statement from Marjorie Yellow he did not suspect the girls.

Mr. Birkett: 'On October 24th, when Marjorie was arrested, she had been under examination by police officers for fifty-two hours?'—'She had been under certain examination.'

'I put it to you that it was fifty-two hours?'—'I should say not.'

The police had taken the extraordinary and highly irregular step of giving witnesses for the prosecution copies of the statements they had made in the lower court so that they could learn them by heart and repeat them in the Assize Court. Thomas Lawrence, a foundry manager, his brother William and William Andrews, a dental surgeon, had all been given copies.

The Judge asked Detective-Inspector Vince: 'Did it occur to you that in this case, these people would be cross-examined as to the detail of their recollections?'—'It was pretty obvious they would be.'

The Judge: 'Don't you feel that what the jury has heard in the witness box has not been the recollection of witnesses at all, but the recollection of what they read twenty-four hours before?'—'They were not given for that purpose.'

Norman Birkett took up the same challenge: 'You took a statement from Marjorie on October 9th. You did not even give a copy of that to the defending solicitor until the prosecution was in full swing?'—'No.' The copies of statements supplied to prosecution witnesses had not been given to the defence, either.

Birkett: 'She never gets a line of what she has said until her case for murder is prepared at the police court?'—'That is so.'

'Do you think that right and just?'—'Certainly they did not get it.'

After Sir Bernard Spilsbury declared that it was possible, but not probable, that Marston's wound was self-inflicted, Birkett rose to make two submissions. The first was that whereas the two sisters were charged with being jointly concerned, there was no evidence of common design. The second was that there was not sufficient evidence to warrant the case going to the jury. Against Emily Thay, he said, there had not been a line of evidence.

Birkett had been helped by the fact that in talking of 63 Willows Crescent he knew the place like a book, for he had visited the house and inspected it. It was a shockingly sordid *ménage*, bereft of furniture except for a single bed, the floor littered with debris and cigarette ends. He was not helped by the fact that, in the case of one highly strung witness whose memory he wished to prove unreliable (and did), the weaving of his eloquent hands literally hypnotised the woman. Optical fatigue, coupled with a melodious, rhythmic voice, can hypnotise, and because she had kept her eyes fixed on his hands, she passed right out.

It was clear from Mr. Justice Humphreys' summing-up that he favoured an acquittal. The evidence, he said, was so unsatisfactory that he was perfectly certain no jury in the world would dream of acting upon it. There was a *prima facie* case that one or other of the accused did strike the blow which caused the death, but that would not do. In his opinion, there was no evidence at all against Emily Thay. He strongly condemned the action of the police in giving copies of evidence to witnesses.

The two girls listened intently. Marjorie Yellow, dark, pale and lively, whose eyes roved everywhere in court, and Emily more stolid, whose eyes never left the crimson-robed Judge looked lost and helpless amidst all this panoply of justice. '*We may be out tonight*,' Marjorie whispered excitedly to her little sister. But when the jury returned a verdict of Not Guilty, Yellow looked as though she would faint.

'Let the two girls be discharged,' said Mr. Justice Humphreys. They made to descend the steps to the cell again, but a wardress opend the side of the dock and they were free.

Mr. Healy had earlier expressed the satisfaction of the prosecution—a satisfaction which all must feel, he said—that the two sisters, living in humble circumstances, had had the best legal talent in the country. Both sisters thanked Mr. Birkett profusely before returning to their mother's house and running the gauntlet of a vast crowd of 2,000, part hostile and part simply curious.

CHAPTER XXI

The Impressive Mr. Gregory

In the course of a long career Norman Birkett certainly had some unusual clients, from Mrs. Merrick to the litigously-minded Count Reventlow, one of Barbara Hutton's numerous husbands; from the humble quarryman's wife to an ostentatious, homicidal, homosexual ex-spy and honours tout—the remarkable Arthur John Peter Michael Maundy Gregory.

It is a sad reflection on the stratification and structure of English society that Maundy Gregory could ever had prospered as he did; snobbery must have been rife indeed for Gregory to have maintained two houses (one in Hyde Park Terrace and another at Thames Ditton), a flat in Brighton and two motor launches, on which he gave lavish parties, all on the proceeds of selling honours.

To ordinary people the Honours List is a mystery. How does anybody get on the List, and who puts them there? There are two Lists, the Departmental List and the Prime Minister's List. The former is compiled from the Civil Service and the Armed Forces, honours being awarded according to grade, as an almost automatic reward for long and unsullied service; thus a Permanent Secretary on a salary of £7,000 can expect a K.C.B. or a G.C.M.G.; an Under-Secretary, at slightly more than half that salary, can hope for a C.B. or a C.M.G. Top brass in the Armed Services may get a G.C.B. and bottom brass can hope for an O.B.E.

The Prime Minister's List includes hundreds drawn from all walks of life who are not in the public service. Charities, the arts, social work, science and such fields are 'rewarded' by this public and nicely graded method of bestowing official approval.

A great many honours, such as that awarded to a dance-band leader, are simply given to people who just do their jobs. Civil Servants who have not been caught publicly beating their wives or have not gone bankrupt are more likely to be honoured than, say, one who is outspoken or bubbling with original ideas.

Honours come early or late—mostly late, and often too late to matter, recognising ability long since acclaimed by the public. Somerset Maugham had to wait until he was eighty-one to become a Companion of Honour; Sir Compton Mackenzie was knighted at the age of sixty-nine.

Political honours are very carefully assigned by the Political Honours Scrutiny Committee, whose job it is nowadays to ensure that recommendations are not made because of donations to party funds. And therein lies a story.

Forty years ago the Right Honourable David Lloyd George was doing a considerable trade in the sale of peerages. The First World War had spared, among its survivors, a large number of war profiteers whose swollen bank balances had lost their novelty, and who longed for status symbols. Badges of respectability are invariably sought most frantically by those whose money was not earned respectably.

Lloyd George was not proved to be filling his own personal pocket in this way. But in 1919 he had divided the Liberal Party. There was more sympathy and support for Asquith, his predecessor as Prime Minister, a man of complete integrity, and if Lloyd George wanted to have a political party behind him he must start a new one. This could be achieved by raising a political fund and having sole control of it.

Willing touts, including the unsavoury Mr. Gregory, were readily forthcoming. Acting as intermediaries, they approached the newly rich, the profiteers or the merely mediocre, and made it known that they could acquire titles for a price. It is strange that so many were willing to do this, since an honour bought cannot give the satisfaction of an honour conferred. Social climbers, however, did not care; those who were not in the know could infer that the honour *had* been conferred.

The scale in the sale of honours can be gauged from the phenomenal growth of the Lloyd George Fund, which at one time reached £3,000,000—worth, at present monetary values, more like £10,000,000.

Feeling ran high in both the House of Commons and the House of Lords, for under Lloyd George's Premiership far more peers had been created than under the Premierships of Campbell-Bannerman and Asquith. The matter was frequently debated, but it was Lloyd George's list of 1922 that aroused the fiercest controversy, for not only did it include many whose 'services' to society were not outstanding but one or two names whose personal back-grounds were positively dubious. It included one man who had been fined half a million by the Supreme Court of South Africa, and his petition to the Judicial Committee of the Privy Council for leave to appeal was refused only seven months before Lloyd George selected him for a peerage. The disclosures that followed discussion of the 1922 Honours List brought King George V's pent-up concern to a head, and he wrote to Lloyd George in forthright terms about this gross abuse of the honours system.

After debate in both Houses, the Honours (Prevention of Abuses) Act of 1925 was passed. It is against this background that the activities of Maundy Gregory must be seen.

Gregory was born in 1877 of a humble but respectable family in Southampton, had a modest run of success as an actor and im-pressario and turned, before the First World War, to running a detective agency.

When war broke out Gregory is alleged to have joined MI5, the anti-spy organisation. Services that are secret attract a fair proportion of people who are bizarre, eccentric and of dubious moral fibre; the mere fact of being engaged on secret work makes some of them feel separate from, and by inference superior to, their fellow-mortals ('Ah, if you knew what *I* know!'). Wil-liam J. Morgan, who trained people in secret work in the Second World War, has said in his memoirs that their job was to 'lie, cheat and kill', and most sensible people would agree that pro-ficiency in these things, in however worthy a cause, implies some erosion of the moral fibre.

If Gregory was engaged on hush-hush work—and there is no proof of it—it would be completely in line with his vanity, greed and love of intrigue.

In 1919 Maundy Gregory started a publication called the *Whitehall Gazette*. The mere choice of the title shows his sense of showmanship and love of deceit, for it had, as he intended, an official ring. Distributed free to clubs and Government offices, it contained blatant puffs for people in diplomacy, commerce and Government service, for which the people concerned frequently paid large sums of money.

Gregory prospered, and as he did so became more florid and flamboyant. He dressed in immaculate purple serge, and from his ample stomach hung a gold chain with a priceless diamond

attached. His offices in Parliament Street were within easy reach
of Parliament and Downing Street, and everything about them
conveyed a spurious air of officialdom. Uniformed flunkeys wore
a crown in their lapels. His own red-leather chair aped the
furnishings of the House of Lords. Bell-pushes, telephones and
switches littered his massive desk, while the walls of his huge
office were hung with portraits which included one of Bloody
Judge Jeffries.

The *Whitehall Gazette* was a very useful means of making influential contact in the fields of diplomacy and the Government
service. He owned a sumptuous lunch and dining-club, the Ambassador, which was the mecca of the rich and influential, and a
useful operating ground in which to find potential victims.

He would sandwich his name between distinguished names
when preparing seating plans, the others not realising that he
owned the club. The Faber dinners, held on the eve of the Derby
and once initiated by Lieut.-Colonel Walter Faber, were trans-
ferred to the Ambassador, adding to his social prestige.

Gregory's genius lay as much in what he left unsaid as what he
actually said. The quasi-official decorum of his offices is an example of this. He was helped, of course, by his uncritical acceptance by peers, Members of Parliament, prominent Civil Servants
and generals and—of course—by frequent visits to his offices of
Lloyd George himself. Certainly Gregory had unusual connections among Continental royalty, and was a close friend of the
Montenegrin royal family, King Alfonso of Spain and King
George of Greece. Their signed portraits lined his office.

Of pronounced homosexual leanings, he liked collecting
statuettes of Narcissus, but he shared a house with a Mrs. Rosse,
wife of a composer he had met in his theatrical days. Perhaps as a
hang-over from his MI5 days, he loved an air of mystery, using
black blotting-paper so that it couldn't be read, having a scrambler
on one telephone and using a taxi so that he could arrive and de-
part from places without attracting attention. He greatly admired
Hitler and Mussolini, and (how I do not know) possessed Mussolini's early passport. Altogether he was a mysterious and unsavoury figure, but he understood too well how to exploit the
vanity inherent in everyone and the snobbery common to many.

Gregory's lavish and flamboyant manner of living meant a constant financial strain, even though his mistress had substantial

means of her own. The changing political climate and the wide
publicity given to the sale of honours had depressed the market
just a little, and he—or his agents—became less discreet. In 1932
a man died who had given Gregory £30,000 in mere anticipation
of honours he never received. His executors demanded the return
of the money and actually instituted court proceedings, to prevent
which Gregory paid up at the last moment.

At last he really over-stepped himself in an approach, through
an intermediary called Moffat, to Lieut.-Commander Edward
Leake, a retired Royal Navy officer. Leake had no desire to
pay for an honour of any kind, and reported the matter to the
authorities. In due course, Maundy Gregory was summoned at
Bow Street Police Court in February 1933 for:

> 'Having on January 23rd attempted to obtained from
> Lieutenant-Commander Edward Whaney Billyard Leake,
> R.N., retired, of Lowndes Square, S.W., £10,000 as an induce-
> ment for endeavouring to procure for him the grant of a dignity
> or title of honour contrary to the Honours (Prevention of
> Abuses) Act 1925.'

This was the first prosecution of its kind under the Act. The
Attorney-General, Mr. Thomas Inskip, K.C., and Mr. Eustace
Fulton conducted the case on behalf of the Crown; Mr. Norman
Birkett, K.C., and Mr. Valentine Holmes defended. The Director
of Public Prosecutions, Sir E. Tindall Atkinson, occupied a seat
with counsel.

Inskip outlined the facts leading to the prosecution. Lieut.-
Commander Leake, a holder of the Distinguished Service Order,
had no previous acquaintance with Gregory, but in December
received a letter from Moffatt, written on Sports Club notepaper, asking for a private interview. Leake, not knowing him,
asked what it was about. Moffatt wrote again, but Leake, un-
interested, ignored it, but on a second attempt to contact him by
telephone he answered himself and arranged to see Moffatt on
January 23rd, 1933.

Moffatt told Leake, after some hedging, that his name had been
mentioned in connection with a knighthood, which would cost
£10,000. In accordance with what had become Gregory's streamlined technique, Moffatt produced the *Whitehall Gazette* and
pointed to a report of a Derby Eve Dinner at the Ambassador

Club. 'That is the man,' he said, singling out Gregory's name, 'you can see the sort of people he associates with. He can get the knighthood for you.'

The same afternoon Leake and Moffatt went to Gregory's house, where Gregory told Leake that he could procure him a knighthood, but that, 'Of course, you will understand that certain doors require unlocking and the sinews of war are necessary to unlock them. We are gentlemen and understand one another.' He added that he could include Leake's name in the King's Birthday Honours List to be published in June. He was a consummate name-dropper, and mentioned in passing his friendship with Mussolini, his possession of an order permitting him access to the Pope at any time, his secret service work and his friendship with the King of Greece.

Leake reported the matter to the police, and two days later lunched with Gregory at the Carlton. Gregory said he had discussed the matter with the parties concerned, and the knighthood could be arranged for £10,000. Gregory suggested a lunch two days later, at which a friend of his, Lord Southborough, would be present.

'I have no information,' the Attorney-General stated, 'to justify the statement that Lord Southborough would be at the lunch or that Mr. Gregory had Lord Southborough's authority to say he would be there.' On January 26th Leake received a letter from Gregory referring to Leake's 'great sporting effort' and asking him to lunch. Leake did not lunch with him or phone him. What he did was to make a very full statement to a Treasury solicitor.

Leake, giving evidence, confirmed this account of the overtures made to him, and told how, when he told Gregory of his decision to drop the matter, Gregory had said: 'It is very regrettable, as the matter is now practically completed. If you adhere to your decision the matter must drop and I cannot revive it again. Cannot you give, say, £2,000 on account to keep the pot boiling?' Leake said that his decision was final.

Gregory had entered a plea of Not Guilty, and the alarm and despondency among those who had bought their honours and now feared exposure was considerable. Editions of the evening newspapers were snatched from street sellers by distinguished-looking men who would normally send a chauffeur or messenger to buy a paper. Mr. Birkett, who had been brought into the case hurriedly, asked, and was given, an adjournment.

Looking at the facts in the intervening fortnight, Norman Birkett advised Maundy Gregory that there was little point in him persisting with a plea of Not Guilty. The facts as stated would be difficult to deny, and there was reason to think that other prosecutions would inevitably follow, even if, as was unlikely, this one should fail. He did not think the court would believe for a moment that a man of Leake's obvious and unshakeable integrity and record of public service would make such serious statements irresponsibly. Maundy Gregory admitted that the accusations were true. 'In that case,' said Birkett, 'you will have to plead Guilty. To plead Not Guilty in face of incontrovertible evidence would be to invite a sterner penalty.'

It was disagreeable advice to take, but Gregory agreed. The sale of honours would be finished for him, he knew, but he had had the foresight hurriedly to canvas wealthy and distinguished clients during the adjournment, and get from several £2,000 on the promise to keep their names out of the case!

On the resumption of the case Birkett rose. 'Before the proceedings are resumed,' he said, 'perhaps I might say that the adjournment has given me an opportunity of consulting with Mr. Valentine Holmes and the solicitors instructing me, and of giving the most careful consideration to every aspect of this case . . . we have tendered certain advice to Mr. Maundy Gregory . . . and I am, therefore, instructed to withdraw the plea of "Not Guilty" and to substitute a plea of "Guilty" to this summons.'

The object of this gambit was to have the matter dealt with summarily, to minimise publicity and possibly lessen the penalty and cost.

The Attorney-General had no objection to this suggestion. Too much fishing in troubled waters was likely to embarrass holders of honours in the Civil Service, the Armed Forces and many spheres of public life. Nobody wanted a full-scale trial at the Old Bailey, least of all the Government.

Inspector Askew, who served Gregory with the summons, said that he had not been in trouble with the authorities before, but that 'the police, however, have had a number of complaints similar to this one'.

The Magistrate (Mr. Graham-Campbell): 'What do you mean

by that?'—'The police have had a number of complaints that persons have paid or been asked to pay sums of money in similar circumstances.'

Birkett was quick in the uptake on this innuendo. 'I do not propose to detain you more than a few moments,' he told the magistrate, smoothly. 'The only point which now remains, in my opinion, is the appropriate penalty. As regards the evidence of Inspector Askew, I am suggesting that had these matters to which he made reference been the subject of detailed investigation in this court—which they have not—I am instructed that Mr. Gregory would have been able to tender explanations of those particular matters. I venture to submit that the fairest way of dealing with the question of penalty would be to eliminate all consideration of those matters referred to by Inspector Askew.' He pleaded for the imposition of 'a monetary penalty' as being adequate to the offence.

Birkett had hoped to get Gregory off with a fine, but he did not succeed. Gregory was fined £50 and fifty guineas costs and sentenced to two months' imprisonment in the second division. In his speech to the magistrate Birkett had said that: 'As far as Mr. Gregory is concerned the object of the prosecution has been fully achieved, and I am asked to say that so far as his activities in this direction are concerned they are wholly at an end.'

A conviction did, indeed, bring Maundy Gregory's sale of honours 'wholly to an end', but the case was followed by an uproar in Parliament and the appointment of a Royal Commission: 'To advise on the procedure to be adopted in future to assist the Prime Minister in making recommendations to His Majesty of the names of persons deserving of special honour.'

And what of Mr. Gregory when he came out of prison? He still had his elaborate pedigree, compiled by the College of Arms, tracing his ancestry back to Edward III and proving that the blood of eight kings of England, John o'Gaunt and the Black Prince beat in his heart. He still possessed fantastic jewellery, including a huge rose diamond once owned by the Romanoffs. If anyone asked him to a banquet he could still sport the insignia of the Royal Montenegrin Order, the Grand Cross of the Equestrian Order of the Holy Sepulchre, the Order of the White Rose of Finland, Knight of Grace of the Order of St. John of Jerusalem, a Papal Order and the Order of Pius IX.

While Gregory was in prison a more sinister rumour was being investigated. Relatives of Mrs. Rosse, and her husband, from whom she had been separated for eight years, were suspicious of the circumstances in which Mrs. Rosse had died. She had been taken ill suddenly in August 1932, when Gregory was desperate for money following the peremptory demand for the repayment of that £30,000 from the executors of a man he had swindled. On that occasion she had hastily prepared a will leaving all her money, about £18,000, to Maundy Gregory. Within weeks she was dead, and Gregory lost no time in cashing her securities.

Maundy Gregory had been secretive with Mrs. Rosse's family, and the circumstances in which she was buried were most peculiar. Her last illness, with all the symptoms of poisoning, came upon her after eating a meal with him. Gregory had supervised all the arrangements for her funeral, rejecting the usual wooden coffin and having one with a lead shell which, instead of being soldered and sealed as usual, was left open. He then went to inordinate trouble to find a burying place near the water; he tried Pangbourne, near the Thames, but being refused there, he found a site in Bisham churchyard, within a few feet of the river, where the ground is frequently flooded. The coffin was then buried in extremely shallow ground.

All this suggests that Gregory desired the coffin to become waterlogged, as it did the same winter when the river overflowed into the churchyard. Poisons were found in his house. When he came out of prison he fled the country—just before the Home Office, at the urgent request of relatives, ordered an exhumation. But no positive evidence as to cause of death could be given, despite nearly three months spent on analysis and investigation, and in the end an open verdict was recorded.

One sinister fact is that having been refused permission to have Mrs. Rosse buried by the waterside at Whitchurch, near Pangbourne, he agreed to pay a very high burial fee of one hundred pounds for the privilege of having her buried at Bisham—a fee imposed to discourage further demands on the very limited burial space remaining. Since Gregory never paid the undertaker, his generosity in this matter is interesting.

Was Maundy Gregory a murderer when Norman Birkett defended him for selling honours? If so, his approach to Leake was a desperate throw of the dice, for having agreed to repay the

£30,000 to the executors of the man he had swindled, £18,000, which Mrs. Rosse left him in her will, got him only partly out of the wood. He had asked Lieut.-Commander Leake for £10,000, but added that for £12,000 it could be done much quicker. The two sums together make exactly the sum he was required to repay, and which he had to find quickly to avoid exposure and ruin.

Until the outbreak of war Gregory—who had now given himself a title without payment, and called himself Sir Arthur Gregory—lived in style on money sent by friends in London. During the German occupation he was interned, fell ill and died in a Paris hospital in 1941.

CHAPTER XXII

The Brighton Trunk Murder

THE YEAR WAS 1934. Norman Birkett was enjoying every minute of his well-earned success. The ill-health that had dogged him in youth lay far behind, his energy seemingly inexhaustible. 'Try and get Birkett; he's expensive nowadays but he's worth it' was the general cry in solicitors' offices; sometimes months would go by without the break of a single day, yet Birkett's enthusiasm, coolness and powers of concentration remained unimpaired.

He had left politics behind, too. When he was defeated at the General Election in 1931 he decided not to stand again. He was never truly a politician, and having struggled so hard to make a success late in life, he could not afford to throw away the fruits of success for an uncertain political career. But he foresaw the menace of Fascism at a time when many right-wing Tories were saying, 'Britain needs a Mussolini.' Mussolini was certainly admired by many influential right-wingers—the late Lord Rothermere, the newspaper proprietor, for one—but Birkett, speaking at the National Liberal Club, warned against both Fascism and Communism as menaces to liberty. 'In Russia, Germany and Italy democracy and liberty have fallen at the feet of the dictator,' he declared, and warned his hearers that the evil could not be localised and that 'the menace to the things we cherish, such as personal liberty, is great and overwhelming'. Years later, sitting as a Judge at the Nuremberg trials, he was to realise how horribly prophetic his words were; millions upon millions were to die terrible deaths because of the moral and political contagion he had so accurately diagnosed. 'Are we sure,' he asked, 'that in our country at the present time the same kind of menace is not present?'

Later in the year Birkett found himself studying in some detail the purposes and principles of Sir Oswald Mosley's British Union of Fascists, for in the course of an action for libel which Sir Oswald brought, successfully, against the *Star* he cross-examined him in considerable detail. Sir Oswald's complaint was based upon an article in the *Star* following a debate between him and

(*Left*) 'Mrs. Isabella Ruxton', mistress of Dr. Buck Ruxton (*right*), whom he murdered and dismembered at his house in Lancaster. (*Below*) The lonely ravine near Moffat where portions of her body and that of Mary Rogerson were found

Judgement day at Nuremberg. Mr. Justice Birkett, one of the two British judges on the international tribunal, reads the historic judgement. Mr. Justice Lawrence is on the right

With Mr. Dag Hammarskjöld, Secretary-General of the United Nations, to receive an honorary degree at Cambridge University in 1958

Mr. Maxton, M.P. He said that the words of the *Star* imputed that he and the Fascists would be ready to take over the Government of this country with machine-guns when the moment arrived.

There is little doubt that this is what the *Star* imputed and fully intended to convey in its words:

> 'Sir Oswald warned Mr. Maxton that he and his Fascists would be ready to take over the government with the aid of machine guns when the moment arrived.
>
> 'Mr. Tom Mann was recently thrown into prison on the mere suspicion that he might say something ten times less provocative than Sir Oswald's words.'

In this action Birkett fared rather badly at the hands of Sir Patrick Hastings, whose handling of the case was more able and showed a readier appreciation of realities. Mr. Birkett relied too heavily on the unpopularity of Fascism as an idea, whereas that was not the issue. There was absolutely no legal justification for suggesting that Sir Oswald Mosley was ten times more deserving of imprisonment than Tom Mann.

His action in cross-examining Sir Oswald as to credit (on matters not strictly relevant, with a view to throwing discredit on his evidence and character) did not help the *Star*'s case at all. Sir Oswald was the aggrieved party, and was bringing the action. Mr. Birkett behaved towards him as if he were the culprit, questioning him severely for the best part of the day. The following sample is typical:

Mr. Birkett: 'The reference to machine-guns in your speech involved training in the use of them?'—'No, it involves the use of machine-guns in circumstances in which it would be legitimate to use them—to save the State and the Crown from a Communist uprising.'

'When the crisis comes and you bring your machine-guns in the streets and shoot people down . . .'—'I didn't say "shoot people down".'

'Then what are you going to do—use blank ammunition?'—'We should have to deal with the Communists.'

'But aren't they people?'—'They represent a tiny minority.'

'Who are you to say, "I will take machine-guns into the street and shoot people down during a crisis"?'—'No more and no less

o

than any other British citizen,' retorted Sir Oswald, 'who sees the State in danger of being overthrown by any organised rising.'

'You are organised to meet them?'—'Organised on properly legal and constitutional methods. . . .'

Addressing the jury, Mr. Birkett said he did not propose to discuss damages, because he felt they should not arise; but if they did arise, he said, 'there is one coin of the realm which will meet the case, and that is the smallest one'.

Sir Patrick Hastings criticised severely Mr. Birkett's action in cross-examining Sir Oswald as to credit. 'It certainly seems a dreadful thing that the *Star* should have instructed their counsel in open court to say that they were going to cross-examine Sir Oswald as to his credit, and then have the whole of the cross-examination directed to that.'

Lord Hewart's summing-up made it clear that Mr. Birkett's plea for damages of no more than a farthing was not likely to succeed. Dealing with the libellous passage in the *Star*, he asked: 'What is the fair meaning of those words to a reasonable reader who has not the advantage and pleasure of listening to instructions so ably given by Mr. Norman Birkett? What do those words mean if they do not mean this: "Mr. Mann has been thrown into prison for something ten times less bad. How much more it is the duty of the Director of Public Prosecutions to take steps to put Sir Oswald Mosley into prison." '

Although Lord Hewart acknowledged that the case had been argued by 'two of the best advocates of this or any other generation', he rejected Birkett's argument that the leader complained of in the *Star* was a plea for liberty of opinion. 'Toleration of free speech only begins,' said Lord Hewart, 'when persons listen decently and fairly to opinions with which they profoundly disagree.'

The jury returned a verdict for Sir Oswald Mosley against the *Star*, awarding him £5,000 damages and costs.

It was not, of course, Birkett's fault that this case could not be won. He had followed the *Star*'s directions as to the line to be taken, and both Judge and defending counsel well knew that, as an advocate, he must follow instructions. Even so, it is strange that Birkett did not profer different advice to this newspaper. The *Star* was not alone in regarding the general aims and ideas of

Fascism with aversion, but it is difficult to see how they could enter a plea of justification for a libel which was based on an inaccurate report of what Sir Oswald Mosley had said. Political attitudes are no justification for attacking the integrity and character of individuals.

The trial of Mrs. Ethel Lillie Major at Lincoln Assizes before Mr. Justice Charles on a charge of murdering her husband by administering strychnine was one of the most difficult—one could say hopeless—cases Birkett was ever called upon to defend.

The Majors were living at No. 2 Council Houses, Kirkby-on-Main, but Mrs. Major and her son of fourteen went every night to sleep at the home of her father, Tom Brown, a retired game-keeper. There had been incessant quarrelling and bickering between Mr. and Mrs. Major.

Mrs. Major claimed to have 'discovered' two love letters written to her husband by Mrs. Rose Kettleborough, a next-door neighbour, but their authenticity was never proved, and there seems a strong supposition that Mrs. Major wrote them herself.

On May 24th, 1924, after a short and agonising illness, Arthur Major died, the doctor giving the cause as 'status epilepticus'. Mrs. Major appeared to be in rather a hurry to get him buried—the vicar, who called, demurred at this—and the funeral arrangements were stopped when the local police received a letter from 'Fairplay' asking: '. . . have you ever heard of a wife poisoning her husband? Look further into the death of Mr. Major of Kirkby-on-Main. Why did he complain of his food tasting nasty and throw it to a neighbour's dog, which has since died? Ask the undertaker if he looked natural after death. . . .'

The stomach organs of Mr. Major and the dog showed, on analysis, 1·27 grains and 0·12 grain of strychnine, a poison which Mrs. Major's father bought four years previously to kill vermin and kept in a locked cupboard in his house. He had a key to this himself, but a spare key disappeared, and he 'never knew the going of it'. It was found in Mrs. Major's possession.

Interviewed by the police, Mrs. Major mentioned strychnine poisoning before being informed of the pathologist's findings.

There was little Birkett could do to defend Mrs. Major, who prepared the meal that made her husband violently and fatally sick. He established that she had been a good mother, and spoke of a

'house divided against itself'. A sad feature of the case was that
the son was in the terrible predicament of having to give evidence
in court against his own mother.

One puzzling feature of the case was that according to Dr.
Roche Lynch, the Home Office Analyst, Major had been given
two heavy doses of strychnine—one on May 22nd and another,
presumably in water, on May 24th. But strychnine is almost
incredibly bitter, and the second dose would have taken two and a
half pints of water to dissolve it. 'It is difficult to imagine,' com-
mented the Judge in his summing up, 'that you could administer
things so frightfully bitter without the man expelling it directly.'

Mrs. Major was found Guilty and condemned to death, the
jury adding a recommendation to mercy. The passing of the
death sentence was a terrible ordeal, most of all for Mrs. Major,
but harrassing alike to Mr. Birkett and everyone else in court.
The forty-two-year-old widow had to be supported by two
wardresses as the words of doom were said to her, and wept
freely, collapsing as the Chaplain added his 'Amen'.

The jury's strong recommendation to mercy was rejected by
the Court of Criminal Appeal, and Ethel Major was hanged at
Hull on December 19th, 1934. Birkett could not have thought
her innocent of the charge, but there were serious doubts as to her
mental balance, which, while not constituting insanity, might
have affected the degree of her culpability.

There is a chain reaction in human affairs as well as nuclear
physics; one thing sparks off another. When, for instance, a man
in a blue suit called at the left-luggage office at Brighton Station
and deposited an unusually shaped trunk over six feet long, a
little more than two feet wide and about a foot deep, he thereby
involved Mr. Norman Birkett in the most sensational and unusual
murder trial in his career.

Not that Birkett ever had any connection with the man, whose
identity was never discovered, or was concerned with the fate of
the anonymous, cruelly murdered woman whose dismembered
body lay concealed inside the trunk. The cloakroom attendant,
Mr. Vinnicombe, paid it no special attention; it was just another
piece of left luggage. Eventually, however, its foul emanations
betrayed it, and the horrible secret was out. The remains were of a
woman of about thirty, well nourished, five months pregnant.

Her head, arms and legs were missing, but the legs, found in a case at King's Cross Station, suggested a woman of fastidious habits, for the feet were pedicured.

The identity of the woman was never discovered, but in the course of police enquiries the list of missing people were carefully combed and the number of possible victims reduced by elimination. Hundreds of people disappear every year, so that this was, inevitably, a slow process.

Enquiring into the whereabouts of women missing from the Brighton area, the police eventually called at the Skylark Café on Brighton front and interviewed Tony Mancini (alias Hyman Gold or Jack Noytre), a petty thief known to have been living with a forty-two-year-old prostitute known locally as Violette Kaye, but whose real name was Saunders, and who was known to have disappeared. The questioning was continued at the Town Hall, but as Violette Kaye was twelve years older than the woman in the trunk, he was allowed to go.

Even so, the police decided to visit his room at 52 Kemp Street, where he had been living for the last five weeks; they were curious to know why he had changed lodgings just at the time that Violette Kaye had disappeared. Mancini had meanwhile left his room, for reasons that were appallingly plain. At the foot of his bed stood an old trunk. The overpowering stench in the room warned them of what it contained—the putrifying corpse of Violette Kaye.

It was a million-to-one coincidence that in investigating one trunk murder case the police should happen upon another, in the self-same town, and at more or less the same time.

Mancini had lost his nerve after the questioning, stayed up all night with friends in a dance hall, visited an all-night café, caught an early morning train to London and spent Sunday and Monday there, staying at a Salvation Army hostel in the East End. He was arrested on Tuesday while trudging along the London–Maidstone road, whisked back to Brighton and, as holiday-makers in gay beach attire hissed and booed outside the Magistrates' Court, was committed for trial at Lewes Assizes, where he appeared before Mr. Justice Branson on December 10th, the case lasting five days. Mr. J. D. Cassels, K.C., and Mr. Quintin Hogg (now Lord Hailsham) appeared for the prosecution. For the defence, there were two silks, Mr. Norman Birkett and Mr. John Flowers, with Mr. Eric Neve.

Birkett was under no illusion that this would be an easy case. Mr. F. H. Carpenter, the Brighton solicitor who had defended Mancini in the Magistrates' Court and placed the brief with Birkett, knew that too. For instance, during the hue-and-cry for Mancini one newspaper had described his lurid past in terms that were partly accurate but substantially false. Inevitably, the jury would have read such reports or heard about them.

It was a hectic period for Birkett, with libel actions, a sensational divorce case and a load of other work all coming at the same time. But he allowed no other work to overlap with his defence of Mancini.

Armies of reporters and special writers invaded Lewes. The public galleries were full to overflowing, while huge queues waited in case a seat became vacant.

Mr. Cassels outlined a case that looked grim indeed. Mancini was twenty-six years old, a waiter by occupation. Violette Saunders (known as Kaye) was forty-two. Her decomposed body had been found in a trunk in the basement of 52 Kemp Street, Brighton, on the morning of Sunday, July 15th. Until a few hours before that room was occupied by Noytre (Mancini).

A post mortem made by Sir Bernard Spilsbury and two other doctors had revealed a fracture in the skull produced, in Sir Bernard's opinion, by a violent blow with some blunt instrument, and had caused death by shock. Mancini had met Violette Kaye when he was working in a café near the Alhambra in London; they had moved to Brighton and lived together, describing themselves as man and wife and changing their address no less than thirteen times. One of those addresses was 44 Park Crescent, where they took a basement flat at sixteen shillings a week.

Mr. Snuggs the landlord there would tell the court that Mancini and Violette Kaye were on affectionate terms, and that he heard no quarrel while they were there. An elderly gentleman, Charles Moores, known as 'uncle', visited them regularly.

On May 5th Mancini obtained employment at the Skylark Café as handyman and waiter. Miss Kaye had called at the café on May 10th and made a scene, being jealous at what she imagined to be the too-friendly attitude of Mancini towards a waitress there, Miss Attrill. That afternoon, too, Mr. Kerslake, driver of 'uncle's' (Charles Moore's) car, called at the basement flat to see her—to tell her, in fact, that Moore had been taken to a mental home. 'He will tell you,' said Mr. Cassels, 'that she seemed to be in a very distressed condition, very excited, nervous and shaken. She was twitching in the hands and face. So far as he is able to judge, she presented the appearance of being under the influence of drugs.'

Violette Kaye had a sister, Olive Watts, who had written to say she was coming to Brighton on May 14th. On the morning of Friday, May 11th, a telegram was handed in at the Head Post Office at Brighton addressed to Olive and saying: 'Going abroad. Good job. Sail Sunday. Will write. Vi.' Who, asked Mr. Cassels, had sent that telegram? The writing in capital letters was similar to that used by Mancini in writing the menus at the Skylark Café, and Violette's sister could say that her sister had never written in that way. From the moment that telegram was sent, Mancini told everyone lies about what had happened to Violette Kaye. He told Miss Attrill, a waitress at the Skylark, that she had gone to Paris, and when he took her back to the basement flat gave her some of Violette's clothing, 'because she could not get them into her case'.

Miss Attrill, womanlike, was puzzled that Violette Kaye had left her slippers, and that there were no blankets or linen on the bed.

Mancini bought a trunk in Brighton market—the trunk in which Violette Kaye was found two months later. He moved with it to Kemp Street, telling others that Violette had gone to Paris, adding, in his talks to a woman called Joyce Golding, 'I hope she is not coming back, as I do not want her to follow me about in the streets shouting names after me.' He said he had received a letter from her.

There was, continued Cassels, an incident in an amusement arcade called 'Aladdin's Cave'. Three witnesses were waiting to recount what happened. Mancini said he had given his wife 'the biggest hiding she had ever had', bashing her from pillar to post. 'What is the good of knocking a woman about with your fists?' Mancini bragged, 'you only hurt yourself. You should hit them with a hammer, the same as I did, and slosh her up.'

With blood-chilling detail Mr. Cassels described the trunk, and the landlady's complaint that a fluid was seeping from it.

Mancini said it was french polish, cleared the fluid up and put sacking underneath.

Following the discovery of the trunk by the police, and the post mortem on the body, a hammer was found among some rubbish at 44 Park Crescent. Sir Bernard Spilsbury would say that a fracture of the skull could have been produced by a hammer. Traces of morphine were found in the body.

Dr. Roche Lynch, said Mr. Cassels, had examined the prisoner's clothing after his arrest, and on three shirts and two pairs of trousers there was human blood. Blood had also been detected in a cupboard at 44 Park Crescent. Furthermore, on meeting a girl, Doris Saville, in Stepney on July 15th he had asked her to concoct a story which would absolve him from any complicity in Violette Kaye's death. She was to say she had met him, returned with him to Park Crescent and seen a woman, and that they then went for a walk and, on returning, found the woman dead.

Fifty witnesses had been lined up to corroborate the Crown's contention that the couple had quarrelled, that Mancini had killed her, concealed her body and told lies to account for her disappearance. Nor was Mancini's own background calculated to help his case. He was a squalid *souteneur* living on the immoral earnings of this ageing, fiercely possessive prostitute, a man with a criminal record, a man who could bear to sleep—and even entertain—in a room where the huddled body of his ex-mistress was putrifying. 'Do you keep rabbits?' one friend asked, puzzled by the overpowering stench.

Altogether a sinister catalogue of circumstantial evidence. Again and again Birkett made hurried notes. Could he convince the jury that this young man had simply concealed the death of Violette Kaye, but not encompassed it? Mancini had told the police in a statement: 'I went into the bedroom and she was laying on the bed with a handkerchief tied around her neck, and there was blood all over the sheets and everywhere. *Well, I got frightened. I knew they would blame me, and I couldn't prove I hadn't done it* . . . I hadn't the courage to go and tell the police what I had found, so I decided to take it with me . . . there was always men coming to the house . . . I don't know who killed her; as God is my judge I don't know . . . I am quite innocent except for the fact that I kept the body.'

What had Mr. Birkett to concentrate upon; what points would be worrying the jury most? There was the paramount question of how Violette Kaye met her death. There was that mysterious telegram. There was the discovery of that hammer, its head dulled as though it had been held in a flame to destroy some tell-tale evidence. There was the blood on Mancini's clothing. . . .

Mr. Birkett first questioned Chief Inspector Donaldson about the basement flat where Violette was killed, or died.

'You prepared this plan of the basement flat at 44 Park Crescent?'—'Yes.'

'Did you observe the steps from the street level to the area?'—'Yes, sir.'

'Were they very worn?'—'Yes, sir.'

'Were they steep?'—'Fairly so.'

'Were they narrow?'—'Yes, sir.'

'Did they call for care?'—'A little.'

'And the area floor; had that a hard, stone surface?'—'Yes.'

Mr. Snuggs, the landlord at Park Crescent, confirmed that Mancini and Kaye had lived there as 'Mr. and Mrs. Watson'. Birkett set out, by cross-examination, to prove two things—that Mancini and his mistress were not in the habit of quarrelling, and that she was accustomed to receiving many callers who might or might not be seen by others.

Birkett: 'Whenever you saw Mancini and the woman, did they appear not merely friendly but affectionate?'—'Yes.'

'I want to get this plainly before the jury; at no time, from start to finish, did you ever see anything, of any kind, to the contrary?'—'No, sir.'

'Did you ever see any men going down the basement flat with this woman?'—'Once.'

'You saw her going there with a man?'—'Yes.'

'Did she go down first and the man follow afterwards?'—'Yes.'

'Do you know who he was?'—'No. He was a tall man. That's all I can say.'

'How long did he stay?'—'About half an hour.'

'What time of day was this?'—'It was at night, between ten and eleven.'

A man had come at night, and the landlord did not know who he was. How many others might have come, at any hour, who the landlord did not see at all? One visitor, a regular visitor, had since been certified insane. Was it so improbable that some other visitor, who had come and gone unobserved, was also unbalanced?

Birkett questioned Snuggs on the frequent visits of the now insane bookmaker, who had given her a wireless set and had the flat wired for electric current. Then he asked: 'Have you heard of a man called Darkie?'

'No' was the answer.

'Of a man called Hoppy?'—'No.'

'You tell the jury, do you not, that your opportunities for observing the number of men who came to the basement flat were limited?'—'Oh, yes.'

Mancini's second landlord even permitted himself a certain enthusiasm for his former tenant. 'All the time he was living with us,' he said, 'he was a perfect gentleman.' Kerslake, chauffeur to Violette Kaye's bookmaker 'uncle', told how he called on her after her scene with Mancini at the Skylark.

Mr. Birkett: 'Are you familiar with the effect of drugs on people?'—'Yes.'

'Would you say that the appearance of this woman was like that of someone under the influence of drugs?'—'Yes—drugs and drink.'

'Was she agitated and twitching?'—'Yes.'

'Did she seem extremely frightened?'—'Yes.'

'Her condition was really remarkable, was it not?'—'Yes, sir, it was.'

Kerslake had heard the voices of two men, as he stood in the doorway. Who were they?

But there was the hammer. A witness who declared that when he gave up the flat at Park Crescent he left behind a hammer, whose head was bright and shining, could not pass unchallenged. Otherwise the jury could assume that somebody had put it through fire to destroy stains. With a casual air Birkett rose to question.

'Isn't it a common type of hammer?'—'Yes, I suppose it is.'

'A standard type, used everywhere by shoemakers?'—'It's rather old-fashioned.'

'There are plenty of old-fashioned things remaining, are there not?'—'There are.'

'Look at that hammer head. Look at the state it is in. Can you really say that *that* is the hammer head you left?'

The witness thought hard. He had felt so sure of himself, but Birkett's grave demeanour, as he asked this last crucial question, made him realise that a man's life was at stake in court. 'Well, no,' he said at last, 'it isn't possible to say.'

Another witness, Joyce Golding, told Mr. Cassels in reply to questions that Mancini had told her Violette had gone to Montmartre, and that he asked her to live with him. She had refused. But within minutes Birkett had discredited her as a witness. He asked: 'Where are you a waitress now?'

Golding: 'I am not working now.'

For a split second Birkett waited, giving her the chance to amplify this statement if she wished. Then he said gently: 'I am sorry to have to do this. I am very sorry indeed. But you haven't been a waitress, in any sense of the term, for years, have you?'

The woman's voice could barely be heard in court. 'No,' she whispered.

Birkett: 'How do you live?'

Golding: 'On the streets.'

'You had known Mancini well for five or six years?'—'Pretty well.'

'In London?'—'Yes.'

'I suppose you read a great deal in the papers about this case?'—'I didn't read much about it.'

'Look at the jury and tell them. Did you not read every single word about the man Tony you had known?'—'No. I wasn't interested that much.'

Birkett adjusted his spectacles as he looked at her, as though to be sure he was looking at the right person. For the first time a note of distinct reprimand crept into his voice. '*Interested*, madam! You had known him all those years! I put it to you that it is a deliberate lie to say that the prisoner ever invited you to go and live with him?'—'He invited me for the simple reason that he knew what I was.'

'And your story that he had quarrelled with his wife—with Violette Kaye—that is not true either, is it?'—'He *did* say he had quarrelled with her. I could bring witnesses to prove it. There's one here."

'Who is that?'—'Mrs. Summers. She'd tell you.'

'Do you know that Mrs. Summers has sworn on oath that Mancini and Violette Kaye were on very affectionate terms?'— 'It might have slipped her memory.'

The three witnesses from 'Aladdin's Cave' next told their story. John Cochrane, a skittles attendant, said that Mancini had told him 'he had trouble with the missus' and 'he'd given her the biggest hiding she'd ever had'. Frederick Coftrey told of sinister comments Mancini was alleged to have made: 'He said he'd bashed her from pillar to post and when he woke up she'd packed her trunk and gone . . . he said, "What's the good of knocking your woman about with your fists? You only hurt yourself. You should hit her with a hammer, the same as I did, and slosh her up."' George Boxall, a sanitary engineer, had been in the funfair at the time and heard this conversation.

Birkett disposed of these witnesses with expedition. The proprietor had since sacked Coftrey for theft. Further, although all three were supposed to have heard the conversation, only *two* had heard the reference to the hammer. Their evidence didn't make sense. If any was unreliable on one matter of memory he could be inaccurate on another.

His cross-examination of Doris Saville, the young girl who said she had been asked to make an alibi for Mancini by pretending to have been with him on the evening of Violette Kaye's death, was brilliant. She had said: 'He told me we were supposed to have gone to tea with a woman at 44 Park Crescent and while there she told us she was expecting three men to come and see her about some business, so we left her alone with the three men and went for a walk, and when we came back we found the woman dead.'

Birkett: 'You said in the course of your evidence that you had agreed to do what he asked because you were afraid of him?'— 'Yes.'

'Is that true?'—'Yes.'

'Then why did you go to meet him at half-past eleven that same night?'—'Because I was afraid. Well, I was frightened something might happen if I did *not* turn up.'

Birkett, with quiet insistence, demolished this story. Why, if she really feared this strange man, did she leave the security of a Salvation Army hostel, where she had friends whose protection she could have sought? Birkett also elicited by questioning that she knew the detectives wished to see her because Mancini was wanted for murder, and that she had not done any work since, being maintained at police expense.

He read from her evidence to the police: '. . . he said the murder was done and that he was entirely innocent of it and I was supposed to have met him at the front.'

'Did you say that?' Birkett asked.

'Yes.' The eyes of the jury were on the girl, every nuance of expression being carefully watched.

'He was saying, then, "There has been a murder, *and I am innocent of it*, and I want you to help me." Is that what it was?'—'Yes.'

Birkett relished nothing better than a battle with experts. Dr. Roche Lynch the Home Office Analyst, questioned by Mr. Cassels, said that there was morphine in Violette Kaye's body; the fact that he found *any* quantity indicated that more than a medicinal dose had been taken. He added that Violette Kaye could not have been an addict, since in that case he would not have expected to find any morphine at all. Birkett challenged this assumption.

Birkett: 'Dr. Roche Lynch, why would you not have expected to find any morphine?'

Dr. Lynch: 'In the case of addicts, morphine is so quickly destroyed by the body that it is with the greatest difficulty that one finds it at all.'

Birkett: 'Can you say *with certainty* that it would not be found in the decomposed body of an addict?'—'I am certain that it would not.'

'Is morphine contained in some patent medicines?'—'Yes; in all sorts of patent medicines, but only in very small amounts.'

The Crown's case looked less and less impregnable. For Dr. Lynch had said that there was more than a medicinal dose of morphine in Violette Kaye's decomposed remains. But what of those bloodstains alleged by the Crown to be on Mancini's clothing? Birkett had arranged for a microscope to be available on a table in court, together with the suspect clothing. He asked Dr. Lynch: 'Now let us turn to the question of blood spots. What is the general principle upon which you analyse these?'

Dr. Lynch: 'Human blood is divided into four groups, and every member of the population belongs to one of these four groups.'

'And of what value is that principle to you in criminal work?'
—'Well, if an alleged murderer has blood on his clothes, and the
group of that blood is the same as his victim's and different from
his own, he naturally has to make an explanation.'

'Was it possible in the case of the articles we are now concerned
with, the trousers and the shirts, to distinguish the blood group
to which the spots belonged?'—'As a matter of fact, no. Owing
to the decomposed state of the body, we were unable to discover
the blood group of the dead woman.'

The bloodstains were therefore of no value as evidence. In any
case, the garments had been bought *after* the death of Violette
Kaye. Birkett had studied a mark on a shirt through the microscope. 'You say these marks indicate that the blood was splashed
upon it?'

Dr. Lynch was quite adamant about it. 'Yes,' he said.

'How long after death would blood splash from a dead
person?'—'It might a few hours after, if there had been extensive
bleeding.'

'It's a very minute spot of blood, isn't it?'—'It *is* small.'

'Could it have been caused by a finger on the lining of the
pocket?'—'Yes, it could.' But it was clear from the tone of Dr.
Lynch's reply that he did not think it had.

'Do you know when this shirt was bought?'—'I do not.'

'Or when these trousers were?'—'No.'

'If I were to establish that they were not in the accused's
possession during the woman's life would it be clear, do you think,
that the blood could not be hers?'

The deflation of the expert was complete. The court, however
incongruously, roared with laughter.

In the course of the prosecution's case Birkett sprang a surprise
on the court. Newspapers had been saying freely that Mancini
had a record. Normally such details are only given in court if
and after a prisoner has been found guilty, but in this instance
Birkett decided to grasp the nettle. He asked Inspector Donaldson: 'Are there any convictions against the prisoner?'

Donaldson: 'Yes, for stealing silver in London, for loitering
with intent to commit a felony in Birmingham; and for stealing
clothing in London.'

Birkett: 'Any convictions for violence?'—'There is no record
of any convictions for violence.'

'Had Violette Saunders—or Kaye—been convicted in connection with prostitution?'—'Yes.'

'Is it within your professional knowledge, doing your duty, if
there have been any false statements in the Press relating to this
prisoner?'—'Yes, sir. From the accounts I have read I am
satisfied that many of the stories that were told in relation to this
matter were untrue.'

Just as Birkett had deflated Dr. Lynch the Home Office Analyst,
he now turned to Sir Bernard Spilsbury, who produced in court
the exact piece of bone forming the depressed fracture of the dead
woman's skull. He had told Mr. Cassels that it could have been
produced with the hammer head, and that death would probably
follow the fracture in a few minutes. He said that the woman had
not died from morphine poisoning.

'Your views,' Birkett asked politely, 'are rightly described as
theories, are they not?' (Applied to post mortems I am not certain
that the question could be called a fair one, for what can a pathologist do except to reconstruct the past on the basis of present
evidence? He can only examine a corpse and speculate as to what
happened during its life.) Sir Bernard Spilsbury hesitated, then
answered: 'I am not quite sure that is right,' he said evenly,
'when my opinion is based on experience.'

'They are the results of your experience but are mere theories
without question?'—'They are, in the sense that they are not
facts.'

Sir Bernard was in trouble again when he produced a small
piece of skull.

'How long?' demanded Birkett, 'have you been in possession
of the small piece of bone which has been produced here for the
first time on the third day of the trial?'—'Since my first examination.'

'Your first examination—on July 15th?'—'Yes.'

'Five months ago?'—'Yes.'

'Did it not seem to you that the defence might have been
informed that that small piece of bone was in your possession?'—
'I am afraid it did not occur to me.'

Next, to the manner in which Violette Kaye might have
died.

'Take morphine. Dr. Roche Lynch has said that he could not
be sure whether a fatal dose had not been taken. Assume it *was*

a fatal dose. Does not that account for death?'—'Why, certainly, if nothing else were done.'

'A person can get severe injuries on the head, be unconscious, and recover?'—'Yes.'

'A person can get injuries akin to the injuries here, and recover?'—'Akin, yes.'

'Postulating these injuries, from which you say a person may recover, and a dose of morphine which is described as a fatal dose, death may be due to morphine, though the injuries to the head are apparent?'—'Yes.'

'Do you agree that a person slightly drunk, or under the influence of drugs, might trip over a stone brace at the top of steps leading to the Park Crescent basement, might lose consciousness and then recover and do all sorts of things—difficult things—before death supervenes?'—'It is possible.'

A person, said Birkett, could trip or stumble against that stone brace, and fall nearly twelve feet, striking a projecting stone window-sill below. That could have produced the fracture.

Addressing the court for the defence, Birkett castigated the publication of false reports of Mancini in the Press. It was, he said, 'a crime akin to murder'. He pointed to the contradiction between a witness's statement that Mancini had told him he 'bashed her from pillar to post' and Sir Bernard's evidence that the body bore no bruises. Violette Kaye, he said, could have fallen down the steps while under the influence of drink or drugs, staggered to bed and died; or she had been killed by somebody else. He examined Mancini himself on life at the flat:

Birkett: 'Were you in any way responsible for the death of Violette Kaye?'—'I was not, sir.'

'Did you ever use that hammer in any way at all?'—'I have never even seen it.'

'Where did she [Violette Kaye] get her money?'—'She was a loose woman and I knew it.'

'What was Violette Kaye's general manner ...?'—'She appeared to be in fear.'

'In fear?'—'Yes. Some evenings she'd come home and say, "Quick, pack up your clothes, we've got to go." We were always moving, and she appeared to be in fear all the time.'

'Did she have any particular habits?'—'She used to drink—sometimes too much.'

A friend of journalists and authors, Lord Birkett was a frequent guest at the Press Club, London. His ready wit made him the most sought-after of after-dinner speakers. This picture was taken in 1959

In the garden of his country home at Chalfont St. Giles, Lord Birkett relaxes with a biography after successfully acting as arbitrator in the printing dispute of 1959

Lord Birkett (then Sir Norman Birkett) in the black and gold State robes of a Lord Justice of Appeal. The adjusting of his spectacles was a characteristic gesture when he was cross-examining as a barrister

'Anything else?'—'I don't know if she took drugs. She had a bottle in a drawer, but I don't know what was in it. . . .'

'During the whole time you lived with her as man and wife, how did you get on together?'

The court was so silent a pin could be heard drop. Mancini hesitated, aware, as he must have been, of some public feeling against him because of the adverse publicity before the trial. 'Strange as it is,' he said distinctly, 'I used to love her.'

Mancini repeated his story that he had fled because, although innocent of her murder, he knew he would be suspected, and did not expect a fair deal from the police.

Birkett called other witnesses for the defence—a friend of the dead woman, Kay Fredericks, who said Violette seemed sometimes under the influence of drugs, and her mother, who said the same. Walter Blaker, a Kemp Street tailor, testified that Mancini had bought the trousers (later found to be bloodstained) on June 2nd, weeks after Violette Kaye died.

Because of his decision to call witnesses in addition to the prisoner, Norman Birkett was compelled by a rule of procedure to address the jury before counsel for the prosecution. 'You may think one reform that might usefully be made is that counsel for the defence should always speak last, so that he can deal with everything that has been said. . . .'

Where, asked Birkett, was the motive? 'There has not,' he told the jury in ringing tones, 'been a word on that vital question. I submit that that vital omission in the case for the Crown destroys it. All the evidence before the death of Violette Kaye is that they were on friendly and affectionate terms.' The case, he said, was 'simply riddled with doubt'. There was the morphine in the body, more than a medicinal dose. 'Is it not astounding,' asked Birkett, 'that when the prisoner was in the box he was not asked a single question about it?' And would not the prisoner, had he done 'this horrible thing', have thrown the hammer head into the sea?

How had she died? By falling down the steps? Or at the hands of another man? 'It is true,' said Birkett, 'that Violette Kaye was a prostitute, and that the prisoner lived on her earnings. I have no word to say in extenuation—none at all. But you must consider the world in which such people live and the dangers to which they are continually exposed . . . we have been dealing

P

with a class of men and women belonging to an underworld that makes the mind reel. Is it not reasonably probable that in that woman's life—an unhappy, dreadful life; you heard the prisoner say she went in fear—is it not probable that blackmail may have played a part?'

And where were the two men whose voices Kerslake heard when he called on Violette Kaye? 'The finding of the woman's body was proclaimed from the housetops. Those men who were in the flat could tell, but not a word. Does not that put a doubt into your mind?'

His closing words to the jury came as a ringing challenge. 'The ultimate responsibility rests upon you. And never let it be said, never let it be thought, that any word of mine shall seek to deter you from doing that which you feel to be your duty. But I think I am entitled . . . to claim for this man a verdict of Not Guilty. And, members of the jury, in returning that verdict you will vindicate a principle of law, that people are not tried by newspapers, not tried by rumour, not tried by statements born o a love of notoriety, but tried by British juries called to do justice and to decide upon the evidence. I ask you for, I appeal to you for and I claim from you a verdict of Not Guilty.' There was a fraction of a pause, as, facing the jury and running his eyes swiftly from one end of the box to the other, he gave them the admonition: 'Stand firm!'

Mr. Justice Branson's summing-up was admirably lucid and fair. 'According to the prisoner, he went home and found the woman dead, put her in a cupboard and nailed it up. What do you think of that as the action of an innocent man? You should give all the weight you think proper to the prisoner's statement that having been previously convicted—not of any offence of violence—he felt he would not get a fair deal from the police, and must therefore conceal the body. You must ask yourself whether you could imagine an innocent man dealing in this way with a woman whom he said he loved. . . .'

The evidence of the witnesses from 'Aladdin's Cave' the Judge thought in favour of the prisoner, and on the question of the bloodstained clothes he warned the jury: 'You are left in the position of having *no* bloodstained clothes upon which you can safely rely as having been worn by the prisoner before May 10th.'

For two and a quarter hours the all-male jury considered its verdict, mulling over the evidence of prostitutes and pathologists, layabouts and landlords, corner boys, pimps, petty thieves and small tradesmen. Then they returned with their verdict: Not Guilty.

There were gasps and cries from the public gallery, especially from the women. Instantly the court usher called the court to order: 'Silence! Silence!'

Mrs. England, Mancini's mother, wept unrestrainedly, sobbing: 'Thank God!'

'Let the prisoner be discharged,' said Mr. Justice Branson.

Mr. Birkett hurried down to the cell in time to see Mancini being given his belongings. He was so bewildered that he could hardly stammer out a 'Thank you'. All he could say was: 'Not guilty, Mr. Birkett? Not guilty, Mr. Birkett?'

Gently, Birkett took his leave. 'Now go home and look after your mother,' he said, 'she has stood by you and been a brick.'

CHAPTER XXIII

The Excitable Doctor Ruxton

THE TRIAL OF Dr. Buck Ruxton, convicted at Manchester Assizes on March 13th, 1936, for the murder of his Scots mistress, Mrs. Isabella Van Ess (who passed as his wife and was known locally as Isabella Ruxton), was one in which Norman Birkett could not have believed in his client's innocence, and one in which despite every effort he could not save his life.

Dr. Ruxton, whose real name was Bikhtyar Rustomji Ratanji Hakim, was a Parsee born in 1899, and a Bachelor of Medicine of Bombay and of London Universties. There is grisly significance in the fact that he was also a Bachelor of Surgery of the University of Bombay. He had served in the Indian Medical Service at Basra and Baghdad, had practised for a while in London and had since 1930 been living at 2 Dalton Square, Lancaster, where he had a successful practice.

Dr. Ruxton was an hysteric, given to alternate fits of elation, morbid suspicion, outbreaks of violence and aftermaths of lachrymose self-pity. Like many an unbalanced person, he had— if one may put it so—a high degree of low cunning and an ability to rationalise anything he did or wished to do. By our definitions he might not be called mad, but he could scarcely be considered normal.

Mrs. Van Ess ('Mrs.' Ruxton) was living with him at Dalton Square and had borne him three children, aged six, four and two. Living with them as nursemaid was a cheerful, hard-working Scots girl, Mary Rogerson.

Fierce and bitter quarrels were a usual occurrence in that tumultuous household; threats, abuse and attempted assault (he slept with a revolver under his pillow, and was seen by one maid to point a knife at his wife's throat) were part of Isabella Ruxton's daily lot. Twice, in fear of her life, she had sought police protection. A police constable who had called at the Ruxton home in May of 1935 had found the doctor 'in a very excitable state, behaving like a man insane. He said: "I will commit two murders in Dalton Square tonight".' Ruxton added that he would take out a summons against a man who had enticed away his wife's affections—a sinister symptom of a growing and entirely groundless suspicion that was to culminate in the commission of one of the most ghoulish murders of the century.

But for all the appalling misdirection of their emotions, despite the terrifying compound of opposites in Ruxton's psychic make-up (his tenderness in bandaging a child's cut finger; the devilish exactitude with which he dismembered the bodies of mistress and maid), the pair were in love. There could be threats and insults, tension and fear, violence and recrimination and then . . . the door of the surgery would open and Isabella would be standing there, smiling and saying: 'I wonder how I could pick up a row with you.' Or, as Ruxton himself put it: 'We were the kind of people who could not live with each other and could not live without each other. Who loves most chastises most.' The last comment sounds like a sophistic apologia for sadism. In any case, chastisement and murder are two different things.

Sometimes Isabella's forebearance was exhausted, as in 1932, when she tried to gas herself, and in 1934, when she arrived at the house of her sister, Mrs. Nelson, in Edinburgh, with all her baggage, having left Ruxton for good; but he followed her and with paroxysms of self-pity and tearful protestations beguiled her back to the house of doom.

On September 7th, 1935, a week before Ruxton's wife disappeared, Mrs. Ruxton went to Edinburgh to stay with Mr. and Mrs. Edmondson, their daughter Miss Edmondson and their son Robert Edmondson, a municipal clerk. Isabella had intended to stay the night with her sister Mrs. Nelson, but instead she and the Edmondsons stayed at the Adelphi hotel, the brother, sister and Mrs. Ruxton all having separate rooms. Ruxton hired a car, pursued his wife there, and made absurd and entirely unfounded accusations against the young man, whom he suspected of having an affair with Mrs. Ruxton.

On Saturday, September 14th, Mrs. Ruxton borrowed the doctor's Hillman Minx and drove alone to Blackpool to meet her two sisters and see the illuminations, leaving for Lancaster again at 11.30 p.m., the last time she was seen alive. That she arrived at the Ruxton home again is certain, for the car was there the next morning. Nor was Mary Rogerson, the comely, smiling girl who looked after the three Ruxton children and did light work about the house, ever seen again, either. She never went anywhere without telling her father and stepmother; on holiday, indeed, she wrote to them every day without fail. Now she had gone, and there was silence.

Number 2 Dalton Square was a large three-storied house, where the lighter work done by Mrs. Ruxton and Mary Rogerson was supplemented by the sturdy efforts of Mrs. Agnes Oxley, a charlady who came every morning at about 7.10 a.m. and another, Mrs. Elizabeth Curwen, who except for Sunday, when she came at 10 a.m., normally came at 8.30 in the morning and stayed all day, often until late at night. From August 1935 a third char-woman, Mrs. Mabel Smith, was engaged from Mondays to Thursdays, between 2 and 7 p.m.

Mrs. Ruxton went to see the illuminations on the 14th, the day she disappeared. It is interesting that the day before—on the 13th—Dr. Ruxton had told Mrs. Curwen that she need not come to work the following day or on Sunday, that there would be nothing for her to do until Monday. On the morning after Mrs. Ruxton's disappearance, that is on Sunday, September 15th, the other charwoman, Mrs. Oxley, would have begun her work at 7.10 a.m. But Ruxton called at her home at 6.30 in the morning, an unprecedented thing, and told her not to come, as 'Mrs. Ruxton and Mary have gone away on a holiday to Edinburgh'.

On that Sunday morning the girl who delivered the Sunday newspaper made one fruitless call, and on the second, rang per-sistently; the door was opened not, as usual, by Isabella or Mary or Mrs. Curwen. Instead, there stood Dr. Ruxton, agitated, in shirt and trousers and holding his right hand against his body. Mary and Isabella, he said, had gone to Scotland.

At 10 a.m. the milkwoman called. Usually she took the bottles through to the scullery, but today Ruxton told her to put the bottles on a table just inside the front door. Ruxton said he had jammed his right hand and that his wife and housemaid were away with the children. Next, a labourer came with the *Sunday Graphic*, but receiving no answer, pushed the paper under the door. At 10.30 a.m. Ruxton drove his Hillman Minx to a nearby garage and bought two two-gallon tins of petrol; half an hour later he took his car to his regular garage and filled up with four gallons of petrol.

Ruxton took his three children to stay with some friends, Mr.

and Mrs. Anderson, and at four-thirty in the afternoon called on a Mrs. Hampshire to ask her to help with 'a little tidying up' and the reception of patients. But there was more than tidying up to do, she found. Carpets and stair pads had been removed from the stairs and landings, the stairs were dirty and stained, the bath was stained with a queer yellow stain to within six inches of the top; there were wisps of straw scattered about; from the locked doors of the two bedrooms used by Mr. and Mrs. Ruxton protruded more scraps of straw. Rolled-up carpets and stair pads were in the waiting-room, and in the back yard were two carpets and some stair carpeting thick with blood, a bloodstained shirt and some blood-soaked towels.

In the evening Ruxton returned to Dalton Square from the Andersons, with Mrs. Anderson and two of his children, to collect their things. Mrs. Hampshire, whom he had left tidying up, had brought her husband to help her, and he gave them blood-soaked carpets and a blue suit heavily stained with blood as a gift. The Hampshires, fortunately, were not apprehensive by nature or given to uneasy speculations, and accepted these offerings with pleasure. There was so much blood on the carpet that even when she sluiced it with over thirty buckets of water the water still ran red.

From 11 p.m. on the 15th to the morning of September 16th Ruxton was in the house of death. Mrs. Oxley, calling at 7.10 a.m., could not, however, get a reply. At 9 a.m. Ruxton turned up at the Hampshires' home, with unhappy second thought about his gift of the bloodstained suit. He tried to retrieve it, offered to get it cleaned, but Mrs. Hampshire, mindful of his generosity, would not permit him this further expense, and said she would send it to the cleaners herself. But at his insistence she removed the tailor's label.

That day Mrs. Oxley the charwoman, who returned to the house, found certain doors locked, burned material in the yard—which dustmen removed later—and at midday Ruxton returned his Hillman Minx for overhaul and hired an Austin.

The next day Ruxton was involved in a collision with a cyclist at Kendal, did not pull up and was stopped by police at Milnthorpe at 1 p.m. Mrs. Smith began stripping the wallpaper from the staircase, while Mrs. Curwen noticed a bloodstained blanket in the yard. Ruxton asked for a large fire to be lit in the waiting-room, as he proposed to stay up all night.

By September 18th the walls were stripped. Mrs. Smith noticed bloodstained curtains, and one similarly stained curtain among the partly burned rubbish in the yard. He returned the hired car and recovered his own, sleeping at the Andersons until 1 a.m.

On September 19th Mrs. Oxley, arriving at 7.10 a.m., was asked to prepare an early breakfast for the doctor. He shut the kitchen door and made numerous journeys up and down stairs before leaving by car at 8 a.m. Mrs. Curwen arrived to find that the doors that had been locked were now unlocked, and that the house was pervaded by an unpleasant smell. From 8.30 to 11 p.m. fires burned furiously in Ruxton's back yard. Ruxton himself was seen to be stirring the blaze. Incidentally, the charwoman, who had kept fires going in the yard, noticed material resembling a piece of the blue coat Mary Rogerson used to wear and a scrap of her red dressing-gown. There was also a swab of cotton-wool with blood on it.

On wash day, September 23rd, Mrs. Smith emptied the soiled linen basket and found in it a white silk nightgown with a large bloodstain on one shoulder.

One would have thought that suspicion would have fastened on Dr. Ruxton before this. Certainly the family of Mary Rogerson were puzzled and uneasy, and when her brother called to ask if there was news of her, Ruxton asked him if there had been any trouble at home, and implied that she had been having an affair with a laundry boy. The previous day he had told a patient that Mary Rogerson was pregnant (it was subsequently proved that she was not) and that his wife had taken her somewhere for an illegal operation.

Rumours had begun to spread, however. The police were investigating the death of a Mrs. Smalley at Morecambe, and interviewed one of Ruxton's servants. Within hours the name of Dr. Ruxton was being linked by gossip with Mrs. Smalley's death, and he called at Lancaster Police Station to protest. 'Look here, Inspector Moffat, what the hell do the police want enquiring about my private affairs for?'

Next Dr. Ruxton called to see Mary Rogerson's father and told him that a Mrs. Anderson had called his attention to the fact that Mary was pregnant (which Mrs. Anderson denied). Rogerson said he knew nothing about that, but that if Mary did not come back at once he must report it to the police.

On September 29th, 1935, a Miss Johnson was crossing a bridge on the Edinburgh–Carlisle road when, down in the gully below, she espied a bundle. In a ghastly moment of revelation she realised that, protruding from it, was a human hand. She raced back to her hotel and informed her brother, who, returning to the spot, found human remains wrapped in a newspaper and a sheet. Police, in a further search, discovered four more bundles. Two heads were wrapped in children's clothing. The other bundles contained various parts of two female bodies.

With consummate skill these grisly relics were reassembled and examined; they were of two women, although at first one victim was thought to have been a man. The fact that some of the remains were wrapped in an edition of the *Sunday Graphic* sold only in the Morecambe and Lancaster districts narrowed enquiries to that area, and an article on Mary Rogerson's disappearance in the Glasgow *Daily Record* came to the notice of the Chief Constable of Dumfries.

Photographs of the blouse and rompers in which the remains were wrapped were published in the newspapers, and Mrs. Rogerson identified the blouse as one belonging to her daughter, by a patch which she herself had sewn under the arm before giving it to her. The rompers, too, she had given to Mary for the children; a pecularity in the knot which she had tied in the elastic made this certain.

Ruxton meanwhile continued to behave as though he sought the return of his wife. He had reported her missing to the Lancaster Borough Police, and when the bodies were found at Moffat and investigations concentrated on Lancaster, he protested to Captain Vann, the Chief Constable, 'This publicity is ruining my practice,' he said. This was quite true. On October 10th Ruxton asked Mrs. Oxley to stand by him if there were police enquiries.

On October 12th Ruxton went round to several people asking them to make false statements; he asked a Miss Neild to say that he had been at the Anderson's house every day since his wife had gone away; to Mrs. Oxley, whom he had told not to come to the house on September 15th, he appealed to say that he had called again at nine o'clock that day to ask her to come, and she did. Mrs. Oxley refused to say what was not true. He tried to persuade an electrician who had called on September 14th to say that he had come on the night of *September 14th* to mend a fuse, and that Mary Rogerson had opened the door to him. But the electrician had been in bed at the time and refused to be committed. To others Ruxton made requests equally desperate and indiscreet.

On October 13th Ruxton was arrested and charged with the murder of Mary Rogerson, whose body, of the two discovered, had at that stage been more positively identified.

Many remands followed, while pathologists struggled with their technically fascinating but aesthetically revolting task of dealing with the remains. Marks or physical peculiarities had been removed methodically and with surgical skill. Mary Rogerson had had a cast in one eye—and the eyes of body No. 1 had been removed. Mrs. Ruxton's legs were of equal width from the knees to the ankles—and the soft tissues of the legs of body No. 2 had been sliced.

Assembling the remains, it was clear that body No. 1 had been of a young woman, about five feet in height (Mary Rogerson was five feet in height), while body No. 2 was of a woman of about thirty-five years of age and about five foot 6 inches in height.

The mutilations, by a supreme irony, helped to identify the victims rather than ensure their anonymity. Mary had a birthmark on her right forearm; the skin where it would have been had been removed. Mrs. Ruxton had a prominent nose; the nose had been removed from body No. 2. Her toes were humped; the toes were missing. She had a bunion on one toe; an excision had been made on that toe.

But more tangible evidence identified these tragic remains. Finger-prints were taken from the left hand of body No. 2 and compared with finger-prints found on articles handled by Mary Rogerson in the home. They were identical. Photographs of the dead women were enlarged to life size, and superimposed on to photographs of the skulls found; they fitted exactly.

And so the gruesome jig-saw was completed, the damnatory evidence assembled and this cunning hysteric was tried for the murder of Iabella Ruxton at Manchester Winter Assizes before Mr. Justice Singleton. Counsel for the Crown were Mr. C. J. Jackson, K.C., Mr. Maxwell Fyfe, K.C., and Mr. Hartley Shawcross. Norman Birkett and Philip Kershaw, K.C., appeared for the prisoner.

Birkett knew that in this case there was little hope of securing an acquittal for Dr. Ruxton. There were far too many witnesses, there was the melancholy testimony of the dismembered corpses, the furnishings drenched with human blood, the contradictory lies told to account for the two women's disappearance, the strange happenings at the house from the night they vanished. Why should a man with three servants spend his time trying to remove carpets and dirty stair pads?

There were witnesses a'plenty to prove that Dr. Ruxton was a man of violent temper, and that he had been seen with his hands on Mrs. Ruxton's throat—and she had died by strangulation. As Mr. Jackson put it to the court:

'On April 6th, 1934, Mrs. Ruxton went to the police station, and from what she told the detective-sergeant it was necessary for him to go across to the Ruxtons' house. The police officer invited the doctor to come over to the police station, which he did, and when he saw his wife there he went into a violent temper, accused her of being unfaithful and said he would be justified in murdering her.' The next day she called at the station again, Ruxton followed her there, and once again, in an excitable scene, used threats of murder.

'In May 1935,' continued prosecuting counsel, '. . . a police officer called at the prisoner's house, and on arrival found the doctor in a very excited state. He was behaving like a madman and said that he felt like murdering two persons in Dalton Square. He mentioned that his wife was going out to meet a man, and you will probably come to the conclusion that he was frightfully jealous with regard to his wife and any man she met, danced with or spoke to. At this time he mentioned the name of Edmondson as one of whom he was jealous without, I submit, any justification whatever. There is no justification for murder, and the prosecution does not seek to prove any motive, but I shall ask you to bear in mind the evidence of this jealousy. . . .'

On the morning of September 16th, when Mrs. Oxley had called at 2 Dalton Square and received no reply, Ruxton had been out all night getting rid of the bodies. Among the rubbish taken away by the dustman was a blue silk dress with glass buttons worn by Mary Rogerson. 'You may well ask,' said Mr. Jackson, 'why he should burn her clothing, unless he was desirous of getting rid of it to support his story of her going away. There was the

blood-soaked carpet, so saturated that even when thirty buckets
of water had been thrown over it the water ran red; no cut finger
could account for that.'

Mrs. Ruxton, the prosecution declared, had received before her
death violent blows in the face, and had been strangled. It seemed
likely that Mary, the housemaid, had tried to save her mistress or
at least witnessed the crime, for her skull was fractured, and she was
probably killed by some other means, perhaps a knife, as a trail
of blood led from the two bedrooms on the top landing to the
bottom of the staircase.

Despite the formidable case against Buck Ruxton, Mr. Birkett
did his best for his client, never letting a single point pass unchallenged if it were possible to dispute it, and allowing no point
in Ruxton's favour to go by default. The history of Ruxton's
previous threats and violence was a sinister one in view of later
developments, and Birkett tried—not very successfully—to mitigate some of the stories told, as in his cross-examination of Isabella
Ruxton's sister, Mrs. Nelson, to whom Mrs. Ruxton had once fled
for refuge, and for whom she had so often sent in her fear and
distress:

Birkett: 'You were very fond of your sister, I take it, and in the
various disputes that arose between your sister and Dr. Ruxton I
think you rather sided with her?'—'Naturally, but not altogether
or unjustly. I sometimes reasoned with her. The disputes were
fairly frequent.'

'Would you describe your sister as highly impulsive and excitable?'—'Yes, I would. Excitable to a point.'

'Apt to act on the spur of the moment?'—'Not without someone behind her. She was impulsive, she had impulses, but she
was not one that acted very often on her own.'

This attempt to apportion equally any blame for the tension
and quarrels had not succeeded. But Mr. Birkett now tried to
establish that the couple, despite their disputes, were on affectionate terms:

'At first, when the association began between your sister and
Dr. Ruxton, they were fond of each other—in fact, it would be
right to say that they were passionately fond of each other?'—
'They were; I know that my sister was passionately fond of him.'

'We are one about this, that in the early days that was the relationship that existed? Now unhappily that changed, did it not,

and there were disputes and quarrels from the time she went to Lancaster in 1930?'—'Yes.'

'Would you say that in your experience of Dr. Ruxton he was very excitable, and that when anything upset him his conversation became almost unintelligible?'—'That is right. He spoke at an immensely rapid rate, rather incoherently, and kept running from one subject to another at a tangent.'

'When anything upset him he used very extravagant language —rather ridiculous language.'—'Yes.'

Birkett hoped by these points to take the edge off some of the damaging and threatening things which Ruxton had said about and to Isabella Ruxton. He turned to the incident in 1931, when Mrs. Nelson was urgently summoned to Lancaster by telegram, and where Ruxton, beside himself with excitement, alleged that his wife had tried to gas herself. She was pregnant at the time, and in April 1932 gave birth to a child that was dead.

Birkett: 'The dispute there was that Dr. Ruxton was saying she had deliberately tried to gas herself, and she said it was an accident. He had been without doubt tremendously upset about it, and was upon that occasion very excited?'—'Yes.'

'Again, spoke very incoherently and very rapidly and used wild words?'—'In the bedroom. It was in the bedroom that he said he would cut all our throats.'

'Was there some suggestion then that the children would be taken away?'—'No, there was no suggestion.'

'He was passionately fond of the children?'—Yes.'

'After that excitable time, still on the subject of gassing, he calmed down quite quickly, did he not?'—'Not quickly; he finally said he believed her and became very nice. He was always very nice.'

'The position, then, was this, that on one day he was highly excitable, using these wild words, and on the next day was as nice as could be?'—'Yes, to me.'

William Thompson, Chief Constable of Clitheroe, said that when Mrs. Ruxton came to the station and made a statement in 1934: 'Ruxton came in accompanied by Detective-Sergeant Stainton. He waved his arms in the air, commenced to shriek and foam at the mouth. I tried to calm him, and he said: "My wife has been unfaithful. I will kill her if it continues. . . ." On that occasion Mrs. Ruxton wanted to leave him, but they made it up.'

Mr. Birkett: 'Take the expression "foamed at the mouth". Is that not a figurative expression?'—'He did actually foam at the mouth. As a matter of fact, I got very concerned about him and thought he was going to have a seizure. He was hysterical, almost incoherent at times. . . .'

'I suppose the phrase "I will kill her if it continues" was put down afterwards?'—'Yes, about half-past four when I came back to the house.'

'I am sure you would agree that you could not possibly at four-thirty record the whole of that conversation. I suggest that in the events of the afternoon you got that phrase wrong?'—'No, he actually did use these words.'

Birkett tried to minimise if not negate the highly damaging remark made by Ruxton to Police Constable William Wilson, who went to the house in answer to a desperate telephone call from Mrs. Ruxton. The doctor 'was behaving like a man insane. He said: "I will commit two murders in Dalton Square to-night." '

'When you saw Dr. Ruxton with Mrs. Ruxton,' Birkett asked the constable, 'did Mrs. Ruxton say that the man who had been referred to would kill Dr. Ruxton, and was it then that Dr. Ruxton said: "Well, if he does, that will be two murders?"'—'I never heard Mrs. Ruxton say that.'

'That is how I suggest that the suggestion of murders came in. But quite generally he spoke extremely rapidly?'—'Yes.'

'And most incoherently and very wildly?'—'Yes, I am afraid he did.'

'I suggest that the murders came in the way I have mentioned?' —'No, I am afraid not.'

'You mean you do not recall Mrs. Ruxton saying that? She did say something presumably?'—'She never said anything about anyone doing any murders, killing anyone.'

'Did she not say: "The man who has been discussed, he will kill you."'—'No, she did not.'

'She was highly excited, too? Did she appear to know what she was saying?'—'She was in a very distressed condition. She appeared very frightened.'

When Mrs. Hampshire, who had helped to tidy up the house at Dr. Ruxton's urgent request, gave her evidence it included the fact that an uneaten meal for two lay on the table in the lounge.

There was straw on the staircase ('Not a lot; just as if someone had been carrying an armful of straw and bits had fallen off as the person walked up the stairs.') She saw two locked bedrooms at the top of the stairs. 'I looked for a key, as I wanted to get the bits of straw from under the doors when I was sweeping up.'

The straw was significant, for one of the torsos had straw attaching to it.

There has never been any question of Dr. Ruxton being responsible for the death of the Mrs. Smalley whose body was found at Morecambe. But because of rumours of excessive bloodstains in his house, the police had interviewed Mrs. Curwen, a charwoman employed by Ruxton. To Mrs. Hampshire he had said: 'I have a great joke for you, Mrs. Hampshire. The police have been questioning me about the Mrs. Smalley business.'

Norman Birkett, cross-examining Mrs. Hampshire, made a good point—that when Ruxton called at his house with the two children to get their night attire he had gone upstairs with them. But upstairs, according to the prosecution, the bodies of two dead women were in the locked bedrooms.

Mr. Birkett: 'It is quite clear that with his two children the doctor went upstairs, and must have gone into the room of Mrs. Ruxton for the children's night things?'—'He must have gone into one of the rooms, because he came down with the nightdresses in a case.'

'How long do you think he was up there?'—'About three minutes.'

'It would have been a simple thing for Dr. Ruxton to say to the children: "Stay here with Mrs. Hampshire while I go upstairs"?'—'Yes.'

'But he did in fact go with them?'—'Yes.'

Mr. Justice Singleton: 'Do you know whether they went right to the top of the house?'—'I do not know, but the fact that Elizabeth came down carrying the case . . .'

'Rather points to the fact that she had been to the bedroom to get the case herself?'—'Yes, I thought so.'

There was, however, no shaking her evidence of how she had been given the blue suit and how Ruxton had tried desperately to get it back again, because it was bloodstained. But in two questions to Mrs. Hampshire, Mr. Jackson, for the prosecution, undid what meagre benefit might have derived from Birkett's cross-examination:

Mr. Jackson: 'When the prisoner told you that the police had been questioning him about the death of Mrs. Smalley in Morecambe, I understand he was highly amused?'—'Yes, he was.'

'When he told you that they had questioned him about Mary Rogerson, was he amused then?'—'No.'

'What was his state then?'—'He was frantic.'

It was a dramatic moment in the trial when Mr. Birkett rose and said: 'My Lord, I call the prisoner.' An anxious one for Birkett, too, because Ruxton's hysteria and uncontrolled volubility might prove a grave handicap to the defence.

The cross-examination was mainly directed to eliciting denials of the damaging things he had been heard to say and seen to do. He denied that, as one witness alleged, he had said he would bring Mrs. Ruxton back to the mortuary. He denied Eliza Hunter's evidence that she had seen him with his hands round his wife's neck. He denied that he held a knife at her throat. He repudiated the evidence of P.C. Wilson, who had heard him say: 'I will commit two murders in Dalton Square tonight.'

At first Ruxton was inclined to be hysterical in the box, but gained confidence as the cross-examination proceeded. His description of how he cut his hand while opening a tin of peaches was particularly lucid, although it was odd he should throw away the opener with the tin.

In his long speech for the defence, Birkett emphasised that much of the evidence was circumstantial, which could 'be highly dangerous'. He implied that Ruxton's mental processes should be considered in assessing the value of anything he said in a state of excitement (meaning, of course, that his threats should not be taken at face value). The evidence of the garage was that there was no record of whether Ruxton took his car out on the night of September 16th, when the prosecution claimed he was depositing the human remains in the ravine at Moffat. An important point was that the night was wet and the car was clean.

'There is,' continued Birkett, 'no witness to say that there was anything unusual at 2 Dalton Square, that there was a car in front of the house at a given time, and that articles were being packed into the car. . . . It is said that he went to Moffat with the dismembered bodies and threw them down into the ravine, skull, bones, limbs and flesh, and yet never a spot of blood was found on that car.'

But Mr. Justice Singleton's fair and balanced summing-up on the eleventh day of the trial had little to include in the prisoner's favour. Why had neither Mrs. Ruxton nor Mary Rogerson, if either were still alive, contacted the children, to whom both were devoted? Why had not Mrs. Ruxton got in touch with her sister Mrs. Nelson? Why had Mary not written to her father and stepmother?

Ruxton had said that Mary Rogerson was pregnant. There was irrefutable physical disproof of this, nor did her remains indicate pregnancy in any stage.

Birkett must have realised the case was lost when the Judge said to the jury:

'In the course of his remarks yesterday Mr. Birkett, in dealing with Mr. Jackson's address to you, said: "My friend said that if you were satisfied that those remains in the ravine at Moffat were proved to be the remains of Mrs. Ruxton and Miss Rogerson your task was well-nigh completed"; and he proceeded to question that, and said that if they went away that morning from 2 Dalton Square—as the prisoner said—why should he be accused of their murder merely because they were dead?'

But, said the Judge, if they did go away, who else might have murdered them? 'They cannot,' said Mr. Justice Singleton, 'have been cut up very well in the ravine. They had been treated, again one imagines from the evidence, by a person of some anatomical skill. Again . . . if those two women were murdered by some-body of whom we have not heard, can you see the reason for the removal of signs of identity or possible means of identification? Does the condition in which they are found point, or does it not point, to disarticulation by somebody with skill in such matters, and to a desire, and a complete desire, to remove, not only signs which would give the cause of death, but also to remove signs of identity?'

The evidence of how he tried to retrieve his bloodstained coat, having at first given it away, was heavily against him. So, too, was the evidence of a pathologist who found that blood had run down, in stream form, from the top of the bath down the sides— vastly in excess of what could be expected of a cut hand. A carpet had on it not only blood but also some human tissue. The identity

Q

of the two women *had* been established. But if they simply went away, *without the children*, why did they take the children's rompers, in which some remains were found?

'It is most important, as Mr. Birkett has said to you,' the Judge continued, 'that no innocent man should suffer—most important. It is equally important that the principles of justice as administered in this country should be carried out and that juries shall not shrink from doing their duty when a case is proved. . . .'

The jury found Ruxton Guilty, and his appeal against the sentence of death was dismissed on April 27th, 1936. He was executed at Strangeways Prison, Manchester, on May 12th.

Subsequently a Sunday newspaper published Ruxton's confession, for which they had paid over £3,000, from which part of the expenses of the defence were paid.

From Lord Birkett's comments on the Ruxton case in his television interview with John Freeman in *Face to Face* it is clear that he cannot have believed in Ruxton's innocence. Every man, however, is entitled to a defence, and Birkett did his very best in an impossible case.

Freeman raised an interesting point. He asked: 'There's another question on the same subject, also Dr. Ruxton. You know the practice which has grown up recently of great newspapers paying for the defence of criminals in return for their confessions? Do you approve of that?'

Lord Birkett said he did approve, but did not know if it had been done in Ruxton's case, and rather thought it had not been. At any rate, he had no knowledge of it.

This seems a little extraordinary. Is it conceivable that, with all the intense day-to-day interest in this sensational case, Birkett never saw the published confessions, and could not even remember them having been published?

Ruxton, incidentally, was grateful for Birkett's efforts and wrote from his death cell a letter of thanks. He also left Birkett a legacy of a set of fish knives and forks. Politely, Norman Birkett refused to accept it.

CHAPTER XXIV

Near the Crossroads

By 1936 Norman Birkett had reached the summit of his real career, and knew it. He had already been offered a judgeship and declined it—as he was to refuse for a second time before finally accepting it in 1941—because his children were growing up and he begrudged the inevitable long absences from home while on circuit. 'I suppose I shall have to one day,' he would say, 'but not now. Not now.' He would like to have added 'never', but was too ambitious and too respectful of the machinery of government and of justice to postpone too long demands or requests made in the name of duty. There was, of course, the financial aspect; Birkett had a sound sense of money, and knew that once he turned his back on his high earnings as an advocate, it would be very unlikely that he could ever again reach such a level of income.

Although Birkett preferred to defend in murder trials, he proved in the Rouse trial that he could be formidable as prosecuting counsel, and was equally relentless in securing a verdict of Guilty against 'Nurse' Dorothea Waddingham for the murder of Ada Baguley in a Nottingham nursing home.

'Nurse' Waddingham was living with her lover, Ronald Sullivan, in the home in Devon Drive. With her protruding teeth and unintelligent stare, she was not attractive, and her almost hypnotic hold on Sullivan was not easy to explain. However, in January 1936 a Mrs. Baguley, aged eighty-nine, and her daughter Ada, aged fifty, moved into the home, suffering respectively from senility and disseminated sclerosis. Nurse Waddingham grumbled incessantly at the poor pay and the burden of work, saying continually that they 'ought to be in hospital'. It was to lever more money out of the couple, and she succeeded. Mrs. Baguley owned property, and, to her solicitor's disquiet (he had an almost uncanny prescience of disaster), made over her money to Nurse Waddingham in consideration of treatment for life.

This signed, Mrs. Baguley lived only a few more days, dying after a Royal Silver Jubilee Day celebration which included tinned salmon. A few months later Ada Baguley, on a day when she had received a visitor and appeared to be in reasonable health—allowing for her complaint—also died suddenly. A death certificate was given ascribing death to weakened heart arteries, but a strangely worded letter, written by Sullivan and alleged to have been signed by Miss Baguley, reached the Nottingham Medical Officer of Health. Miss Baguley asked to be cremated, adding 'and my last wish is my relatives shall not know of my death'.

This unusual request naturally aroused suspicion. The Medical Officer ordered a post mortem, which revealed that Miss Baguley had died from a fatal dose of morphia. Both Dorothea Waddingham and Sullivan her paramour were charged with murder, but at Nottingham Assize Mr. Justice Goddard (later Lord Chief Justice) ruled that there was insufficient evidence to proceed against Sullivan.

Morphine had never been prescribed for either of the Baguleys, and Norman Birkett had little difficulty in proving that Miss Baguley must have been given morphine supplied for other patients. Nurse Waddingham, a mother with three children, one of them only four months old, was found Guilty and condemned to death. The jury added a recommendation to mercy, but she was hanged on April 16th, 1936.

A murder trial at the Old Bailey was to give Birkett ample scope for that skill in cross-examination for which he was deservedly famous.

Albert Hadfield, a confectioner, aged sixty-nine, was charged before Mr. Justice Greaves-Lord with the murder of Mrs. Laura Chapman, an elderly woman of independent means. Both lived in Twickenham.

Mrs. Chapman was found dead in her home on July 9th, 1936, with forty-six stab wounds in her body, lying under a heap of burned clothes. Neighbours had noticed that the milk had not been collected, and others claimed to remember having seen Hadfield in the house round about the time when it was supposed she had been attacked. One neighbour had seen him using a small cloth and cleaning 'a very small thing'.

Mrs. Chapman lived alone. A policeman called while Hadfield was in the house, and claimed that Hadfield had told him that he managed some of Mrs. Chapman's property, and was trying to sell a house for her. Then, according to the policeman, Hadfield had said, pointing to a heap, 'You may find a body under there.' Two postcards from Hadfield to Mrs. Chapman were found, one allegedly bearing a bloody thumb-print. But the thumb-print was too blurred to identify, and the detectives had, foolishly, taken no scientific steps to prove their contention that the print *was* of blood.

By challenging their contention and proving that the recollections of witnesses were vague and inconclusive, Norman Birkett secured Hadfield's acquittal. He had interrupted his holiday to conduct this defence. Now, having saved the man's life, he calmly took off his wig and gown with the comment: 'Now I can go back to my holiday.'

The mystery of the murder of this elderly lady, whose forty-six stab wounds indicated a paroxysm of savagery, has never been solved.

In the meantime a civil and constitutional drama was beginning to unfold. London was seething with rumours about the growing friendship of King Edward and Mrs. Wallis Simpson. In the United States and on the Continent fact and speculation were printed with uncensored and uninhibited abandon. In England, though not without a plain hint from authority, the Press imposed a voluntary censorship upon itself. Officially the crisis round the monarchy did not exist, and most people hoped it would blow over.

Mr. Birkett found himself caught up in this gathering drama, and with superb diplomacy Mrs. Simpson's proceedings for a divorce against her husband were conducted with a speed and precision unusual in cases of this kind. At Mr. Birkett's suggestion, although Mrs. Simpson was a resident of London at the time, the case was somehow heard in Ipswich, a fact which puzzled and irritated the Judge.

Inordinate preparations had been made to obstruct and exclude the Press. Mrs. Simpson's Buick, driven by the King's chauffeur, raced into Ipswich at a speed which, according to one observer, easily outdistanced a cameraman's car moving at 65 miles per hour. Police opened the courthouse gates for the car to enter and smashed two press cameras. To the amazement of some Ipswich lawyers, they could not get into the court, while even the Mayor had to explain and justify himself in seeking admission.

The courtroom gallery seats immediately facing Mrs. Simpson were left empty, tickets being given only for those public seats behind her.

Sir John Hawke, the Judge, asked irritably, 'How did the case come here?' There were frantic whispers to the Judge from the clerk and Sir John was heard to reply, 'Yes, yes, I see.'

Witnesses differ as to Mrs. Simpson's demeanour. A Hearst correspondent was impressed by her 'queenly composure', while the *New York Times* correspondent observed that her tongue moved rapidly in nervous movements from cheek to cheek.

Mr. Birkett drew her story from her in thirty-one carefully prepared questions, in answering which she observed a most commendable economy of words. It was 'Yes', or 'No', or 'Yes, I did.' Her letter to Mr. Simpson, also a model of brevity, was read:

'Dear Ernest,
  'I have just learned that while you have been away, instead of being on business as you led me to believe, you have been staying at a hotel at Bray with a lady.
  'I am sure you realize that is conduct which I cannot possibly overlook and I must insist that you do not continue to live here with me.
  'This only confirms suspicions which I have had for a long time. I am therefore instructing my solicitors to take proceedings for divorce.
                                                        'Wallis.'

A few employees of the Hotel de Paris at Bray gave the usual evidence of Mr. Simpson's stay there with another woman. Usually in such cases the 'other woman' is named, but in this instance she was not.

Mr. Justice Hawke, fidgeting with his handkerchief, said, with a bored air, 'Well, I suppose I must come to the conclusion there was adultery in this case.'

Mr. Birkett: 'I assume what your Lordship has in mind.' For a moment it looked as though Birkett's usual felicity of expression might have deserted him. The Judge's face clouded. 'How do you know what is in my mind?' he asked bleakly, 'What is it I have in my mind, Mr. Birkett?'

With exemplary patience, Birkett took the implied rebuke with good grace, verging almost on the obsequious in his anxiety not to jeopardise his client's case by any want of self-control on his part. 'I think, with great deference,' he added quietly, 'that Your Lordship may have in mind what is known as "ordinary hotel evidence", where the name of the lady is not disclosed. With respect, I thought that might have been in your Lordship's mind.'

Visibly, the Judge thawed. 'That is what it must have been, Mr. Birkett. I am glad for your help.'

Birkett: 'The lady's name, My Lord, was mentioned in the petition, so now I ask for a decree nisi with costs against the Respondent.'

Mr. Justice Hawke: 'Yes, costs against the Respondent, I am afraid. I suppose I must in these unusual circumstances. So you may have it, with costs.'

Birkett: 'Decree nisi with costs?'

Mr. Justice Hawke: 'Yes, I suppose so.'

Gallantly, Mr. Birkett proferred his arm. She took it, and they sailed out of court, the Ipswich police slamming the doors after them to delay everyone else in court and allow Mrs. Simpson to get clear. Her car sped out of town, the police swung one of their cars across the road and blocked further traffic for ten minutes.

Seldom can Mr. Birkett have had a briefer case—the whole thing had taken less than twenty minutes. Now the King's abdication was inevitable, for the woman he loved would now be free, if she wished, to marry him.

Although Birkett often worked for seven days a week, and although many cases dealt with such depths of degradation and horror as to make the mind reel, he himself was seldom depressed by the subject-matter with which he had to deal. He could always keep his objectivity, speaking, arguing and pleading with all the vehemence and logic he could muster, on behalf of his client, with his client's interests in mind, and never himself personally involved.

But there was frequently a lighter side, such as that of the policeman's impeccable, odourless, irreproachable feet.

On a bright summer's day a newspaper photographer took a good picture of Police Constable Plumb on point duty. He was in the act of removing his helmet and mopping his brow.

This human study was used in an evening paper with an innocuous caption.

A few years later, when Plumb had left the police and become a Civil Servant, he saw the same photograph of himself used in an advertisement with the words: 'Phew! I am going to get my feet into a Jeyes' Fluid foot-bath.' A relative sent this to Plumb, and many friends and relatives noticed it.

Civil Servants must not court publicity, although it is difficult to believe that His Majesty's Treasury would have thought that Mr. Plumb had initiated this advertisement. Mr. Plumb thought they might. Some could imagine, he said, that he had authorised this use of the photograph or even been paid for it. The truth is that policemen and ex-policemen are touchy about their feet; for example, they detest being called 'flatties'. Mr. Plumb was hurt to the quick by the implication that his feet might be smelly. A Statement of Claim was drawn up, the case (*Plumb* v. *Jeyes Sanitary Compounds Co. Ltd.* (1937)) was heard, and the following dialogue ensued:

Birkett: 'Do you entertain some dim recollections of your days as a policeman?'—'Yes.'

'Happy days?'—'Some were.'

'Do you seriously suggest that anybody looking at this advertisement would say that you had got bad feet?'—'Yes. The advertisement for Jeyes' says it is good for feet or smelling feet.'

'Is anybody going to think a penny the worse of you because you have a foot-bath?'—'No, but this is associated with disinfectant. I would use a foot-bath because my feet ached and not because they were smelly.'

'Supposing they did smell, do you think they would be unique in the world, or that ordinary people's feet smell as a common thing?'—'They do. But it is possible to use bath salts—quite different from Jeyes' Fluid.'

'Do you think your reputation would be enhanced if you washed your feet in scented salts?'—'Oh, no.' Nevertheless, said Civil Servant Plumb, a reader of the advertisement would think that he had feet that smelled highly—so high that he needed Jeyes' Fluid. It had led to jokes that made him angry and it had caused 'bad feeling in the family'.

To this, addressing the jury, Norman Birkett said that he had heard of families being broken up for many reasons, but never by Jeyes' Fluid.

However, Mr. Plumb's wounded susceptibilities were assuaged by an award of £100 damages, with costs.

But from the gaiety of that case to the grim tragedy of Mona Tinsley was but a matter of weeks. This sweet little girl, only ten years of age, should have returned to her home and parents at half-past four after leaving the Wesleyan School in Newark on January 5th, 1937. It was a dark, cold, blustery night, but her parents did not start enquiries until 7 p.m., or report her disappearance to the police until 9.45 p.m.

The following day, after diligent police enquiries, witnesses were found who had seen a man loitering near the school, while others had seen Mona with this same man board a bus near the school. Enquiries centred on Frederick Nodder, a labourer of dubious character who lived alone in a house called 'Peacehaven'. One neighbour had seen Mona framed in the doorway at midday on January 6th, but not since.

Nodder claimed that he had not seen Mona for fifteen months —as 'Uncle Fred' and using an assumed name, he had once stayed as a lodger in the Tinsley household. The police, suspecting murder, searched the house, dug up the garden and tried every avenue of enquiry. But the little girl could not be found. Nodder, however, was arrested on a warrant for non-payment of a bastardy order, as a means of keeping him in custody while the search continued. Gravel pits were dug, ponds and canals dragged and drained. Nine hundred volunteers combed empty premises, waste land, fields, ditches and roads.

Nodder eventually changed his story and admitted meeting the girl near her school, taking her to his home and later putting her on a bus from Retford to Sheffield because she wanted to visit her aunt, who lived there. That this little girl would have such a desire without informing her parents, that Nodder would not know how worried the parents must have been, that to send her on this dark and blustery night, alone, with a prospect of a long walk in a town she had last visited as an infant, was an unlikely story.

Nodder was tried at the Warwick Winter Assizes on March 9th, 1937, before Mr. Justice Swift, Mr. Birkett leading for the Crown, with Mr. R. E. A. Elwes, and Mr. Maurice Healy, K.C., with Mr. N. F. M. Robinson appearing for the accused.

That Nodder was hiding something, that he had abducted the girl and brought her to some harm, nobody in court could doubt. That he did not elect to go into the witness box made a profoundly disturbing impression on the Judge. 'Why,' the Judge asked the jury, 'does he give us no information? Why is he silent when we are wondering and considering what has happened to that little girl?'

Nodder was found guilty and sentenced to seven years' penal servitude. But Mr. Justice Swift, like the police, had the gravest misgivings about Mona Tinsley's fate. 'You will probably spend many of your nights while you are serving this sentence wondering if this little girl has been found,' he told Nodder sternly. 'This thought may spoil much of your sleep. For you may rest assured that if she *is* found, and if harm has come to her, you will be brought back into that dock again.'

Some weeks later the body of Mona Tinsley was recovered from the River Idle, a ligature around her neck showing that she had been strangled before being put into the water. True to Mr. Justice Swift's grim prophecy, Nodder was tried again, at Nottingham Assizes before Mr. Justice MacNaghten. Again the same counsel led for the prosecution and defence. The jury found Nodder Guilty of murder. The black cap was placed on the Judge's head. 'Frederick Nodder,' said Mr. Justice MacNaghten, addressing the prisoner, 'the jury by their verdict have found that you murdered Mona Lilian Tinsley. Justice has slowly but surely overtaken you, and it only remains for me to pronounce the sentence which the law and justice require.' He then pronounced the death sentence, which, after the dismissal of Nodder's appeal by the Court of Criminal Appeal on December 13th, 1937, was duly carried out.

CHAPTER XXV

On the Brink

TWO MORE YEARS, two precious, adventure-packed years now remained to Birkett before Europe was to be enveloped in the flames of Fascist aggression, the evil tyranny whose real nature he had foreseen and warned against years ago. The golden age of the advocate was fading, and he remained its greatest and most faithful exemplar.

In 1938 he once again refused a judgeship. The King, however, approved his appointment to be a Commissioner of Assize on the Midland Circuit, where he first practised as a junior barrister, in the place of Mr. Justice Finlay, who was presiding over a Commission in London. When there is particular pressure of business a distinguished barrister may be made a Commissioner of Assize either for a single occasion or, as in this case, under a more comprehensive commission with the same status as an Assize Judge.

The year had started with a very moving case, in which Birkett defended, at Leicester Assizes, a seventeen-year-old boy, accused of murdering his father. The boy was found Not Guilty of murder, but Guilty of manslaughter 'under great provocation'. It had been an unhappy home, and women wept in the public gallery as Birkett spoke of the home 'where misery, long-drawn, reigned day in and day out. It is impossible to measure the slow corrosion of the years, and I ask you to think, as the head and front of this matter, that the dead man was the author of that misery.

'Here is this boy, not yet eighteen, whose only fault was this overmastering love for his mother, whom he believed to be in danger.' The boy, terrified for his mother's safety in face of incessant attacks and threats from the dead man, had killed his father with a hatchet.

Mr. Justice Finlay, in sentencing the boy to twelve months in the second division, paid tribute to Mr. Birkett, who, sought after by every solicitor and able to command over 1,000 guineas for an Assize Court case, had at the urgent representation of a friend, Mr. R. P. Marchant, a Mansfield solicitor, undertaken this defence under the Poor Prisoners Defence Act for a fee of £15 15s.

The Judge said: 'I rejoice, and everyone must rejoice, at the tribute to English justice that the accused, having no means, had been defended in such an admirable and skilful manner.' Defending counsel and solicitor had, said Mr. Justice Finlay, rendered a public service.

Birkett's first job as a Commissioner of Assize was to try the case of a servant girl of twenty-three whose muddled, wayward life was going from bad to worse despite six reformative months in a Borstal Institution. For her own good—to give her time to think and re-orientate—Birkett sentenced her to six months imprisonment, telling her in a fatherly way to mend her ways 'because otherwise I can see before you a life of very great misery'.

A special juror summoned to serve at Bedfordshire Assizes was so impressed by Birkett's handling of the cases before him that he wrote to him a personal letter saying: 'Your kindness and humanity to those in the criminal proceedings and patience in all, greatly impressed me and made one proud of British Justice.' The reference to 'humanity' touched Birkett deeply, and in a charming reply he assured the juror that of all the descriptions that could be applied to his work as a Judge, there was none he could value more.

It is a fact that in early life Birkett's health gave rise to anxiety, and that periodically he was ill for weeks and even months on end in the years ahead; yet in between these spells of ill health his vitality was amazing. It was not simply the mass of paper work, the time taken in consultations and so on, but the actual physical exertion of travel and rush. Late in 1937, for example, he had given himself a tiring first visit to North America as the guest of the Canadian Bar Association. A few weeks later he interrupted his busy practice to be a Commissioner of Assize; he found time to inspect and buy eighty-four acres of sheep farm in Lakeland to save it from speculative builders. He campaigned for national parks; presided over the Dickens Fellowship celebrations, speaking for forty minutes without benefit of a note (a feat which brought him a tribute from the Lord Chief Justice); found time to attend sittings of a Home Office committee on abortion, and presided over the sixth annual meeting of the Institute for the Scientific Treatment of Delinquency.

The last two activities were fitted into a day when he was defending Edward Chaplin in a sensational murder trial at the Old

Bailey, which monopolised his morning and afternoon. In the early evening he attended the Inter-Departmental Committee on Abortion, as Chairman; at eight-thirty he spoke at the Institute for the Scientific Treatment of Delinquency.

His plea to make Lakeland a National Park was one which he was to make with insistence and eloquence for the rest of his life. By 'National Park', he explained, he meant just leaving Lakeland as it was. He also inveighed, prophetically enough, against the arbitrary and all-too-comprehensive powers of the Official Secrets Act of 1911, especially Section 2, which made it an offence to disclose without authorisation any information to which a person had had access by reason of holding office under the Crown. Such information need not be confidential; it was sufficient that its disclosure had not been specifically authorised. It meant, he said, that journalists, M.P.s, Civil Servants and policemen were committing offences every day of their lives, by giving information which was not confidential but had not received express authorisation.

That the powers conferred by this Act, whose original purpose was to prevent and punish espionage, are inordinate is true even today; an emergency measure, permitting the State arbitrary powers in times of exceptional and grave crisis, has become an inherent part of the country's legal system, ensuring that wherever the real or imaginary interests of the country are concerned, the State has the last word.

Norman Birkett did not pursue this line of thought as energetically as he did some of his other interests, such as the protection of Lakeland; the same may be said of his association with the Institute for the Scientific Treatment of Delinquency. Although a kindly man, Birkett felt that while justice must be measured with mercy, society must be protected against those who were too 'far gone' to benefit from psychiatry. Some crimes were too appalling to justify any hope that the culprit could or should be rehabilitated.

The Institute for the Scientific Treatment of Delinquency was at the time of its formation in 1932 the only organisation in the world devoted exclusively to scientific research into the causes and prevention of crime. It maintained (as it still does) an observation centre in Mayfair for the diagnosis and treatment of delinquents, the workers, including scientists and psychiatrists, being unpaid. Cases referred to the Institute ranged from juveniles to adults, from sexual perversion to shoplifting, from violence to attempted suicide.

Much aggression is psychiatric in origin, and many a child's mind (and an adult's, for that matter) has been untangled by this pioneering organisation.

Birkett gave the Institute moral support and was in general sympathy with its objects. Dr. Edward Glover, M.D., LL.D., Chairman of the Institute, told me, 'I found he had little interest in the deeper aspects of modern psychology and perhaps thought we were a rather cranky body. But he was sympathetic to "good causes" and carried out his duties with his accustomed charm and efficiency. He was essentially a lawyer, although with a breadth of cultural interest unusual in lawyers. He was also a "liberal" in the general as well as the political sense of that term, and it was perhaps because he realised the liberal aspirations of the I.S.T.D. that he was ready to support it. I would have called him "one of our good friends", but not in any sense a "revolutionary", and in its time the I.S.T.D. has been a quietly revolutionary body. He was curiously enough quite conservative on the issue of "criminal responsibility" and was not too keen on extending the authority of the psychiatrist in criminological matters.'

Where law and order and the stability of society were concerned, Birkett could be very conservative. He upheld capital punishment for certain offences, condemned several people to death by hanging, sentenced one man to be flogged and—in wartime—sentenced a young man of twenty-three to death after a secret trial. In all these cases, I do not doubt, he wished to make the punishment as salutary as the crime was heinous, for the protection of the majority. Even so, the point is worth noting; there was mettle behind the mildness.

Increasingly, before war broke out, Birkett was drawn into voluntary Government work. He was appointed by the Lord Chancellor a member of the committee, under Mr. Justice Hodson, to consider the administration and working of the Poor Persons Rules and report whether any amendments were necessary. Meanwhile, after two hard years of voluntary effort as Chairman of the Inter-Departmental Committee on Abortion, its report was made public.

Its main recommendations were that the law should be clarified to make it plain that abortion can be legal where it is necessary to save life or avert permanent damage to health. It expressed its strong opposition on ethical, social and medical grounds to any broad relaxation of the existing law, and although it would have welcomed any feasible means of terminating pregnancies resulting from rape, it could suggest no workable formula by which this could be done.

At the same time Birkett joined yet another committee—the Libel Law Committee, which, under Lord Porter, was asked to examine the law of defamation and to report on any changes it might think desirable in the existing law. Few members of that committee could have had more, if as much, experience of libel actions as Norman Birkett; they had always been an important and lucrative part of his practice.

It was on the eve of war that Mr. Birkett met his match in court and was thoroughly out-argued by a litigant who had only recently studied law in her spare time.

Mrs. Florence Borders and her husband Jim had bought a house on mortgage, and found it showed a number of unexpected faults: cracks appeared in the ceiling, floors squeaked and plaster began to fall. Mrs. Borders, dissatisfied, formed a federation of tenants and tenants' associations, studied law in her spare time at the London School of Economics and determined to challenge the building societies, some of which were putting up 'jerry-built' houses. Meanwhile, she withheld mortgage payments.

Being too poor to afford a lawyer, she defended herself when the building society brought a claim against her, bringing a counter-claim for £500, alleging misrepresentation on the value of the house. The Judge dismissed both actions, leaving Mrs. Borders clear title to her house, but disallowing her counter-claim. Soon 500 tenants intentionally defaulted.

Norman Birkett was at a loss how to handle this intelligent, fast-hitting witness when, in a later action, her husband sued the building society for libel in connection with a letter sent to the building society by their solicitors. The crowded court enjoyed the interchanges between Birkett and Mrs. Borders:

Birkett: 'You have acquired the title of "The Tenants' K.C."?'

Mrs. Borders: 'I have heard of it.'

'All the world knows of it?'—'Thank you.'

'You are a woman of strong, independent mind?'—'I would rather let the world say as to that.'

'You have a head for these things?'—'I have a head for many things.'

'A business head?'—'I have always considered myself merely as a housewife.'

Replying to another question, Mrs. Borders caused roars of laughter in court by retorting: 'There may not be any difference between Mr. and Mrs. Birkett, but there is a difference between Mr. and Mrs. Borders!'

Birkett was near to losing his temper, something that never quite happened. 'Do you think it smart to introduce the name of my wife?' he asked sternly. 'No,' said Mrs. Borders calmly. 'You were suggesting a particular relationship between husband and wife, and I was trying to explain it.'

'You are getting accustomed to litigation?'—'This is the first time I have had the pleasure of meeting you, Mr. Birkett.'

Some were amused at the spectacle of a woman who had learned law in her spare time getting the better of the most brilliant master of cross-examination at the Bar. Norman Birkett was not, least of all when Jim Borders won the day with an award of £150. However, his annoyance did not last. He was too magnanimous a man to begrudge a woman the rewards of her persistence and study.

CHAPTER XXVI

War—and Change

WITH THE COMING of the Second World War the entire pattern of his life was changed. His life was as crowded as ever, but some strains were greater and the satisfactions fewer. It wasn't simply the austere rations, the lugubrious blackout that seemed a symbol of Europe's fate, nor the air raids and the streets littered with rubble, crazily tilting timbers and broken glass. The change he had so long dreaded could no longer be delayed; he must leave the Bar, which had been his love during the most fruitful, exciting and satisfying years of his life.

In September 1939 Norman Birkett was made chairman of the Home Office Advisory Committee which dealt with cases of detention under Defence Regulation 18b. He was chosen deliberately because of his exemplary patience and sense of humanity, and some such influence was needed to mitigate, at least, the operation of a regulation alien to most concepts of British justice. It is obviously repugnant that any Home Secretary, however enlightened, should have the power to order the detention of people without trial, but the harsh realities of war demanded it.

With Birkett on this committee were Dr. J. J. Mallon, Sir A. G. Hazlerigg, Professor W. E. Collinson, Miss Violet Malcolm and Sir George Clarke.

It was a prodigious task, because although not everyone detained asserted their right of appeal to Mr. Birkett's tribunal, a great number did—and in the early days of the 1940 invasion scare 27,261 'enemy aliens' were interned. That number included, quite certainly, many who were aliens but not enemies— it was an unfair aspect of this regulation that many might think it implied a stigma, although the grounds on which detention was made were seldom stated or sustained. There were political detainees, too. Sir Oswald Mosley and eight other prominent members of the British Union of Fascists were arrested under this regulation.

It is a strange coincidence that Sir Oswald Mosley, who had

coped effectively with Norman Birkett's searching cross-examination during the libel action against the *Star*, should find himself arguing once again the merits of his beliefs and the purposes of his Fascist Party before Norman Birkett. In fact, he argued his case for a whole day—without avail.

Birkett was equally adamant in upholding the Home Secretary's right to detain Captain A. H. M. Ramsay, M.P., whose arrest was the subject of a protest to the Committee of Privileges. Captain Ramsay claimed that although he appealed to Birkett's committee on the day of his arrest, eight weeks elapsed (in prison) before he appeared before them, that he was not permitted a solicitor to speak for him or allowed to call a witness in his defence. However, in his case, as in the case of Mosley, the Advisory Committee recommended that his detention should continue.

Such measures must, of course, be judged against the background of circumstances prevailing at that time; it is certain that they were administered with more tolerance and respect for the individual than would have been the case, in time of war, in any other country in the world. Indeed, by November 1941 only 8,663 aliens remained interned, and Norman Birkett liked to say, with pride, that of those released, none had given any trouble.

In consultation with the Ministry of Information, the wartime clearing-house of official information and the medium for censorship, the B.B.C. asked Norman Birkett if he would broadcast to home listeners on different aspects of the war. Basically, his talks —given under the pseudonym of 'Onlooker'—were meant to help morale.

Some thought Birkett a poor choice for the role of propagandist, lacking fire and punch and altogether too academic in his approach to the problems raised by war. This criticism was misconceived. Despite air raids and the imminence of Nazi invasion, morale in Britain was very good, even in London, then reeling under the blitz. Birkett stood for certain values that were quite the opposite of everything that the Nazi creed embraced. His thoughtful, quiet, confident appraisals, with their sprinklings of apt quotation and reasoned optimism, had a large and appreciative public.

It was considered policy, too, not to compete with Mussolini or Hitler in frenzied polemics.

So Birkett's routine was changing fast. He was still in practice, but had less time to devote to litigation. He lived at his country house at Chalfont St. Giles with Mrs. Birkett and his daughter Linnea, relaxing occasionally with his books or in the garden, or helping his wife and daughter to care for the evacuated children to whom they gave refuge from the air raids until more permanent accommodation could be found for them. Michael Birkett was at Stowe School. Linnea, a keen musician, would play on the pianoforte once used by Rachmaninoff and Toscanini.

The Birketts kept open house to Canadian airmen whose bomber squadron, commanded by Wing Commander L. F. Fraser, D.F.C., a former Canadian bush pilot, was stationed in the vicinity. Sometimes they would pay a return visit to the officers' mess, to which they presented a dozen silver tankards.

Soon, inevitably, the word got round the Temple that 'Onlooker', who broadcast on the B.B.C. was Mr. Birkett. Who could doubt that voice? It had been heard in courts all over Britain; its well-modulated inflexions, the contrast of the rise and fall in tone, the eloquent pauses and well-clipped enunciation (a legacy of the days in his youth when, with iron persistence, he had all but obliterated his Lancashire accent) were unmistakable.

War breeds hysteria, but happily there were none of those public disturbances that disgraced Britain in the First World War, where any German or foreigner with a pronounced accent might find his furniture pitched through the windows of his home. There had been such an influx of refugees from Hitler before the war that the British were well used to foreigners in their midst. But some of these refugees, deeply ashamed at the enormities committed in the name of the country from which they had had to fly, felt uneasy—might not the British public think they were spies? Norman Birkett appealed, in one of his broadcasts, to people not to regard these 74,000 Germans and Austrians as spies. Most were victims of Nazi oppression, he said, and felt the most burning hatred of the Nazi system.

It was essential, he said, that unreasoning panic should not be allowed to get control. The hounding and persecution of helpless individuals, and the stigmatising of foreigners as 'spies' did not help national security. How many other men, I wonder, would have spoken up for the nationals in our midst of the country with which we were at war? His action was typical of his sane sense of values; we must keep our humanity, he insisted. The war was being fought to preserve it, not to risk contamination by the very evils we sought to abolish.

The strain of long hours and the difficulties of wartime travel began to tell on him, and in 1940 he was taken ill, the B.B.C. fixing a microphone in his home at Chalfont to save him the fatigue of a journey to the studio.

In June 1941 came the announcement that the King had conferred a knighthood on Mr. Birkett. At the same time Lord Halifax, British Ambassador in the United States, was repeatedly urging upon the home Government the need to send out to America some distinguished speakers who could put over Britain's case. America needed to realise that Britain was straining every sinew against the Nazi onslaught; that, with her Allies, she would certainly turn the tide and carry the battle into the enemy's camp (it sounds feasible now, but at that time all Europe had been engulfed, only bomb-battered Britain holding the flag of defiance aloft). The mission was not as simple as it looked. Sentimental and historical bonds do indeed bind and link America and Britain, but finance and politics often operate according to laws of their own. There were elements not exactly displeased at the prospect of Britain's empire facing disintegration. Even Roosevelt was at times more preoccupied with this thought than with the possibilities of post-war Soviet expansion. In some parts of America Nazi propagandists played cleverly on isolationist sympathies.

Norman Birkett had never flown before, and although enthused by his mission, was already rather tired before he began his long and arduous journeyings. He travelled 30,000 miles in a few weeks, in a succession of plane flights and train journeys, often arriving at his hotel late at night, keeping on the move for seven days a week.

Certainly Birkett put immense work and thought into the speeches that he gave, even though he gave the impression, in delivery, of effortless spontaneity. He quoted, with great effect, part of a speech made by Mr. Hughes, President of the American Bar Association in Westminster Hall in 1924:

'We come here to tighten the bonds of friendship . . . we come in the spirit of fraternity . . . because it is in truth the spirit of the larger fellowship represented here today, in which differences of particular interest and environment cannot avail to obscure the

community of tradition of those who have been trained according to the standards and the methods of the Common Law. We
come with even a larger aim than the enjoyment of fraternal association in order that by these agreeable interchanges and a more
intimate knowledge of each other, we may promote a clearer
appreciation of our privilege, opportunity and responsibility
as ministers of justice in a world which needs justice and the
reasonableness which makes justice possible.'

In his speech 'The Ties That Bind' to the American Bar Association at Indianapolis Birkett spoke for over two hours without
a single note. He outlined Britain's struggle, showed by example
how Britain and America have common standards of freedom
and justice and finished, as Mr. Winston Churchill did, with the
lines:

> *Say not the struggle naught availeth,*
> *The labour and the wounds are vain,*
> *The enemy faints not nor faileth*
> *And as things have been, they remain . . .*

> *If hopes were dupes, fears may be liars;*
> *It may be in yon smoke concealed*
> *Your comrades chase e'en now the fliers*
> *And but for you, possess the field.*

> *For while the tired waves vainly breaking*
> *Seem here no painful inch to gain,*
> *Far back through creeks and inlets making*
> *Comes silent, flooding in, the main.*

> *And not by eastern windows only,*
> *When daylight comes, comes in the light,*
> *In front, the sun climbs slow, how slowly,*
> *But westward, look, the land is bright.*

Those who heard that speech, and Birkett's mellifluous render-
ing of Arthur Hugh Clough's beautiful lines, included many a
hardened American lawyer visibly in tears. The poet's words had
acquired a prophetic ring, declaimed by a lawyer who in many
ways was at heart a poet. As Norman Birkett finished, his audience rose with one accord and applauded loud and long.

Sir Norman's talks were favourably reported upon by the
British Embassy, although Lord Halifax, at whose initiative the

whole thing had been arranged, must have been amused to hear that some Americans had suggested to the British Government that Birkett ought to be their Ambassador in the United States.

Later in 1941 came the announcement that Sir Norman had been made a Judge of the High Court on the death of Mr. Justice Hawke. Birkett had long dreaded it. Now, in wartime, he could not possibly refuse a third time. It meant, as he well knew, a final and irrevocable break with the Bar as an advocate; his position would now be more remote. By temperament he was an actor, finding in law the perfect medium for his talent; he liked to hold the floor, to answer as an individual the challenge of a difficult problem, to win a jury over to his client's point of view.

It was a sad day he had to tell Edgar Bowker, his faithful clerk, that he had accepted the judgeship and that for them this must be the parting of the ways. But it was not the end of their long and happy association. Bowker asked to go with him as Judge's clerk. As this would mean a financial sacrifice to Bowker, Birkett could not possibly have suggested such a thing himself; but he was relieved and delighted at Bowker's decision. For Birkett, too, his elevation implied a very heavy financial loss. The judge's salary of £5,000 was fixed when taxation hardly existed, and when money was worth several times what it was then. At one time indeed £5,000 a year was a fabulous income, the idea being that judges must be beyond all financial care, and so invulnerable to corruption.

A drop from £30,000 a year to a mere £5,000 did not worry him.

Lord Halifax had requested that Birkett should pay the United States a return visit, and in April 1942 Birkett flew to Lisbon *en route* to America. It is probable that, even as he passed through Lisbon, a drama was being enacted which was later to involve him; for Lisbon was, like Stockholm, a busy spy centre, a rare piece of neutral territory. A spy was at about that time wresting secrets from a pitiably amateur traitor who was, within a few months, to appear on trial for his life before Birkett at the Old Bailey.

Once again Birkett assayed the tiring Atlantic flight—he had made a pre-war visit to North America by passenger liner—and again he found himself caught up in a restless whirl of plane-catching, hurrying for trains and coaches, living in one suit and out of one suitcase, gulping down scratch meals and rushing from studio to lecture-hall. He told a San Francisco audience that when he arrived at New York in the one and only suit he was allowed to bring, he 'looked like a tent after a high wind'.

In Detroit he addressed two hundred members of the Detroit Bar Association, where he impressed them immensely by his understanding of American history and superb spoken English. He stressed Anglo-American responsibility for maintaining 'real democracy in the world that will follow the peace' and also convulsed his audience with laughter as he described his bewildered reactions to an American baseball match.

During his stay in Detroit Sir Norman was shown over the Chrysler plant and Ford's Willow Run factory, and, it would seem, was either misled by his escorts or misunderstood what he heard and saw. For in a talk to the Overseas League in London on his return, he declared that American production would stagger the world. 'I was invited to factories which staggered the imagination,' he said. 'At Willow Run I saw endless miles of machinery turning out a Liberator every hour.'

Clearly Sir Norman was trying to encourage his home audience, but it is certain that he did *not* see a Liberator an hour being turned out at Willow Run, because only a few weeks before his visit Lieutenant-General Brehob B. Somervell, United States Army Supply Chief, had spoken sharply to Detroit, saying: 'Not a man, machine or plant is producing to full capacity.' Willow Run certainly was and is a breathtaking sight, but at the time Birkett saw it, it had not completed one plane on its assembly lines and was working at only a fraction of its normal capacity. Detroit, always a city of violent extremes, had been seething with industrial disputes, and shortly after he left a labour squabble caused the closure of three war plants employing 10,000 men.

Birkett's statement was cabled back to the United States by the London office of the *New York Times*; it ill accorded with the statement published at the same time in *Life* magazine that 'wildcat strikes and sitdowns, material shortages and poor planning at the top have cut into Detroit's production of war weapons'. On tanks and guns, Detroit was ahead of schedule; on planes it was woefully behind. *Life*'s comment on Birkett's speech was: 'Sir Norman was seeing things that weren't there.'

CHAPTER XXVII

Death of a Spy

As a Judge Norman Birkett may not be remembered for any outstanding judgements. But he brought to his elevated task a humanity, knowledge of human frailty and passion, and patience which made a memorable impression on all who saw him at work. The scarlet and ermine robes, used when trying criminal cases, seemed expressive of responsibility rather than of power. There was rapt attention in his manner, a quiet concentration; no longer so much projection of his own personality, but still that immense capacity for detail.

The first case he tried, at the Old Bailey, was of an unmarried mother charged with infanticide; it was a particularly sad case of an inexperienced woman torn between love and despair, and Mr. Justice Birkett, feeling that her cup of sorrow was already brimmed over, bound her over. A soldier, too, caught in the toils of a pitiful emotional entanglement, and charged with attempted murder, he sentenced to only two days imprisonment—which meant his immediate release.

As a Judge, however, Birkett could distinguish between sentiment and sentimentality. To Alexander C. Scott-Ford, a twenty-one-year-old merchant seaman, tried before him under the Treachery Act for betraying defence secrets to the German Intelligence Service, he had no mercy to offer.

It is difficult to imagine a more base and more futile act of treachery.

Scott-Ford a native of Plymouth, while serving in the Royal Navy before the war, fell desperately in love with a young German girl, and had indeed been discharged from the Royal Navy with ignominy after a sentence of imprisonment for falsifying his pay-book—a piece of dishonesty occasioned by his desire to impress the girl.

When war broke out the girl returned to Germany, and Scott-Ford, was desperately anxious to get in touch with her. He joined the Merchant Navy, and one day, when the ship put in at Lisbon, he made a round of the night clubs and was accosted by an enemy agent. The agent, hearing of his difficulty in getting in touch with his sweetheart, guaranteed that she would receive any letters Scott-Ford chose to write to her.

In return, Scott-Ford gave the agent information not only about his own ship but of the movements of convoys between Lisbon and Great Britain. One convoy was attacked with loss of life, including some of his former shipmates. For this appalling act the young man received (in addition to the favour of his letters being delivered to his German girl-friend) a mere £18 in cash. On his return to Britain, Scott-Ford, on German instructions, toured public-houses, mixing with seamen and pumping them for information, which, on his next visit to Lisbon, he handed over to the enemy agent.

On asking for more money, however, he was curtly told that he must do as instructed without making demands, and that if he did not he would be exposed to the British authorities. Having no other means of livelihood, he had, perforce, to continue in his job and, at the same time—under the double threat that he himself might be exposed and his girl friend in Germany maltreated —pass on information to the Germans.

Lisbon was well known, like Stockholm, as a clearing house of spies of all nations, but as attacks on convoys were stepped up, so security measures were tightened. Suspicion fell upon Scott-Ford; he talked too much in drink, and on return to England he was arrested.

The trial at the Old Bailey was held *in camera*. The prisoner was ably defended, under the Poor Person's Rules, by Mr. Anthony Hawke, was found guilty and sentenced to death by hanging. At that time (October 16th, 1942) he was the third British subject to be hanged for treachery during the war, the other two being a sea-going engineer and a native of Gibraltar. Eight other enemy agents had been executed—four German, two Dutch, one Swiss and one Belgian. Scott-Ford was hanged at Wandsworth Prison eighteen days after his trial. He did not appeal to the Court of Criminal Appeal, for at the time of his arrest the evidence of his guilt was overwhelming. He was in possession of memoranda which gave the position and names of ships and their escorts in the convoy in which he returned for the last time to Britain. There were also particulars of the speed, course, distance travelled, a log of the voyage, description of weather conditions and the aircraft protection provided.

How did Norman Birkett feel as the black cap was placed upon his head and he found himself uttering the dread words of doom upon a fellow-mortal? He said afterwards that he felt no emotion whatever. There was, Birkett declared, something remote about the Judge's role.

During 1943, probably as an aftermath of the two exhausting tours of Canada and the United States, Birkett was taken very ill in court at York, and for the next eight months was nursed by his family slowly and patiently back to health. The bitter winter found him fit again, but with a depleted stamina that limited, irrevocably, his recreational activities for the rest of his life, going the gruelling rounds of a circuit Judge, out in all weathers, rushing from town to town, walking with measured and dignified gait in the processions to the Assizes.

In the King's Bench Division Birkett gave judgement for Mr. Learie Constantine, a British subject from the West Indies and a famous cricketer, who had been refused accommodation at a London hotel. He held that the hotel was a common inn duty bound to provide accommodation to travellers, and that although Constantine was a man of colour, no ground existed on which they were entitled to refuse him.

In the box Leary Constantine conducted himself with great dignity and modesty, Sir Norman declared, dealt with all questions with intelligence and truth, was not concerned to be vindictive or malicious, but was obviously affected by the indignity and humiliation which had been put on him and occasioned him such distress.

Birkett had given much anxious thought to this case, which he regarded as a serious one, for the plight of coloured British subjects of good character when they applied for accommodation was far from satisfactory. But he awarded only nominal damages.

How often must Birkett have wished that he was on the floor of the court, fighting the case, rather than sitting in judgement! He admitted as much later in life. Being a Judge was in some respects a disappointment for him, the loss of something precious, something necessary to him, for which there was no substitute. Yet there was still scope for imagination, for his special gift of getting beneath the surface of things. In a tragic case at Birmingham Assizes of a mother who had gassed her son because he was suffering from an incurable disease he bound the mother over, feeling she had suffered enough.

Later, however, he tried a case in which the degree of inhumanity displayed was as bad as any of the enormities of the Nazis. At Denbighshire Assizes he sentenced a husband to twelve years in gaol for the manslaughter of his wife by neglecting her. 'I have been stunned almost beyond expression by the revelation of human suffering in this case,' he declared. 'Here was a woman dying slowly of starvation, the only person in the house being a man of very low intelligence, who left her without food, clothing and attention. Yet nothing was done. She was removed to hospital only one day before she died. No official warnings of any kind were addressed to the husband.' The wretched woman had fractures of both legs, neither of which had been treated, and had died of starvation.

That Birkett, though holding fast to those principles of justice and order considered essential to well-organised society, was a merciful judge, is generally accepted. He *was* capable of great kindness when he believed the circumstances justified it; one cannot imagine Mr. Justice Avory, for example, binding over a woman who had pleaded guilty to killing her son because he had an incurable disease. More unusual still in a Judge, Sir Norman Birkett would cheerfully admit himself to be in the wrong if he subsequently discovered that he had been.

A case in point occurred at Chester Assizes in 1945. A twenty-two-year-old sailor from Manchester had pleaded guilty to office-breaking and larceny, and Birkett had ordered him to be sent to a Borstal institution for three years. Having made this order, Birkett found on reading the Probation Officer's report on the young man that he had never previously been in trouble, that he had been serving in one of His Majesty's ships when it struck a rock in Norwegian waters, was in the *Ark Royal* when she was sunk and was severely wounded and suffered from frostbite while on convoy duty.

Birkett knew what grim hazards sailors had accepted throughout the war, and his heart warmed to this man, who, when his whole future could be affected by the court's decision, had been too modest to mention his praiseworthy war record. Birkett changed his mind. Why, he asked the young man, when he was once more brought before him, did he not reveal those facts?

'I did not want to rest on my laurels,' the young man replied. Birkett looked straight into that open, frank face, pondering why it was a man of principle should have drifted into crime; here was an instance where good and evil were at war in the individual, but where, in a personal crisis, self-interest had been subordinated to principle. Birkett decided to stake his faith on the better side of the man's nature, changed his mind, quashed the order to Borstal and bound the man over for two years. He left the court a free man, telling a friend, 'If ever there was a gentleman in England, it's that Judge. . . . I couldn't drag the Navy in. I was too proud of it.'

In his judgement on three anarchists tried at the Old Bailey for conspiracy 'to endeavour to seduce members of the Forces from their duty' Sir Norman Birkett was rather more severe. Anarchists, despite the sinister implications of the word, are in Britain at least harmless people whose vehemence is confined to the printed word. Disliking all authority, anarchists do not acknowledge the validity of the Armed Forces of any nation and one feels that the authorities were lacking in humour and rather heavy-handed in bringing this particular prosecution. Nobody was 'disaffected' by the paper circulated in a very limited way to a few members of the Forces. However, there was a war on, and Norman Birkett, with uneasy memories of the spy trial, which had shown him where disaffection could lead a man, passed sentences of nine months imprisonment on three of those concerned.

Shortly before the war finished, Birkett made legal history with one judgement. It was to the effect that a trade union can be libelled. In hearing a complaint from the National Union of General and Municipal Workers concerning a circular issued to officials of the Chemical Workers' Union he held that a trade union can be libelled. It is a legal entity and 'it would be strange if this trade union was unable to come to court to claim redress for something which most vitally and most injuriously affects its true interests'. It had long been considered that a trade union could be libelled, but Birkett's was the first positive ruling.

At this time, too, Birkett had some experience of crime from another angle—his country home at Chalfont St. Giles was robbed.

CHAPTER XXVIII

Justice at Nuremberg

IT IS A tribute indeed to Norman Birkett's amazing career that, when the Second World War finished, he, the draper's son, should have been chosen together with Lord Justice Lawrence, to represent Britain at the Nuremberg Trials—the most spectacular tribunal ever assembled—to consider the most hideous catalogue of crime ever compiled.

The Lord Chancellor's choice fell upon Birkett because he embodied all those requirements, seldom found in combination, necessary to a task so immense and unique. His flair for applying himself to great masses of detail and bringing them into due form; his unassailable fairness and common sense; his feeling for humanity, for the millions of dead, injured and wronged who might not speak for themselves; his clear-headedness and lack of excitability; all these were sorely needed.

That such a trial would follow the war was forecast in a statement issued by President Roosevelt on October 7th, 1942, from the White House that 'the successful close of this war shall include provisions for the surrender to the United Nations of war criminals'. A Soviet note a week later underscored this decision, while the Moscow Declaration of 1943, signed by Mr. Winston Churchill, President Roosevelt and Stalin, confirmed that 'the major criminals whose offences have no particular localisation will be punished by joint decision of the Governments of the Allies'.

Again, at Yalta, the Allies declared that 'war criminals shall be justly and swiftly punished'.

But did Britain *really* want the Nuremberg trial? An *aide-memoire* from Sir Alexander Cadogan of the Foreign Office to Judge Rosenman on April 23rd, 1945, suggested that 'the preferable course in the case of Hitler and a number of arch-criminals associated with him' would be execution without trial. Whose views did this *aide-memoire* reflect—those of the Foreign Office, the Cabinet as a whole or Mr. Winston Churchill? Mr. Churchill has since written that the idea of executing a nation's leaders after defeat 'will certainly stir them to fight to the bitter end in any future war. . . .'

America, France and Russia wanted the trial, however, and at the San Francisco Conference in May 1945 Mr. Eden, on behalf of the United Kingdom, accepted the principle of the trial of war criminals by an international tribunal. Each of the four Governments should prepare its prosecutions, each would contribute two Judges to the tribunal.

The 24,000-word indictment was of planning and waging aggressive war, committing war crimes and of crimes against humanity. Apart from the testimony which the four countries could produce from their own witnesses and documentation, a mountain of damnatory evidence was available from the Germans themselves—nearly 500 tons of crated papers from the German Foreign Office were found in a castle at Marburg, 300 crates of German High Command files and all the files of the German Navy, to mention only a few sources.

Besides this tremendous volume of documentation, reports came in from the occupied countries, illustrated by photographs, as with the French album *Crimes Hitleriens*, of crimes against civilians.

For a year—from November 1945 until October 1946—Sir Norman lived in Germany, in a house about ten miles from Nuremberg, often sitting in the courtroom for more than twelve hours at a time. Often in his lifetime he had prosecuted or defended individual murderers; the trial of an individual might take weeks. But here millions upon millions of murders were at issue, and the mountains of evidence would appal any man.

The physical strain of this extraordinary trial apart, can anyone estimate the *mental* effect of all this horror upon a man of Birkett's sensibility? The annihilation of villages; the killing and torturing of millions of civilians; the gas chambers, the concentration camps —could anyone have believed that human nature could sink so low? I myself wondered, during the war, whether some stories might not have been exaggerated; later, seeing for myself the pyramids of human ash at Terezin concentration camp in Czechoslovakia, I knew it had really happened; there, too, were thoussands of little cardboard boxes like sugar cartons, each containing the remains of one human being, each numbered and named and kept until the statistics of destruction were accepted by Berlin.

The trial was a nightmare of hellish photographs, horrifying films, appalling statements; the danger was that with such a surfeit of horror one might cease to feel, cease to react any more.

Yet with all this strain Norman Birkett remained cheerful, clear-headed and patient, and earned the admiration of Americans, Russians and French alike. At first the two Russian Judges, who alone of all of them wore uniform, Major-General I. T. Nikitchenko and Colonel A. F. Volchov, were stand-offish, but Birkett's quiet, friendly demeanour soon thawed them. He sat next to Nikitchenko throughout all the hearings, and the two became firm friends. Eventually, when the trial was over they parted with promises to keep in touch. Birkett sent him a magnificent volume of photographs, fountain pens and other gifts, but these, like his letters, were never acknowledged. The cold war was on.

Lady Birkett kept house for her husband, and once Linnea, now twenty-one years old, who had latterly been working in a war factory, came to Salzburg for the music festival, and stayed with her parents. Michael Birkett was still at Stowe.

Birkett visited Hitler's ruined chancellery. With Mr. Francis Biddle and Mr. John J. Parker, or the Soviet Judges, or M. Donnedieu de Vobres and M. le Conseiller Falco, the French delegates, he would meet off duty and discuss everything from politics to art late into the night. And except for a bout of sunstroke caught while trout-fishing, which put him out of action for a day, Norman Birkett kept very fit, despite the fact that 40 per cent of the lawyers were ill at some time during the trial, and 55 per cent of the journalists had been ill, especially during an influenza epidemic.

Birkett's relaxed informality came as a surprise to the Americans, especially the G.I.s who guarded the court. He would often stop for long, friendly chats with them. With the local barber, too, he was a familiar and friendly visitor. 'I shan't give you much trouble,' Lord Justice Lawrence used to say, 'but wait till you get busy on him!'—indicating Birkett's ginger mane.

With all the strain of the world's greatest trial, Birkett still found time to write to friends. Reading an issue of the *Bournville Works Magazine*, he saw that a correspondent had ascribed some lines, written by an obscure American poet, to the wrong writer. Having no access to his books, and going entirely by memory, he wrote to the magazine and put it right. He had been touched, too, by a Christmas card he had received and hastened to copy it out for the benefit of an old friend in England; it echoed his refusal to give way to despair or cynicism.

> *Oh hurrying years in passing let us keep*
> *Some starry-eyed expectancy aglow:*
> *The thing that children*
> *Waking from their sleep*
> *On Christmas morning know.*

He felt keenly the long exile from England; never had he been away from his country for so long, and the constant recitations of misery and degradation, day in, day out, week in, week out, might have quelled a less-happy spirit.

The course of the trial and verdict of Nuremberg have passed into history; there is no need to repeat them here. But there must surely have been times when Birkett would have preferred to have been an advocate or prosecutor. Judge Jackson, of the United States, was hopelessly outsmarted by Goering. Some of Jackson's questions were far too long, e.g.:

Jackson: 'Now was this leadership principle supported and adopted by you in Germany because you believed that no people are capable of self-government; or because you believed that some may be, but not the German people, or that no matter whether some of us are capable of making our own system, it should not be allowed in Germany?'

Never, in all his forty years at the Bar, did Norman Birkett ask a question of that length. He was a master at asking short, simple questions that elicited vital facts in logical sequence.

In a speech which Birkett made when he returned to Britain, he admitted that there would long be argument as to whether the trial should have been held at all. But during the war, when information of the Nazis' incredible brutalities were known, little more could be done than to warn them that there would be an accounting. He instanced one man who looked like 'an ordinary, respectable citizen, a man with a kindly face, who said that he himself, in one of the concentration camps, had been responsible for the deaths of two million people. His evidence gave a shock of horror to the observers, and taught me never again to rely on the outward appearance as an index of character. People guilty of such things should stand their trial so that the world might know with what horror such behaviour was regarded.'

He thought the trial a fair one. Everyone in court, from Judge to prisoner, could at the touch of a switch listen to what was being said in the language of his choice. No single document was permitted to be used unless it was available to everybody, to counsel and prisoners, in translation. He quoted the boast of Frank, Nazi Governor-General of Poland, who told a meeting of leaders: 'Today, President Roosevelt has said that we are criminals. Gentlemen, we are, we are. But the victor will never be called to account.' Yet I have reason for thinking that on certain aspects of the trial Sir Norman was not entirely happy.

The judgement that made history was typed by Birkett himself on an American Army typewriter. He did it to preserve absolute security. When the trial was over and the judgement delivered (he, like the other Judges, reading part of it) Birkett tried to secure the typewriter as a personal souvenir. Strangely, the U.S. Army would not part with it; he asked the lieutenant in charge of office equipment if he could buy it. The lieutenant referred the matter to his captain, who refused. Birkett approached the commanding general, but red tape still triumphed. He let it go at that.

Sir Norman received no extra payment for these excessively heavy duties. Answering a question in the House of Commons, Sir Frank Soskice, Solicitor-General, said that the cost of sending Mr. Justice Birkett as an associate judge to the Nuremberg Trials was £7,250, of which £5,263 was the personal salary of the judge and his staff—his ordinary statutory salary.

Sir Norman kept an enormous dossier of paper relating to the Nuremberg Trials, intending to make them the basis of a book. Like the writing of his autobiography, it was an ambition he never achieved. As he grew older demands on his time and services increased all the time, making the sustained concentration necessary to the writing of a full-length book impossible.

S

CHAPTER XXIX

Lord Justice of Appeal

BIRKETT LOVED A busy life. The strain of the Nuremberg Trials had come only two years after a long and exhausting illness. Yet on his return to England he became, for the second time, Master of the Curriers Company, one of the City of London's ancient guilds, which dated back to the reign of Henry III. The currier's job was to dress and level leather by the use of the currier's knife, and would seem to have little connection with law. But, like most guilds, it admits people outside the craft, particularly distinguished judges and advocates. Lord Hewart, Lord Chief Justice, was also a currier.

Birkett loved tradition and even ceremony, if it was the means of keeping tradition alive (such as, say, the custom of handing the Judge at the Old Bailey a posy of flowers, originally to counteract the appalling smells from the adjacent cells). He liked the social conviviality of the livery company because, as he once told fellow-liverymen, 'I have found there a refuge from the exhausting labours of my own profession.' Though the function of many of these guilds has either ceased or become attenuated, he did not think their survival an anachronism. 'I think myself that one of the most valuable things in life is a sense of tradition, and I in the fullest sense of the term am a traditionalist, so much so that I do not like people interfering with well-established things.'

He took his son, Michael, into the Currier's, and Norman Birkett's first year of Mastership is commemorated by two loving cups which he commissioned from Omar Ramsden, the distinguished silversmith, bearing on them the words: 'We few, we happy few, we band of brothers.' Sir Norman was Master four times.

The older he became, the greater the range of interests and the demands on his time. As Chairman of the Standing Committee on National Parks he campaigned continually for the preservation of beauty spots 'for the recreation, enjoyment and instruction of the common man'. The Pilgrims Trust, of which he became President, gave scope for his warm feelings towards America, a country he again visited in 1947, accompanied by Lady Birkett and his son Michael.

On that trip he was, in Toronto, the guest of D. L. McCarthy, K.C., Dean of the Ontario Bar, and his address on the art of advocacy at the Law Club attracted the largest gathering ever assembled there. He spoke for over an hour entirely without notes, yet the transcription shows not a wasted or inappropriate word. 'We in Britain,' he told his audience, 'have an unwritten law . . . that every counsel, whoever he may be, has no right to decline any brief that may be offered to him except for good and sufficient reason. I have frequently had to undertake murder cases of the greatest complexity and difficulty, not because I wanted to but because of the unwritten law that I could not refuse them.'

Birkett believed, in the words of Lord Erskine, who undertook the defence of Tom Paine, when he said: 'When the day comes that the advocate in England is permitted to choose whom he will and whom he will not defend, and becomes not the advocate but the judge in the cause, at that moment the liberties of the citizens of England are at an end.' The ideal, said Sir Norman, is that 'the ordinary citizens shall always have at their disposal the man who can protect them, who can defend them, who can stand up before arbitrary power from whatever quarter it may come and assert the inalienable rights of the individual to the eternal freedoms'.

Birkett knew that this was the role of the advocate, and one of the reasons why lawyers as a class can never be very popular, because of the accusation that lawyers affect views which are not their own and champion causes in which they do not personally believe.

The freedom of the Press was one of Birkett's constant themes. He had seen the disastrous results, in Germany, of a press subservient to and shackled by the State, 'As long as that great instrument of freedom, the Press, is allowed to go unfettered in our land, the more hope we have of avoiding these terrible things,' he told members of the Press Club in London. He told the Newspaper Press Fund that 'the importance of a free and fearless Press cannot be over-estimated'.

His views of Press freedom were amply demonstrated by his hearing of the trial at Liverpool Assizes of Mr. James Gaunt, editor-proprietor of the *Morecambe and Heysham Visitor*, for seditious libel following the publication of an article in which he severely criticised the Jews. The views expressed in that article

must have seemed alien to Birkett's ideas, but Gaunt was found
Not Guilty and discharged, following a summing-up in which
Birkett made it clear that the issue was not one of Jew or non-Jew,
but a question of whether a newspaper had the right to say what it
believed to be true, whether it were true or not.

On the subject of the death penalty, Birkett was not wholly
against it, while accepting its limitation to the more atrocious
cases. In 1948, for the first time since the House of Commons
voted to suspend the death sentence for murder and after the
House of Lords rejected the suspension clause in the Criminal
Justice Bill, he passed sentence of death on George Epton, an engineer, for the murder of Miss Winifrid Mulholland. On this occasion, instead of the long and lugubrious address to the prisoner
which ends '. . . and may the Lord have mercy on your soul', he
used the shorter version: 'The sentence of the court on you is the
sentence prescribed by law, namely, that you suffer death by
hanging.'

In 1949 Birkett underwent a dangerous operation, and the
following year was ill yet again.

To young people who had broken the law but whose lives
could be more happily directed by understanding, Birkett as a
Judge showed infinite kindness. At Cambridge Assizes he heard
the case of a girl below sixteen years of age, against whom a
nineteen-year-old soldier had committed an offence; her parents
were willing for her to marry, his would not agree. 'I am not a
marriage broker,' said Birkett, 'but it seems a pity where two
young people are fond of each other and the man is of good character that a bar should be put in their way, particularly where a
child has been born.' After these remarks the soldier's counsel
said that he would apply in court for permission to marry, and
the soldier was conditionally discharged. In another case a girl of
fourteen was expecting a baby, Birkett asked the father: 'Do you
think there is a chance that they will marry?' The father was
against a marriage, and again Birkett discharged the youth conditionally, saying, 'I am not here as a moralist, but you know what
your duty should be with regard to this girl.'

To an eighteen-year-old tractor driver who had married the
the girl, who was fifteen at the time of the offence and had since
had a baby, Birkett spoke words of charity and hope: 'I have
been impressed,' he said, 'by the character you displayed and your

loyalty to the girl. Now that you are man and wife I hope that you will forget all the unhappiness of these past few weeks.'

In all these cases, where the law had been broken, Birkett showed that he could be impatient of forms and practice when these seemed a denial of justice and humanitarianism.

After he was made a Lord Justice of Appeal in 1950—an office he held until his retirement in 1957—Sir Norman Birkett continued to apply the law as an instrument of justice, never forgetting that its purpose was to protect the individual. On one occasion he overruled the Lord Chief Justice, whose award to a workman for the loss of a thumb he considered inadequate. The case of a man suffering from an industrial disease without any legal right to compensation he denounced as a 'monstrous injustice'.

One quirk Birkett did permit himself as a Judge. He would not permit the use of slipshod English if he could prevent it. He hated pretension in language. Why, he asked a Ministry of Works witness, use a non-existent word such as 'finalise'? And to pupils at a Queenswood school he once said, 'I cannot tell you what misery it causes me when I hear said: "Then, my Lord, they were evacuated to alternative accommodation." Nobody thinks of saying: "They were taken to other homes."' In the Court of Appeal the word 'exclusivity' occurred. 'This,' said Birkett 'is a new word to me.' Counsel said it was a word that might come into use, when Birkett said: 'I hope not. Let us stamp on it now.'

To pupils of Leighton Park School he gave, in 1951, a talk to 230 boys on the uses of English. Jargon, he said, was the use of technical words to conceal meaning. But lawyer's jargon, he warned them, could not always be avoided, because he often had to confine himself to the drab, dull and inelegant solely to make his meaning clear. He dismissed the idea that a sentence could never end in a preposition; Bacon, Lamb and some of the world's greatest stylists had done so. He liked simplicity in language, and maintained that the power of Abraham Lincoln's great speech at Gettesburg lay in its simplicity.

Up to the time of his retirement honours came thick and fast. President of the National Book League in succession to Masefield, the Poet Laureate; Chairman of the Court of the University of London from 1946; Treasurer of the Inner Temple in 1956. He was made a Baron in the New Years Honours of 1958.

CHAPTER XXX

Into Retirement

RETIREMENT HAD FEW terrors for Lord Birkett. His life had been so diversified that there was no problem of 'what to do with himself'. There was the Dickens Fellowship—he had always been a lover of Dickens' works, just as he had, only with difficulty, overcome a boyhood revulsion to Sir Walter Scott—and innumerable voluntary societies. Somebody still had to stand on guard against the spoliation of Lakeland, where jerry-builders and pylon erectors would descend in force once vigilance was relaxed. There were his roses in his beautiful garden at Chalfont St. Giles, tended with a gardener's care and love, for memories of the scented rose-shows he attended as a boy in Ulverston lingered with him still.

And, of course, he was in enormous demand as an after-dinner speaker. 'Lord Birkett is coming' was enough to have people stampeding for tickets, with no fear of an empty seat. His humour, urbane, gracious and never malicious, was a delight. Those who heard him give the Foundation Oration at Birkbeck College on the saving grace of humour will long remember him saying that incongruity was often an essential ingredient of humour, and how magnificently he illustrated his point. How, he asked, would Shelley's immortal poem on Ozymandias be diminished if, after the sonorous warning, 'My name is Ozymandias, King of Kings, look on my works, ye mighty, and despair,' the name, 'Emory P. Gray, 17 West 4th Street, Oyster Bay', had been added?

Once, as Chairman of the Court of London University, he was asked to recommend the name of a speaker, the only qualification being that the person chosen had to be a wit. Birkett replied to the effect that he couldn't find a wit, but enclosed the names of two half-wits.

Birkett once described how, when asked to speak to the Law Society at Harvard University, the Dean of the Faculty, in introducing Birkett to the undergraduates, went out of his way to speak about the man who had been invited the time before. He rather bored the audience, because he took the letters of the word Harvard, H for Honour, A for Ambition, R for Reward, V for Virtue and so on, having something to say on each. 'And when the weary undergraduates dispersed,' Birkett related with relish, 'one said to another: "Well, thank God it wasn't the Massachusetts Institute of Technology!"'

But he could tell a joke about himself, too. When he made his first maiden speech in the House of Lords it was not as much an ordeal as the first speech he had made as an M.P. many years before. But he had intended to speak in the debate on crime, mentioning the work of the Institute of Criminology in Cambridge, which had just been founded. One Lord came over to Birkett and said: 'Do you mind if I say a few words before you get up?' 'Not a bit,' replied the new Lord. 'It'll only be a few words,' said the other gratefully, who then got up and said every single thing about the Institute of Criminology which Birkett had intended to say! Hastily, Birkett rejigged his speech on scraps of old envelope.

On one of his visits to America he overheard a piece of repartee which served as a joke at many a dinner (he was apt to get the last bite out of a cherry, and frequently used the same joke for many years). Two Americans were drinking. 'In my State,' said one, 'we have drinks between drinks.' 'In my State,' replied the other, 'we know no such interval.'

Another favourite joke of Birkett's was of the man summoned to pay a bill, who told the Judge, 'As God is my judge, I do not owe the money,' to which the Judge replied in the shortest judgement on record: 'He's not; I am; you do.' In fact, this joke is often wrongly described as having been made by Birkett in passing judgement, but it is not so. Some reports attribute the saying to Judge Cluer, but it has also been ascribed to almost every Judge since Bloody Judge Jeffries.

Twice Lord Birkett was brought out of retirement. In 1957 he was chairman of a committee of three Privy Councillors appointed to enquire into phone-tapping, following the disclosure to an outside body of information obtained by this means by the Home Secretary. Its mandate was: 'To consider and report on the exercise by the Secretary of State of the executive power to intercept communications and in particular under what authority, to what extent and for what purposes this power has been exercised and to what use the information so obtained has been put.'

Subsequently Mr. R. A. Butler, the Home Secretary, assured a restive House of Commons that he appreciated 'the necessity of preventing any abuse of this necessary but distasteful power'. This begged the question that there had already been an abuse. It is bad enough that the modern State eavesdrops on its citizens, but when the information gained is passed to others outside the public service it becomes hardly less than slander by stealth.

Lord Birkett brought to this task the qualities of patience, good humour and common sense this controversial subject demanded. The Committee did not deny the State the right to listen-in to telephone conversations, which it considered necessary to the security of the State, but redefined the circumstances in which such arbitrary action is justified and recommended a tightening up of the conditions under which it is permitted. It was not, incidentally, R. A. Butler's mistake in permitting a report on an intercepted conversation to go to the Bar Council; it was the decision of his predecessor, Lord Tenby.

Two years later, in 1959, Lord Birkett, at the age of seventy-five, and at the urgent request of all concerned, acted as arbitrator in the six-weeks-old printing dispute which put 4,300 firms and over 1,000 newspapers out of action, with great loss to the publishing industry. With infinite patience he explored the situation with everyone, finding the formula on which all could agree. Both trade unions and employers' organisation wanted to show their gratitude to Lord Birkett, but all he would accept was . . . a *Dictionary of Quotations*. He had told the Minister of Labour that he would act as arbitrator 'as a public duty' and with no thought of reward.

In retirement Birkett was in such demand that he had to ration his speeches to one a fortnight, because of the thought and work invariably put into them. As a broadcaster he was perfect, assembling his work with great care, learning it thoroughly and submitting cheerfully and humbly to the inevitable discipline of a B.B.C. radio or television studio. Producers, not unused to celebrities who are difficult and vain, found him easy to work with and amenable to advice and suggestions.

A B.B.C. television interview with Lord Birkett by John Freeman in *Face to Face* (it was the first in this series and established its immense popularity) contained admissions which came as a shock to many of Norman Birkett's old friends. Asked about his religious beliefs, he described himself as a 'Christian Agnostic'— which was a very, very long way from the fervent Wesleyan he was in his youth. He meant that while accepting the Christian ethic, he was less certain on matters of dogma.

Many of his listeners thought he meant by this that he was an atheist, one who specifically denies the existence of a God. This he did not imply. But he had lost the dynamic, positive faith of his youth. The metamorphosis from evangelism to critical neutrality seems extraordinary so late in life, at a time when most men cling tenaciously to those things that give life pattern, stability and meaning. It shows great intellectual courage, yet to me there is something sad at the thought of the young man, who had sung hymns to the early morning air as he raced through the countryside in a horse-drawn wagon, having to say to himself: 'I don't know. I just don't know.' There is a note of genuine sadness in the letters he sent, late in life, to friends, recalling the enchanted days of his childhood and youth, when everything was suffused by the warmth of unqualified faith.

What had caused this disenchantment? Was it a lifetime spent in plumbing the depths of human nature? The horror and disillusionment of the protracted Nuremberg Trials? Where was mercy, intercession, compassion and divine providence to be found amidst all that fear, horror and mechanised slaughter? Was Nuremberg for him the parting of the theological ways? One thing is certain; he respected, and even envied, those who held fast to their faith and never, even by inference, did anything to persuade them to his own point of view, which towards the end of his life could be called Humanist.

Birkett's melodious oratory never flagged. A speech he made at the opening of Ulverston's new library is comparable to Sir Winston Churchill at his best. When, in the House of Lords, he made a speech in defence of his beloved Lakeland—a speech designed to prevent Manchester Corporation drawing water from Ullswater—the House was visibly moved by the passion and the poetry of his appeal. By seventy votes to thirty-six he won the day.

On this note of triumph he passed quickly from the world, dying at London Clinic after an emergency operation. In accordance with his wishes, his cremation at Golders Green was a private affair attended only by his son, with no flowers, service or prayers of any kind. But a beautiful Lakeland Fell, which he saw and loved as a boy, will be named after him by the Ullswater Preservation Society and others who, like him, have a feeling for the wonders of Nature. Until the last, 'Norrie' had retained undiminished his affection for the hills and dales of his home county; his faith in humanity was unshaken by its worst follies and crimes; the trials of body and spirit left him uncomplaining; moving among people in every walk of life, of every religion, creed, colour, degree of intelligence, with diametrically opposed views, he contrived never to make an enemy; and to the last he retained in all its intensity his awe and reverence in face of the works of Nature. Whose divine hand had painted that miraculous canvas? Once he thought he knew. Later he was honest enough to admit that he did not know. But to the end that supreme artistry remained his inspiration, his joy and his faith.

INDEX